Growing Up American: Contempory Children and Their Society

Joan Costello and Phyllis La Farge

Copyright © 1987

Schenkman Books, Inc.
P.O. Box 1570
Harvard Square
Cambridge, MA 02138

Library of Congress Cataloging in Publication Data

Costello, Joan.
  Growing up American.

  Bibliography: p.
  Includes index.
  1. Child rearing—United States. 2. Child
development—United States. 3. Children—United States—
Social conditions. 4. Family—United States. I. La Farge,
Phyllis. II. Title.
HQ769.C753   1985   649'.1'0973   85-1923
ISBN 0-87073-303-6
ISBN 0-87073-304-4 (pbk.)

This book or parts thereof, may not be reproduced without written permission of publisher

Printed in the United States of America

*The Child's Toys and the Old Man's Reasons
Are the Fruits of the Two Seasons.*

—William Blake

for our children
Cathleen
Clare
Tom

Contents

Acknowledgments	xi
Introduction	xiii
Chapter One. Mapping the Territory	1
Julie and Jerry	3
Maps, Roles, and Rules	9
Maps, Roles, Rules, and Cognitive Development	12
The Child under Three	13
The Child of Three to Six	16
The Child over Six	19
Chapter Two. A Family Picnic	23
The Polskys and the Murphys	23
Chapter Three: The Intimate World of Family	35
Stresses on the Private World of Family	38
The Knowledge Explosion	40
Doing Things Together as a Family	42
Women's Roles	44
Linda and Cliff	46
Chapter Four: Seeing the World Through Parents' Lives	59
Works, Workers, and Family Life	61
The Gianninis	64
How Work Affects the Gianninis and Their Children	68
Place, Power, and Possibilities	75
Chapter Five. Finding a Place on the Team	79
Baseball as an Initiation into American Life	80
Chapter Six. Stepping Into a World Beyond Family	89
Church and Neighborhood	90
School	91
Two Days in the Life of Florence Mosby	95
The Preschool Child	105
The Young Schoolchild	110
School and the Markings of Subordinate Status	114
Chapter Seven. Messages from the Modern World	121

Housing and Transportation	128
Government Institutions	131
Families as Inadvertent Victims of Corporate and Government Decisions	133
The Food Industry	136
Learned Helplessness	140
Postscript	149
Notes	153
Bibliography	175
Index	185

Acknowledgments

Work on this book was supported by the Carnegie Corporation of New York through a grant to the Carnegie Council on Children. We are most grateful for the support of the Corporation, in particular Alan Pifer, Barbara Finberg, and David Robinson whose intelligence and humanity have set a standard admired by many within and without the foundation.

Dr. Robert Haggerty and Professors John Demos and William Kessen served faithfully as advisers to the book and gave generously of their time, counsel, and personal support.

The book benefited in many ways from the assistance of the Carnegie Council staff and colleagues at Yale University, especially Professor Kenneth Keniston, Director of the Council, Professor Albert Solnit, then Director of Yale Child Study Center, Professor Irving Janis, Professor John Ogbu, on leave from University of California, Greta Fein, John Gliedman, Marjorie Janis, Linda Hughes, Ellice Forman Peyton, Laurie Rosenbaum, and Bill Roth. We will ever be in debt to many other colleagues and friends who, at various stages, offered what we needed to keep the final goal in sight.

Finally, we are grateful to Alfred Schenkman for giving us voice, and to editor Dalia Lipkin for her efficient and cheerful editorial assistance. And, to our children who weathered the storms, we offer our thanks and beg their forgiveness.

Introduction

> *Within the memory of many living members of even our most modernized societies there existed a view of a society in which virtually every member of the society as far back as could be remembered could count on his children and his children's children growing up and living under conditions roughly similar to his own. Now virtually no one can. The one thing certain is that the future is going to be different and at a constantly accelerated pace.*
>
> —Marion J. Levy, *Modernization and the Structure of Societies*

This book examines the way in which the contemporary American child becomes a member of our society. It explores what children take in from their daily experience and suggests that when they are still very young their experiences begin to shape them mentally and emotionally as people of the late twentieth century. Long before he goes to school a child is shaped by institutions beyond the home. This has been true for children in every society over the centuries, but in modern times the balance of power among the institutions that influence children has shifted dramatically. Those institutions once primarily responsible for rearing children—family, church, and community—have lost power in relation to the professional service institutions—schools, medical centers, social agencies, etc.—and the major economic, governmental, knowledge-producing, and communications institutions of the society.[1] This shift began several centuries ago, but it has speeded up remarkably over the last fifty years bringing unprecedented opportunities for self-fulfillment to young adults and childless couples. Parents, however, are often caught between allegiances to tradition and the pull of contemporary values. While children may be most strongly influenced by parents, everyone in the family relies on modern sources of authority when medical, practical, or personal problems arise. The advice of elders in family, church, and community has to be judged against that of experts in schools, medical centers—or television. Understanding what this implies for the experience of childhood—and the nature of modern parenthood—is the task of this book.

One way of viewing childhood is as a guided tour of social realities where those charged with protecting and preparing us for satisfying and productive lives help us find our way in a succession of more distant and complex social worlds beyond the home. In today's society, as the child's social world expands, he meets people and circumstances that seem more powerful and better informed and that offer more opportunities than the ones parents present. Parents' sense of these attractions generates considerable uncertainty and stress. They find it hard to know what is the best course to steer in guiding children, what issues to do battle over, and what to ignore. Which opportunities should they encourage a child to pursue and which should they urge him to eschew? It is not easy to decide how to protect children from what one does not fully understand; not easy to choose a strategy that will be helpful to a child, one that neither puts him at unacceptable risk nor forces him to retreat from opportunities to grow.

The confusion and stress parents feel is a good indication of the changed balance of influences in their children's lives as compared with those of their own youth. It is not that today's parents are weaker or less committed than those of earlier generations, but that they are confronted with the complex psychological and social dilemmas of childrearing in a changing world.

In discussing the gradual but dramatic changes that have occurred among the institutions that shape childhood experience, we offer no recipes for successful childrearing, although we do offer insights that may help explain why raising children is not easy today. We believe, in fact, that those who think raising children is a breeze are either unusually fortunate or, more likely, out of touch with reality. We are convinced that for parents to feel effective they may need to go beyond techniques for effective management to understand the relationship of the family to other institutions. However, we try to keep one simple fact in focus: the sources of competence and resilience one finds in children are almost always rooted in powerful familial relationships where at least one parent accepts, respects, and encourages the child.

In chapters one and two we explore how children take in the structures and values of their society.[2] The world of everyday life is imprinted with patterns that occur with some regularity—the ways in which we use time, space, things, etc. These patterns are themselves shaped by the institutional structures that maintain a society and by the cultural traditions and imperatives of its people. While growing up, the average child encounters many patterns that carry the imprint of the institutions of the society—their values, the marks of their structures, and their influence on the texture of daily life.

Children grow up among the patterns of a particular material and social world, typically one with sufficient order and consistency so that its character can be expressed in the daily rituals of comings and goings, greetings and meetings, eating and working, talking and arguing. Not every human act reflects a link to societal structures, but there is sufficient consistency between a society's institutional patterns and the lives of families for a child to take in and learn his society's norms from its material and social regularities as he eats his cereal, uses bath soap, or watches television. In particular, he can observe and try on gestures, facial expressions, movements, speech, and emotional expressions and put them together in rituals that will constitute a familiar style to those with whom he lives. This familiar style will make him recognizably French, Japanese, or American by the time he is two years old.[3] Later, much that he has incorporated in gestures, ways of looking, thinking, speaking, etc., will be further shaped and refined by neighborhood peer culture, church, television portrayals of American life, and his school's teaching about the prescribed ways of learning, using knowledge, and practicing social conventions.

In chapter three we describe how the family fulfills its functions of nurture, protection, and preparation of children who will function well in the society and form families of their own. Although the bulk of this book concerns the child's and family's links to institutions of the wider society, we discuss the intimate family world at length because the way a child grows up cannot be separated from an understanding of how he comes to view his family in relation to other institutions, e.g., as strong or threatened, prevailing or beset. Moreover, unless a child has sturdy emotional roots planted and nurtured in a family, his ability to incorporate the influences of other institutions will be shaky.

In chapter four we discuss how families act as the first filters for children's social learning, shaping their first conceptions of the meaning of social events. We give economic status central importance although children incorporate it only indirectly through the messages that come from their parents' work—or lack thereof—and from the social position and material resources that determine the family's leeway in coping with life.

In chapter five we illustrate many of the patterns and key messages of American society by describing a game of baseball.

In chapter six we examine the messages that come from institutions children encounter on their own. Our discussion concentrates on the shaping influence of schools, although we speak briefly of traditional institutions such as church and neighborhood—and of a major contemporary influence, television.

In chapter seven, we look at what children learn from their encounters with the larger institutions that maintain the society. We offer a number of examples of how the patterns of everyday life are intertwined with the ways of thinking, communicating, and doing business that characterize the institutions of public life that maintain a society and chart its future course. These encounters may appear fragmentary and superficial, but we believe they fit together in a mosaic that becomes a powerful context for what children learn about their place in the world. In discussing children's contacts with institutions beyond the home, we describe, at least in general terms, the greater contemporary influence of these institutions on both children and families.

A concluding chapter emphasizes the inevitable struggle families experience as they try to accommodate traditional values and practices with contemporary imperatives. We make a plea for parents to reaffirm and express passionate commitments to values and traditions rooted in the past, whether they can rationalize their passions or not, for these provide a sense of continuity with past generations of families. However, we encourage parents not to pretend they can ignore the nature of contemporary society and its strong influences.[4] It is in combining the knowledge of the present and hopes for the future with the longer inheritance of traditions that our children will have their best chance of standing on firm ground, sure of their roots and ready to reach out and explore new worlds without losing their footing.

Chapter One
Mapping the Territory

> *A Map is not the territory it represents but, if correct, it has a similar structure to the territory which accounts for its usefulness.*
>
> —Alfred Korzybski, *Science and Sanity*

> *Where things are, how to work the system, what to stay away from—this crucial job of social mapping is done by mothers from the moment they first guide the hungry infant mouth to the nipple. Role model and map provider—these are two important aspects of a mother's job with her children in all societies. They are also crucial aspects of the socialization process as it affects the social competence of children.*
>
> —Elise Boulding, "Women as Role Models in Industrializing Societies"

Children become people of their society first through participation in their parents' lives. Trying to make sense of their world, they gradually construct meanings and adaptations based not only on their own direct experience but on daily encounters with parents' words, moods, and actions. They absorb what they can of their parents' knowledge of how things work and how to get things done, what to do about a problem and what not to do, what to suffer and what not to suffer, how to withdraw, when to fight, and when not to fight.[1]

Children learn about their life world in a fashion that is not abstract or a matter of precept or concept, but vivid, involving, and concrete.[2] It is a tale told gradually, one vital detail upon another. They are players but also the audience in a drama of their parents' lives, and their reactions vary according to their individual personalities and their stock of life experience. As they grow older, they develop a view of a life world consistent with their more refined and extensive cognitive and motor skills, an increasingly correct and subtly expressive repertory. The world children perceive and participate in has a certain coherence—that of their family and culture—resembling both the style and vision of a play.

Parents highlight certain actions, reactions, issues, and feelings to the neglect of others; what is emphasized in one family may not be in another. In one family the occurrence of illness may scarcely be mentioned, in another it may be a preoccupation. Or one family may have rituals concerning physical fitness and balanced diets while another may have none. Parents may also disguise their feelings or conceal events so that the child only vaguely discerns what is happening—a professional disappointment, a financial setback, a shady business deal, a sorrow, a betrayal of fidelity, the passion between husband and wife.

Although parents have some conscious choice over what they stress or obscure, their lives are shaped by their socioeconomic class, their culture, and their ancestry.[3] However individual they may be, parents are to a great extent marked by their time, place, and history. Even those decisions that seem purely rational—"we'll discuss this after the children are in bed" or "I think it's time the children knew about this"—reflect both culture and milieu, as well as a conscious choice and less conscious leeway or constraint with which the individual interprets his culture. Parents, like actors, interpret their roles, finding possibilities in them that others may miss. Thus, for instance, even though she sustains their household by cleaning other people's houses and caring for their children, a single mother may fill her children's lives with humor, stories, and ideas and inspire them to study, read, and go to college. But for most parents, interpreting their role is less a conscious choice than a complex interplay of individual personality and life experience. Moreover, the very poor have almost no leeway to play with life's possibilities.[4]

From the age of two the child is increasingly a child of his culture; in his perceptions of the world he will fasten on some aspects of what passes before him and ignore others; that is, he will attend selectively.[5] In a culture that values square corners he will see the corners of the world and neglect the curves. In absorbing the messages of society, the child interprets, filters, and modifies them in a complex way. This process is still far from fully understood, but it clearly involves not only the predispositions of biology and psyche, but the personalities of caregivers, the specific circumstances of his family's life, and the changing circumstances of society at large.

A child's play is vital in this process of assimilating a view of life.[6] It is a visible expression of the active role a child takes in making sense of the world around him.[7] Play is not to be seen simply as a sign of what the child has absorbed of the society or as a kind of metaphor of his life, although in some measure it may be these. More important, play provides the child with an opportunity to construct and test a way of mapping the world that is all his own and in doing so to develop at least an elementary conviction that he can master experience rather than be subdued by it.[8] In an analogous way the artist's creation is not only a depiction or a sign or metaphor for his experience, but the product of an active mastery and transformation of that experience.

To understand how this process works, let us imagine two American children at play. Most play is not nearly so clear-cut as our vignette suggests, but the elements dramatized in this scene are discernible, if more diffuse, in much of everyday play. Our chief protagonist is a four-year-old girl, chosen because we can clearly see how a child of her age selects, interprets, and imitates certain elements of her world when she plays. Among all children at play, the four-year-old is the most daring and resourceful dramatist.

JULIE AND JERRY

Julie is watching television on a rainy day when her mother comes in from the kitchen and says, "No more television." After she turns off the set, Julie sulks for a while, complaining that she doesn't know what to do. Then she has an idea. "Can I have the blanket on your bed?" she asks. "I want to make a house." Her mother consents and, following Julie's directions, helps her spread it over a card table in the living room. Then her mother goes back to the kitchen. Now preoccupied with her game, Julie brings stuffed animals from her room, and a hand towel and some tissues from the bathroom. Her mother asks with some irritation: "What are you doing with those?"

"I'm going to put my animals to bed."
"But why do you need all those tissues?"
"They need their own beds," Julie says.

Taking the tissues and the hand towel into her make-believe house, Julie spreads them out neatly and puts an animal on each. On the towel sleep two bears side by side, the mother and the father.

Julie has just finished arranging her animals for the night when her brother Jerry comes in. He is five. He asks if he can play too and she tells him that he can be one of the children.

"I want to be the father," he says.

"You can't be the father now," Julie says. "Brown Bear is the father. You be a child."

Jerry reluctantly agrees, crawls into the house, and lies down in the spot his sister tells him to, beside a kangaroo. Then Julie, too, lies down. "Close your eyes," she says. "Pretend you're sleeping."

They both close their eyes and for a brief moment there is silence.

Then Julie sits up. "Dinner time," she says. She crawls out of the house, taking two animals with her.

Jerry arranges the rest of the animals, while Julie fetches some plastic margarine cups and covers and sets the table. "But you're supposed to eat breakfast when you get up," he protests. She gives him a scornful glance but gathers up all the dishes again and puts them aside. She goes into her room and brings out her pretty doll's blanket, which she spreads on the floor.

"Their grandmother is coming to dinner," she tells her brother. "They need a tablecloth."

Once more she sets out the dishes, pauses, and looks at her handiwork. Then she goes into the kitchen and gets a tall plastic container (a pitcher for milk) and the salt and pepper shakers. She adds an ashtray—so Dad won't use his saucer the way he usually does.

"They are having real napkins, too," she says, "because their grandmother is coming."

She folds the tissues like napkins and tries with limited success to make the corners meet just right. Just then Jerry knocks several animals down with a toy truck. She explodes and grabs his truck. He grabs it back. She strikes him; he strikes her back. They both scream and their mother intervenes.

"He spoils everything," Julie cries. "He hit me."

When things are a bit calmer, their mother asks what role Jerry was playing in the game.

"I want to be father," says Jerry.

"Julie, won't you let Jerry be father now?" their mother half asks, half threatens.

Julie looks in doubt but finally concedes.

"Come in, hang up your coat, and watch TV. I'm fixing supper," she says.

"But Mom said we can't watch TV," says Jerry.

"Pretend," says his sister with the exasperation of someone forced to explain the obvious.

Jerry sits in an armchair, one leg over the arm, now and then turning the pages of a make-believe newspaper until Julie calls him to dinner. When she summons him he goes on reading his newspaper at the table.

"You can't read. Grandmother is here," Julie says, making a place for another doll.

Jerry accepts her ruling and puts aside his paper.

Julie pours imaginary milk from the pitcher. Sternly she reminds everyone to put his napkin on his lap—not under his chin like a baby.

Brown Bear, a father no longer, misbehaves; halfway through the meal he knocks over his cup and spills. Julie beats him soundly. Then Jerry beats the kangaroo, who will not eat his lima beans.

A lamb is sent away from the table because he is not wearing shoes, something that has always bothered Grandmother. (No one else is wearing shoes but that doesn't seem to matter.)

The meal ends unlike almost any that Jerry and Julie have ever had (or been allowed to have)—in a fit of the sillies with one animal bopping another, the dishes clattering, Jerry grabbing the doll, changing roles, and becoming Grandmother, a silly, noisy Grandmother who talks about napkins and children not wearing shoes.

Julie's World

In her play, Julie constructs, practices, and tests her picture of life at home. She can already depict in broad strokes the world of her family, which is her first model for all social realities she will meet in the course of her life. She also tests her role as a grown-up woman. In her experience so far, being a woman means being a mother. Mother puts children to bed and gets them up; mother plans, cooks, and serves meals.

In doing things mothers do, Julie uses gestures and tones of voice that she has observed in her own mother. There is a certain efficient bustling, a certain tenderness, even a certain harshness.

Her mother's ways express her individual personality and style, part of which derive from past experience—her temperament and its interaction with the style of mothering she herself knew as a child. But her ways also reflect the class and milieu in which the family now lives, the problems and satisfactions of her life with her husband, her kin, her friends, and her job. Julie, with every gesture and intonation, is "raising" her stuffed animals, just as her mother is raising her, to be Americans of a particular cultural group, and the way she does so draws not only on what she has been told or overheard but perhaps even more on the patterned data of sensory experience such as tones of voice, hand and body gestures, how far or how near people place themselves in relation to each other, when and how they look at each other, when they smile, frown, or move in the context of particular social settings.[9]

Moreover, Julie's play reveals that she has absorbed not only a general pattern of tone and gesture but "right ways" of doing things specific to her milieu. She believes that children sleep alone and that fathers and mothers sleep together. In another milieu Julie would accept several children sleeping in one bed, or parents sleeping in different bedrooms.

She also believes that families sit down to eat together and that fathers do not participate in the preparation of the meal. In a less ordered household she might consider family meals an occasional ritual, observed only a few days each week. In another household she might see her father sharing or being in charge of the preparation of the evening meal.

Julie believes that mothers intervene when their children misbehave; she punishes the stuffed animals who "spill their milk." It may be that her mother has never punished her so harshly for such a misdemeanor, but her play portrays the angry feelings she has sensed beneath her mother's self-control.

At four years of age Julie is able to reconstruct specific events, and her play suggests that she knows a good deal about everyday life and its patterns. She knows how a table setting changes for a special guest—with a tablecloth, napkins, a pitcher, and an ashtray for her father. Through changes in her parents' manners, tone, and gestures, as well as in the rules of their behavior (her father does not read his newspaper at the table when Grandmother comes), Julie has learned other messages about the cultural traditions of her family and, insofar as her particular family reflects it, about the society in which they are embedded. Napkins and pitchers are symbols not only of a family tradition but of a certain economic and social status where certain niceties can be afforded.

Julie's experience has taught her about the exercise of power within her family. Grandmother influences mother to ask that Julie and Jerry wear shoes indoors, but once she is gone they take them off and hear no protest from their parents.* Julie's mother can stop her father from reading his newspaper at the table only when Grandmother comes, but in another family a child Julie's age might be getting a different lesson from a different kind of example—a father who retorts, "Mind your own business!" when his wife asks him not to read at the table.

The three- to five-year-old's play is a "phrasing of life," as Margaret Mead has called it. It draws not only on events and relationships in the child's intimate life but on a wider social reality. Everything that has been inculcated in the child and everything he has observed, no matter how casually, can become an ingredient in his play, helping him define who he is as a member of society, who the other members are, what they do and do not do, how they do it, who is one of "us" and who is one of "them," and how, at least in a rudimentary way, the different members can be expected to care for and exert power over others. These elements are all present and often obvious even when the child's overt preoccupation in play is working out—or at least working on—conflicts in his inner world.

The four-year-old's play may draw directly on an experience beyond his immediate family. Although our vignette concentrates on play based on experiences in the private family world, other play episodes might be based on experience in the public world beyond the house. Perhaps Julie has been shopping downtown with her mother and watched while, at the sales clerk's request, she supplied both her driver's license and a major credit card in making a purchase. Playing store with Jerry, Julie may offer him slips of paper—her credit card and license. Her play reflects her

---

*A visit from her grandmother, we might note, is probably one of the few times that Julie sees an old person. She knows no family where more than two generations live in the same house, although some of her friends live in the same apartment or house or down the street from grandparents. She is still too young to draw any general conclusions about this, but they will come in time.

mother's experience with the commercial and credit systems of society which offer flexible services to a wide population but demand a kind of knowledge very different from the kind that might have been acceptable in a small town one hundred years ago. If, however, Julie had gone shopping with her grandmother, who has let her license lapse and who has no major credit cards, her experience might have been quite different.

Turning from Julie and Jerry to a group of nursery school children, we might suppose they play with puppets, one of which is a policeman. A child from a white suburban background who has no reason to be wary of the police might make the policeman a rescuer—helping the victims of a traffic accident perhaps. But a black child from a crowded urban neighborhood might cast the policeman in quite another role. He might show him being paid off by a storekeeper doll, arresting an innocent teenage puppet, or shooting it out with a gang of other puppets. These different representations of a policeman not only suggest different life worlds, they also imply two children's different assessments of their place in society. If both children were playing in the same group, they might get into a heated argument about policemen, each mounting a defense of his newly constructed and not yet firm view of policemen.

For most of us, children's play is not nearly as revealing a spectacle as it could be. We have learned not to attend to the underlying patterns and passions it expresses so eloquently. Most of us feel an obligation to instruct, to help children see the world our way, and to organize their expressions of feeling and thought according to our system of meanings and values. Certainly it can be painful to watch children play out their personal psychological conflicts. To make ourselves feel better about it, we encourage them to play out happy endings, to accommodate to the realities of life as most of us do by looking away.

It is particularly difficult to watch a game that expresses social conflicts—to witness young children in the process of constructing a picture of the world as a place in which certain marks of exclusion or rejection are central to their life choices. One can observe this process among disabled children, among black and other minority children, and, perhaps in a less restricting way, among girls. For instance, although some young black children from poor families express the politics of determined organization and commitment to mastery in their play, giving evidence of the resilience of children even under the burdens of poverty and social exclusion, other children from such families reflect in their play the politics of surrender. Their play reveals their belief in a world that is unyielding, one where their chances for mastery or satisfaction are severely limited, and acquiescence is the only effective response. Not surprisingly, the parents of these children often have a similar outlook, seeing in their lives little possibility of bettering their lot. By and large their outlook is an accurate representation of their options.[10]

MAPS, ROLES, AND RULES

We might summarize how the play of a child like Julie expresses her phrasing of life under three headings: maps, roles, and rules.[11]

By map we mean an individual's effort to make sense of life—to locate himself physically and socially in time and space. In her play Julie follows and tests out a rudimentary map of her world. Her map defines her world not only in physical terms (house, table, dishes, beds) and in time sequences (bed time, time to get up, dinner time), but also—and inseparably—in terms of social meaning. She conceives of a house as a dwelling for a mother, a father, and their children—and no one else. The boundaries of membership determine what can happen there and who is an intimate and who is an outsider. She is defining the social topography of reality as she has experienced it, and it reflects a world specialized for nurture and sociability with intimates. As she charts the physical features and temporal sequences of her world, Julie's map draws on key elements of her culture and her parents' way of life. Her play roots these elements more surely in her consciousness, embedding Julie in that reality more firmly and thus assuring the continuity of her cultural group.

There is no sign in her play of either her father's or her mother's work outside the home, but at the same time, many of Julie's assumptions about resources (money, possessions, space, and time) and social ways of doing things are in keeping with the organization of her parents' work, their income, and their education.

Just as the child's map is shaped by her social milieu, so too is its construction inseparable from her emotional attachments. Julie could not have taken in the essential forms of daily life within her family so elaborately and surely without mutually strong emotional attachments. The crucial link between the socialization process and the child's attachments has been described by Peter L. Berger and Thomas Luckmann in their book, *The Social Construction of Reality*.

> Socialization involves more than purely cognitive learning. It takes place under circumstances that are highly charged emotionally. Indeed, there is good reason to believe that without such emotional attachments to the significant others the learning process would be difficult if not impossible. The child identifies with the significant others in a variety of emotional ways. Whatever they may be, internalization occurs only as identification occurs. The child takes on the significant others' roles and attitudes, that is, internalizes them and makes them his own. And by this identification with significant others the child becomes capable of identifying himself, or acquiring a subjectively coherent and plausible identity.[12]

The play of a four-year-old like Julie offers insight into the process where the "taking on" or "taking in" of a world—external reality—is a building block in the construction of identity. Through her play Julie affirms her inner picture of the world, of how things are—her map. She internalizes what she has observed and participated in, most of which she codes as possibilities for action—what you do when and with whom and, by extension, who you are in your world. At the same time her subjective drama has an objective reality; it "comes from someplace," the external world of her family's life.

Each person's map is idiosyncratic in what it emphasizes or filters out. At the same time it has much in common with the maps of his kin and shows the marks of his cultural traditions, his region, and his time in history. It only imperfectly represents the territory of his life world. An individual's psychic compromises with what is tolerable for him to notice or imagine will influence the accuracy, intricacy, and utility of his map. What underlies the mapping process is the human need for coherence, dependability, and predictability, for a sense of belonging to a reality that one shares with others and in the context of which certain courses of action make sense and become almost automatic. At each stage of development a child may, through play, find his way to a relatively stable version of his map which enables him to see and hear most things the way others in his circle do and play his part in the particular drama of his family, school, and community. It allows him to move among his peers during his school years with some sense of confidence and some freedom from anxiety.

A good part of a person's mental map has to do with roles and rules. *Roles* are ways of being and doing that are defined and bounded by general consent. They are usually based upon precedents. Roles are convenient ways for people who live together—and play or work together—to know what each does and how to respond appropriately almost without thinking. Does mother cook dinner or does father? Or do both? It is confusing and not at all efficient if each act of daily life must be negotiated every time. At the age of four and five Julie and Jerry are very aware of how tasks are divided in their family. If we observed them over a longer period, we would find many examples of role prescriptions that govern their exchanges with others—relatives, friends, strangers, authority figures, storekeepers, professionals.

The roles one plays in life are determined by many circumstances, but the most significant are linked to (though not caused by) race, sex, biology, and socioeconomic class. Take, for example, two women—one a white Manhattan socialite and the other a black Southern farm worker. Both share the biological role of mother and the subordinate status of woman. In this sense they might be seen as having more in common than either would with a man of the same milieu. But their racial difference sets them worlds apart. Even though the Manhattan socialite may choose to slip down the ladder of class—take a job as a sales clerk, say, or shop at a Goodwill store—she will remain a member of a privileged racial and economic group. There is little probability that the black Southern woman can climb even one rung of the social ladder unless the ladder itself is redesigned.

(In describing Julie, we have not been specific about race or class. Although much of her play could occur in any family, her sense of space, time, management of conflicts, notions of propriety, etc., suggests that she is from an average-income white family, or one that shares many of the forms and values of such a family.)

Rules are guides to action and as such are tied to roles—they define who does what and how they do it. When Julie spreads a blanket in a circle formed by her animals, she is rehearsing a rule that has to do with her grandmother's visit. As she grows older it will be refined and generalized into a rule concerning the treatment of honored visitors. In Julie's family it is part of the mother's role to prepare for grandmother's visit. Rules can also be seen as an expression of the conventions of the culture: such and such is done or not done without regard for who does it—visitors are entertained.

The actions that are codified by rules leave a residue in the child's world, and this residue is material for his mental map of how things are—and should be. Thus, for instance, the town officials of a county seat might decide to hold a fair in the autumn to show off the stock and produce of local farmers. It is part of their role to decide how to organize such a fair—to set its rules. One of these rules—tied to the physical realities of harvest time—is that the fair is held only once a year. Another is that special fairgrounds are reserved for it outside of town. This space and its structures are associated with the fair even if unused for months—part of the residue it leaves in the town. A child growing up in the town will have the experience of going to the fair, and this social experience will have its coordinates in time and space: the fair takes place in the autumn after the harvest, and it takes place on the fairground. By the time the child is in school he will have acquired a working sense of some of the rules of the fair: it takes place only once a year and only on the fairground. These rules will help him make sense of explanations he later hears about why certain crops or stock are raised and, more generally, the culture and economy of his town.

MAPS, ROLES, RULES, AND COGNITIVE DEVELOPMENT

Developmentally, children can be expected to take in, organize experience, and assign meaning in keeping with their stage of mental or cognitive development. In this book we consider three developmental stages and draw heavily on Piaget's formulations. From infancy to about two years, during the sensory-motor period of development, children organize experience in terms of actions and reactions. Through an imitation of the motor and gestural signatures of important persons in their life they take in their ways of attending, feeling, acting, and reacting. By two, children have a rudimentary sense of self, firm attachments to those on whom they depend, and a primitive but effective set of schemes for organizing and responding to social situations. From about two through six, children's mental operations are said to be intuitive or prelogical. They learn a great deal about the way the world works, but feel free to play with what they have learned. During these years children develop very clear ideas about intimate relationships—the sharing of loved ones, for example—who belongs with whom and where they stand vis-à-vis important people in their world. They have a sense of personal presence and an elaborate repertory of social roles they have observed and played with. Their personality, like their elementary map of the world, begins to have a degree of coherence and consistency, unless their surroundings have none.

From about seven until early adolescence, children's mental life is characteristically more recognizable to adults as "logical." It conforms more closely to adult ways of thought, although not until they reach adolescence are children able to think about things and ideas without the concrete reference or contexts they depend on when younger. The personalities of children seven to twelve years old express how much and how well they have made sense of the world they live in, how comfortable their place is in their family or among familiar adults and children, and how well they have learned to move surely if cautiously into social situations among relative strangers. During these years children search for, try to understand, play with, and try out the rules that govern material reality and social roles. Increasingly, they become children of a particular physical and social place. Inevitably the possibilities governing the kind of person they will become are narrowed. Gradually the social territories they will explore—and those they will barely notice—are defined.

THE CHILD UNDER THREE

Children under three cannot be said to have a map in the sense we have used it. But they are gradually acquiring a sense of various important landmarks in their life that will become notations on their map once they can code experiences symbolically, especially by means of words.* They are learning about their predictability and dependability, and what they can and cannot do to or with them. Their mother is a landmark, and so are certain people, areas, and occasions of their day, most notably mealtime and bedtime. Their perception of their world does not have the comprehensive or bounded quality associated with the concept of a map. Yet because so much of their learning at this stage of their development

---

*When caregivers are unresponsive, hostile, depressed, or very moody, these and other developments may be suppressed as the child devotes himself to the search for stable, safe, human relationships.

comes through senses and muscles, their landmarks take on a visceral importance. Lifetime attachment to sights, smells, sounds, and tastes, and idiosyncratic ways of moving and touching that grow out of efforts to imitate those who care for and hold them, are established at this age. It is perhaps in tracing back some of our oldest sense and motor memories that we can come closest to recreating for ourselves the very young child's first perception of his world, the beginnings of mapping.[13]

Young children know the world, too, by moving through it and seeing what of it they can move. As adults it is impossible for us to take ourselves back into this aspect of a child's life and imagine what it is to learn, for instance, about the "tableness" of tables by trying to stand up under them and hitting our heads, or to learn about the "woodness" of wood by trying to pick the knots out of a pine floor and finding that it cannot be done. Perhaps only a fun house, space travel, or a suddenly acquired physical handicap—disorienting us from what we know of our actions and their consequences—could give us a taste of these early attempts to construct a life world.[14]

The infant's interest in faces—a preference that begins in the early days of life and appears to be preprogrammed and intimately related to survival—provides the foundation for the emotional attachment that in time develops into an awareness of roles and rules. During the first year, babies begin to discriminate between familiar and unfamiliar faces and discern who has the most power to comfort and hurt them, who holds and cuddles them, who jostles them or throws them around. Fathers and mothers—or other caregivers—may express their caring in different ways; and these different ways will become the basis for an early perception of roles. Most babies learn early that men's play is more physical.[15] Mothers or other caregivers are a source of tenderness or toughness—usually both—engendering warm feelings and frustration.

Between eight and sixteen months the baby's attachment to others and his sense of their power in his life are well enough developed so that he is fussy about strangers and does not easily tolerate separation from those who take care of him. Even then, he registers confusion, withdrawal, or fear in the face of inadequate care.

From a very early age—at least from six or seven months—the baby appears to have a particular interest in other babies and small children. One sees babies mirroring each other's movements in a kind of play that prefigures imitation and suggests that a form of role playing begins in infancy. A baby's imitation of other children may reinforce his sense of who he is; it may contribute to the content of his self-awareness.

The baby of less than a year may begin to imitate gestures of hands, arms, and face, particularly the mouth. These imitated gestures are the building blocks for wider imitation, modeling, and, later, role play. By the age of two, children imitate not just single acts or gestures but patterns of action they observe among those they know and those they encounter by chance, and they begin to model. This means they take on the roles of others and behave like them, but not always imitating them exactly. Those who are powerful in their world—mother, father, older siblings, clever peers, doctor—or those perceived as powerful in the outside world—fireman, truck driver—are the ones they are most apt to imitate at first, with the gradual addition of powerful fantasy figures from television or books. Important neighbors and people whose behavior or appearance appears novel to the child are also imitated.

At this age children are aware of differences between people, and they can sort them and assign qualities appropriately. Men have beards and wear pants. Women have smooth faces and wear dresses as well as pants. Firemen wear special hats and drive red trucks. They distinguish other categories such as race or physical handicaps and know which group is "us" and which is "them." They do not yet attach meanings to different groups, however, beyond liking those associated with someone friendly to them or fearing certain characteristics that are grossly unfamiliar. Or their fear may be based on what they learn from their parents' gestures, facial expressions, or changed tones of voice. Although they can distinguish the attributes that mark people by sex, race, and class, they do not see these attributes as signs of a person's place in society. They may have a rather accurate working sense of how power operates in their own family, particularly with respect to themselves, but they do not yet grasp how power and prejudice work in society.

The child begins to formulate rules during the first three years of life.[16] A toddler who pulls all the cooking pots out of the cupboard may provoke his mother's irritation. His earliest reaction—if it could be put into words—might go something like this: "This very important person on whom I depend so much is angry at me." This perception will soon be modified into, "This important person is angry at me because I am playing with these pots," and then into, "Every time I play with these cooking pots my mother is angry with me." In time this will be formulated into a rudimentary rule: "Don't play with cooking pots in Mother's kitchen." Even at three this rule is still some way from being recast into "Don't play with cooking pots in any kitchen" or, more subtly, "People are apt to be touchy if you fool with their tools."

The toddler's experience with his mother and her cooking pots suggests that learning always takes place in a social context. The most obvious aspect of the toddler's experience is the way he experiments with the physical properties of the pots—which ones fit inside others, what sounds wooden spoons or metal knives make against the pots. Yet what the child learns about the properties of objects occurs in exactly the same context that teaches him about important people's attitudes, and the two kinds of learning color each other.

THE CHILD OF THREE TO SIX

Children of four, like Julie, can express in play virtually all that they have taken in of experience, even what may be taboo. Their play reflects their existing life world at the same time that they selectively modify it, emphasizing some features and ignoring others. They are both exact (each of Julie's animals must have its own bed) and flexible (tissues can be beds and one can have dinner outside the house). Jerry can be the child of two bears, or he can be a father, or even a grandmother.

What is the difference between the map Julie and Jerry are making of their world and the images of the younger child or the map of the older child? For a child of four, landmarks have become part of a whole as they have not for the younger child. A four-year-old's more complete sense of a life world bounded by home and family is revealed in play: he can create a house, a store, an airport, or a garage. But the four-year-old's map is still far from being like an adult's; his concept of reality has not yet taken on fixed boundaries. He has the symbolic landmarks, but he has not reached the point where he believes that they must be where they are or that only certain paths may be taken. In a four-year-old's mental map, landmarks can change their relationship to each other: a father or a mother can sometimes command the entirety of his map, and a once-close relative can recede in importance as he moves away. In many ways the child of four is as free as a creative artist in his experimentation with symbols.

The four-year-old can reconstruct a social role more extensively than he could at a younger age, when he would have played a fragment of a role without regard for sequence or social context. Thus Julie at the age of four plays house, whereas at the age two she might have pretended simply to cook or to put a doll to bed. At four a child can play parent or child, fireman or victim, father or mother, doctor or patient. However, the four-year-old tends to view roles as mutually exclusive; it is hard for him to understand that one can be a fireman and a father, or a mother and a teacher, at the same time. At four a white child will not see any incongruity if a black child plays the father and white children play the other members of the family. The rules that govern social roles and indeed the roles themselves are not definitively set. (By contrast, the seven- or eight-year-old's play is likely to represent social rules as more rigid than in fact, they are.)

The four-year-old, like most children, sees adult roles primarily in terms of power—specifically, the power of those he knows personally to comfort or control him, the power he senses as potentially helpful or pleasurable to him in those he does not know, or the power of certain fantasy figures to transcend the constraints of the everyday world. He may imitate the role of the parent who cares for him, or the doctor who is a source of comfort or pain. He may play at being a fireman, policeman, or possibly a car mechanic or truck driver—people who are actually or potentially helpful in his family's life or who exert visible control or influence over other people or powerful equipment. Or he may take the role of a fictional figure—Super Woman or Batman. There is considerable continuity between his play at four and his play when he was two, but now the figures whose roles he plays have more attributes than they did earlier, and the boundaries of their power are more clearly defined.

By two the child has evolved a rudimentary self-concept based on a sense of what is pleasurable versus what is painful—what he must do and not do to stay comfortable and assure the beneficence of those who care for him. By four this self-concept has grown more elaborate, and the child begins to identify with certain people who are important to him. He elaborates a sense of identification by playing their roles. Little girls grapple with being a "girl like Mommy," sorting out how much of Daddy they can or cannot have. Boys do the same in reverse, playing their role as father. Both persist for a while in wanting to marry their mother or father but eventually give up. A critical experience for a child of this age is learning that those he loves have other loves their own size, and that one can be loved within a circle of intimates without possessing anyone exclusively.

In recent years there are fewer incidental social and physical characteristics that a four-year-old can use in sorting out his roles as a member of one sex. Today children of both sexes can expect to play many more roles than they could in earlier generations, but there is disagreement about the costs and benefits of this role diffusion. Lack of perceptible clues to role definition may make it harder for a child to define roles for himself and therefore acquire a firm sense of himself. It may also be that too great a confusion about roles in childhood can lead to a choice later on of very narrow roles whose rules are rigidly defined, such as the role of a member of a religious or political group that offers definitive answers to life's questions and prescribes a set of precise rituals and norms. However, it may also be that role diffusion allows children to identify with a wide variety of people through their varied role play.[17] They may take in a greater range of their fellow man's activities and feelings than children of earlier generations and thus be capable of extending greater care and concern to more people later on.

The four-year-old's awareness of rules, like his awareness of roles, is more elaborate and more refined than that of a child under three, but rules have not yet attained the degree of abstraction that they have for the older child. Julie is working on a rule about the treatment of honored visitors: her grandmother merits a pitcher, napkins, and her father's full attention. In time this may be generalized into a rule that applies to all visitors, perhaps with certain variations and exceptions; but right now her actions are still part of a rule about her grandmother. Nor does Julie yet know whether all of the details of doing her grandmother honor are essential and, if not, which are and which are not.

Whereas a two-year-old has taken in enough elements of his culture so that an informed observer can identify him as French, Japanese, or American, a four-year-old has taken in much more of his culture. He can dramatize it in his play, although he still feels no constraints about testing its boundaries—about playing with it. The four-year-old's picture of the world is like an artist's preliminary sketch for a painting: the whole thing is there in bold strokes, but he can still experiment and rework the parts. This freedom means that the child does not yet feel compelled to say that the emperor is wearing clothes if the emperor is naked. The rules of social convention, including the social lies that are often embodied in them, do not yet bind him rigidly, even though they do not escape his notice. Suppose, for instance, that his family always picnics in a state park on summer Sundays. If the four-year-old does not think the picnic is as much fun as family myth makes it out to be (too many bugs, no place to swim, a hot drive during which he has to be quiet), he will have no compunctions about saying that he hates picnics and doesn't want to go.

THE CHILD OVER SIX

The seven-, eight-, or nine-year-old is moving into a world bigger than his home, and most societies recognize his capacity to do so either by beginning formal schooling at about this age or by introducing him to work roles and training him in cultural and religious rituals. In our culture, with its extended childhood, the child over six lives in what one might call an "intermediate world"[18]—not yet the world of work but a world beyond the family circle. Life in the intermediate world has much of the form of adult life, although the content is appropriate to a child's experiences, capacities, and fantasies.

The six- to nine-year-old can live in this intermediate world not only because he is sufficiently developed physically to tolerate a full day at school but because his mental and social development has progressed to the point where he can venture beyond the home on his own. His sense of maps, rules, and roles is sufficiently complete to be a reliable guide when he is out on his own. He can tell time and get home from playing with a friend in time for dinner. He can find his way to and from the store or the house of a playmate. He is aware of the differences between friends, enemies, and strangers, and he can be tentatively relied on to discriminate among them as he goes about in his neighborhood.

During this period the child begins to identify with people outside his family—a favorite teacher, a sports figure, or a popular television personality. This is a more difficult process for girls than it is for boys. Although a girl may identify with an actress, athlete, or other woman in the public eye, she may hear many more mixed or critical comments from parents, siblings, and peers about her choice than a boy would. Despite many changes in attitudes in the last decade, our society is still ambivalent about the roles women play outside the home. Responding to this ambivalence, many girls are less likely to identify with figures outside their circle.

Not only are the landmarks of the seven-year-old's map in place, but the topography is more fixed and bounded and, unlike the four-year-old, he is not so inclined to test its limits. He has absorbed not only the rules that govern roles in the society, but the social lies they may entail. Unlike the four-year-old, he will agree to state in public that the naked emperor is indeed wearing clothes if that is what others are convinced must be said or believed. He feels far greater compunction to subscribe to the tastes and prejudices of his family—even to say, "We love going on picnics," although he may still complain about mosquitoes and ask if the family couldn't go to the beach instead. Adults are often pleased because the seven- or eight-year-old "goes along with" the conventionally accepted view of who people are, what they do, and the authority they exercise. He is often a pleasant companion for an adult, well controlled and, especially with strangers, a self-contained, assured person interested in assimilating a variety of experiences and in solving other people's problems according to his rules of life. An adult may not have known such compliance since the time the child became a toddler and may not know it again until after adolescence.

In his play, the seven- or eight-year-old is absorbed in recreating the way things really are. If he were to play house like Julie, he would wish to serve breakfast and not dinner after rising, and to set it up inside the house; if he had to serve it outside he would be likely to call it a picnic. No longer can a boy play a girl's part in a game or a girl a boy's. At this age the child would find it difficult to cast a black child as the father in a white family, although he might not confront the issue head-on, saying something like, "He's not tall enough to be a father," employing a social convention that directs attention away from dangerous topics.

For girls, this is the age of the doll house in which the life of the dolls may be a detailed, almost novelistic re-creation of their own family life, even if intentionally staged in the past or the future. For boys, this concern with detailed re-creation shows up in play with cowboys and Indians or G.I. Joe and super hero figures, for whom they may devise forts, battlefields, or rocket ships. Games, especially those with elaborate rules, appeal for similar reasons. The toy industry has capitalized on the preoccupation of this age group with authentic detail and rules by marketing elaborate stage sets and equipment for the dolls it has promoted, many of which are the toy counterparts of television figures, and by elaborately decorating and diagramming table games and other toys.

The separation of the specialized modern family from work and the nature of work in contemporary society mean that even school-age children rarely have any first-hand acquaintance with their parents' work experience. For instance, the only residue a salesman may have left at home may be papers, a few samples, and ballpoint pens. His children may never have seen him on the job or met his boss. They may come closest to experiencing his work when they listen to his phone calls. If they play "work" they may simply imitate these phone conversations, including the tones of confidence, reassurance, or frustration they have heard in their father's voice.

The six- to nine-year-old's most characteristic preoccupation is the rules of life. His understanding of the rules governing a grandmother's visit are far more detailed than a four-year-old's. He might even have a sense of categories of visitors: those who merit napkins and pitchers, those who drop in and are only offered a cup of coffee, and those who are not invited at all. He may seem rigid or fussy in his perception of rules; for example, he may insist that his mother wear a certain dress to a school function. He will select the dress because he considers it the most appropriate one, whereas a four-year-old may choose one he deems most beautiful, with no concern for its suitability.

The six- to nine-year-old's cognitive development has progressed sufficiently so that in concrete terms, at least, he understands the concept of *invariance,* which is one of the bases for social rules. But there is another reason for his rather strict adherence to rules: they help him feel safe and confident in the intermediate world beyond the home. He is still tentative, and following the rules can help guarantee his physical and emotional safety.

As he steps out into the wider world, the six- to nine-year-old is apt to reveal his individuality in his style of living and learning. Many children of this age pursue interests tenaciously. By becoming experts on whales or baseball or coins, they gain mental control of a sort over one aspect of reality. Other children sample a variety of interests. Similarly, some children have one or two close friends to whom they are devoted over a period of years, while others have friendships that shift and change. Temperament as well as significant relationships and life experience establish individual patterns of mapping and rule making in both intellectual and social areas.

In general, however, children of this age try to learn to handle the world bit by bit. Many of the play activities, hobbies, and clubs they enjoy provide a transition to a wider social world made safe through membership regulations, shared private knowledge, and rules. Who's in and who's out are tightly defined; members may have special passwords or secret codes; they may have a place they always meet and things they always do. Card games and board games are also popular at this age; each offers a small, manageable world defined by rules which the eight-year-old insists on enforcing. (The four-year-old, by contrast, is likely to play cards with an interpretation of rules that is often—to say the least—highly personal.)

In the course of mapping the world beyond the home, eight-year-olds try for bold paths, clear boundaries, immutable rules, learning more and more to see what others claim to see, accepting their semantics and their politics. If they learn to accept sham and bear witness to a well-dressed emperor—who they once insisted wore no clothes—they have not so much learned to put on an act as they have trained themselves not to take notice of what was obvious a few years before. Children who do not or cannot accept the conventions of society are liable to suffer as they try to make their way in the world. But for all their vulnerability, they may, if they have the strength to maintain their vision of things as they are, grow up to be the artists or the movers and shakers of their society.

Chapter Two
A Family Picnic

> *The capacity to see and feel what is there gives way to the tendency to see and feel what one expects to see and feel, which, in turn, is what one is expected to see and feel because everyone else does.*
>
> —Ernest G. Schachtel, *Metamorphosis*

To synthesize the points made in the last chapter about the child's construction of a world, and to set the stage for the next two chapters, we present the story of two families at a picnic.

THE POLSKYS AND THE MURPHYS: A SUNDAY PICNIC

"What shall we serve?" asked Jane Polsky. "I mean tomorrow, when the Murphys come."

It was Saturday morning, and Jane and Steve Polsky were in the kitchen eating breakfast with their two older children, Sarah, eleven, and Dave, nine. Toby, three and a half, had eaten breakfast earlier and sat in the living room watching television.

"Potato salad, hamburgers, a salad, the usual," said Steve Polsky. He was looking out across his own small backyard and into his neighbor's.

"But I'm not sure Bob Murphy can handle a fork," Jane Polsky said. "Remember, I've never met him."

"Why can't he handle a fork?" asked Dave, immediately interested.

"He has something called cerebral palsy," his mother replied.

"What's that?" Dave asked.

"It's a condition that makes you shake," Sarah said. "Don't you remember? Mom told us he had it."

"How did he catch it?" asked Dave.

"Will we catch it?" asked Sarah.

"It's not something you catch," said Jane Polsky. "Some people develop it when they're born and some people get it as a result of an accident."

The children wanted to know which was the case with Mr. Murphy. Their mother told them she didn't know. After all, it was Mrs. Murphy she knew, and they had only recently become acquainted at the church fair.

"Why did you invite them if you don't know them that well?" asked Dave, who was not looking forward to the picnic.

As he listened to his son's questions, Steve Polsky recalled what his wife had told him about the Murphys. Bob had recently been transferred from Houston where he had worked for Delta Oil. Here in town he was assistant manager of a small Delta subsidiary, Newcom Plastics.

"The Murphys are new in our community," said Jane Polsky. "It's nice to be neighborly."

"But they're not our neighbors," said Sarah. "They don't live on our street and their kids don't even go to our school."

"They don't even have kids our age," said Dave. "I don't want to play all afternoon with a kid Toby's age."

"Just this once," his mother said. "We don't ask you to do this kind of thing very often."

"Go get dressed," said Steve, "both of you, Sarah and Dave."

Sarah stood up. "You still haven't decided what we're going to eat when the Murphys come," she said.

"I think I'll make fried chicken," her mother said. "You can eat fried chicken with your fingers. And I'll make a big plate of raw vegetables with a dip."

"You mean we're not going to have potato salad just because these people are coming?" Dave asked.

His mother promised to make some potato salad, even if it did require a fork, if Dave would peel the potatoes.

The two older children left the kitchen to get dressed.

"Have you said anything to Toby about Bob Murphy?" asked Steve.

"Not yet," said his wife. "What do you think I should say?"

"Something so that he doesn't embarrass everybody."

After Toby's TV programs were over, Jane Polsky called him into the kitchen and told him that the following day they would have a visitor whose hands shook when he tried to do things. An accident might have made him that way. And he had a wobbly walk. She cautioned Toby not to say anything about the way Mr. Murphy moved. It would not be kind or polite, she said.

Toby promised not to say anything.

Everything went smoothly when the Murphys arrived. Bob Murphy walked with half-crutches, but he removed his hand from one in order to greet the Polskys. The children noticed his hand trembled.

Jane Polsky greeted the Murphy children, four-year-old Sean and baby Alison, one year old.

"Dave, Toby, Sarah, this is Sean and this is Alison," Jane Polsky said.

Dave said a grudging "Hi." Sarah, who liked babies, went up and held out her finger for Alison. Toby said nothing. He was busy watching Bob Murphy.

"Come round in back," said Steve. "We're all set up there."

His voice was perhaps a little loud, overloaded with welcome. He had not thought about Bob Murphy's disability ahead of time, but now he was concerned that it might be uncomfortably far for Bob to walk around the house to the back yard. But Bob managed well as both families walked to the back where Steve and Jane had set out chairs. Jane brought out glasses, potato chips, crackers, and a cooler of soft drinks and beer.

"Where would you like to sit?" Steve asked Bob Murphy, thinking that Bob might need help when he sat down.

"Any place," said Bob. With surprisingly deft movements he put first one crutch and then the other aside and half sat, half collapsed into a chair.

(Neither Steve nor Jane was aware of the way they involuntarily leaned a little forward, extending their arms ever so slightly while Bob Murphy was sitting down. Nor was Steve aware of the extra heartiness in his voice when he offered Bob and Alice something to drink and told the children to choose their own soft drinks.)

Drinks in hand, the adults began to talk about the church fair where the two women had first met. The Murphys asked about various people who had organized the fair. Conversation branched out.

"You know we're using a lot more of Newcom's plastic tubing; I never thought I'd see the day," Steve said to Bob. Steve worked as a plumber for a contractor in town. "Only ten years back no one would have touched it."

"Yes," said Bob. "That tubing has really taken off. Sales have quadrupled in the last two years."

Bob began to tell Steve about some of Newcom's other products. Eventually Steve asked how come Newcom had decided to locate in town; it seemed to him that the plant was fairly new.

"I'm not sure," Bob answered. "But I understand it was your former mayor who persuaded the chairman of Delta—an old buddy from World War II—to build the plant here."

"Ted Vernon?"

"Yeah, I guess that was his name."

"Yes, I've heard he was the one to bring in Delta. But I'd bet it's a guy called Davies who's responsible for the deal. He's behind a lot of things in this town. He's done more for this town that any ten men. He's president of the First National Bank, but that doesn't tell you the whole story."

Before he knew it, Steve was telling Bob about personalities and politics in town, who was who, what they did, and what influence they had. Jane and Alice joined in.

At one point Steve lit a cigarette.

"Could I have one of those?" Bob Murphy asked.

Steve offered him the pack and, noticing the difficulty with which his fingers took out a cigarette, offered to light it for him.

"I've got it," Bob said.

There was a pause in the conversation as he took out a match. As he struck the match his hand trembled just a little more than usual, and the lighted match fell on his trousers. He quickly brushed it off, but it left a small scorched spot.

"Are you all right?" Jane Polsky asked.

"Sure," said Bob Murphy. "You get used to this sort of thing."

On the second try he lit the cigarette successfully and the conversation resumed.

While they talked, the children lingered and listened, drinking their soft drinks. Alice Murphy set Alison down on the grass where she crawled a few feet away from her mother's chair, returned and pulled herself up while holding onto the chair.

Dave began to kick his mother's chair. She told him to stop.

"I'm bored," he said. "When are we going to eat?"

"Not yet," said Jane Polsky in a low voice. "Why don't you and Toby take Sean and show him your toys?"

He looked at her reluctantly.

"Go on," his father said. "Show Sean some of your toys."

"Okay," said Dave, standing up. He looked at Sean, who got up. Toby, eager not to miss out, stood up, too. The three boys started into the house with Dave in the lead.

"Could I take Alison in?" Sarah asked Alice Murphy.

"If she'll go with you," said Alice. "She's shy these days."

"Sarah is good with babies," Jane said. "I'm sure it will be all right."

Sarah picked up Alison, and together they started into the house. Looking back over Sarah's shoulder Alison kept her eye on her mother. The women watched them and the men went on with their conversation.

A few seconds later they were interrupted by the sound of Alison crying.

Sarah returned and gave Alison to Alice. After a few disgruntled sobs the baby was soon smiling.

"Maybe she'd like a graham cracker," Jane said, half as a question to Alice and half as a suggestion to Sarah to fetch one.

"I'll get her one," said Sarah.

When Sarah returned, Alison took the cracker from her and smiled at her after the first few bites.

The sight of the baby eating the graham cracker prompted Steve Polsky to say, "Hey, what about some food for the rest of us?"

Alice Murphy helped Jane carry lunch from the kitchen, and Steve called the boys out of the house.

"Help yourselves, everyone," Jane said, and then thought of Bob Murphy.

"Can I get you a plate?" she asked.

"I think Alice is fixing mine," he said.

Both families felt more at ease with each other by the time they were through lunch. Jane felt herself relax. She served iced tea after everyone had finished eating. The adults sipped their tea slowly.

"Let's go back and play with your fort," said Sean to Dave. Sean had been very impressed with the boy's fort and soldiers.

Toby stood up at once. His brother did not often allow him a chance to play in the fort.

"Okay," said Dave. With that as a clue, Sarah decided to try her luck, too, and went with them.

Indoors, in the room Dave and Toby shared, the three boys arranged the plastic soldiers for a battle.

Dave put Sean in charge of the attacking soldiers while he himself was in charge of the defense.

"What can I be?" Toby asked.

"You can make this man sneak into the fort. He's a spy and he goes back and tells the general all about what the fort looks like inside." Sarah was told to stand at the back gate and guard it.

Toby was not too clear about what spies did, but he began to move one plastic soldier toward the fort.

"See, he sneaks in this door while the guards are asleep," said Dave. "Hey, why are you making him walk that funny way?" (Toby was making the plastic soldier jiggle as he moved him.)

"He's like Sean's father. He's drunk."

"My father's not drunk," said Sean.

"Then why does he wobble?" asked Toby.

"He was sick," said Dave. "Mom told me. Didn't she tell you?"

"My dad had an accident in his car a long time ago," said Sean. "His brain got hurt. You're mean to say he's drunk." He stood up, kicked over the soldiers he had arranged for the attack, and headed for the door.

"Come on," said Dave. "Toby will say he's sorry and we can play some more. Say you're sorry, Toby."

After a long pause Toby said he was sorry, feeling six cold eyes piercing him and fearing worse if Sean left and told the adults what had happened.

The boys went back to their game, but when they were going downstairs Toby walked in a strange way, tripped, and finally fell down.

After the Murphys had gone home, Dave said to his parents, "Toby said Mr. Murphy was drunk. In front of Sean. He was mean."

"Toby," his mother said. "I thought I told you not to say anything about Mr. Murphy."

"I didn't say anything—Dave asked me about the spy. Besides you told me that man on the street was drunk—the day we went to the dentist."

Later that evening Sarah revealed she had her own confusions about Bob Murphy. As her mother went to turn off the lights in the kitchen, Sarah asked, "Are the Murphy's kids adopted?"

"Not as far as I know," her mother said. "Why do you ask?"

"I mean can they make their own babies with Mr. Murphy that way?"

* * * *

Participating in the picnic, the Polsky and Murphy children—each according to his stage of development—take in from the detail of the experience messages that add to or reinforce their maps of the social world. Although the picnic is an occasion that brings one family to the home of another and at first glance seems a very personal, private occasion, the way the families greet each other, their selection of neutral topics for conversation, their exchange of information about local economic, political, and social issues, and their handling of Bob Murphy's handicap reflect the conventions and style of American culture.

In the course of the conversation with her children about Bob Murphy's disability and about the need to be neighborly, Jane Polsky plays the role of arbiter and instructor in social relations to her children. Dave does not like the idea of visitors he does not know—especially if they have no children his own age. In negotiating with him, his mother gently asserts a social norm and softens its bite: "We don't ask you to do this kind of thing very often."

Her acquiescence, when prodded, to Dave's demand for potato salad suggests something about the politics of family life among the Polskys, but it also suggests something about the way Jane maps her world. Children and, therefore, their wishes and tastes are important to her. She will defer to them and accommodate even if it is inconvenient. She will ask something in return (peeling potatoes), but not a lot. She also demonstrates that she perceives it as a mother's role to ease the children's disappointments. Steve does not accommodate or negotiate: "Go get dressed," he says, "both of you, Sarah and Dave."

Dave, Sarah, and Toby, witnessing and participating in the conversation, take in these messages about their world and its culture. They can expect their mother—and therefore, to a certain extent, other women—to be instructor-arbiters, especially in the social sphere. Sarah may feel obligated to play such a role, and Dave may choose *not* to play it. (Sarah, as an adult, might experience a certain amount of anxiety if she eschewed this role, at least the accommodating aspect of it.) In response to their mother, the children also gain a sense of confidence in their own roles as questioners and plaintiffs.

The mother's role and the children's roles are to some degree reciprocal. If mothers have enough energy and equanimity to answer questions and arbitrate problems, children can ask questions and pose problems. In another social milieu the children's perception of their mother's availability or of her capacity to play this role might be very different. Even in the Polsky family it might be different at another time and in other circumstances.

If the child expects a role as a questioner and plaintiff, this implies that he expects a role in decisions—and a role in decisions entails recognition as an individual. In effect, on the basis of their experience with their mother the Polsky children can expect that they will have an opportunity, perhaps even an obligation, to contribute to decisions through the profoundly American procedure of consensus taking.

Steve recognizes his wife's role as instructor and social arbiter when he asks if she has spoken to Toby, and she accepts the role he casts her in. When she talks to Toby, she takes his development into account, recognizing that an explanation is not enough to guarantee regard for social convention in a three-and-a-half-year-old. She adds a prohibition: "Don't say anything about Mr. Murphy's disability."

When the Murphys arrive Jane handles the introductions, a natural step for her since she is the one who has befriended Alice Murphy, but also very much in line with her mental map for meeting and greeting, her role as social arbiter and hostess. She also takes the initiative in prodding Dave to assume the role of host and show Sean Murphy his toys, and Steve backs her up in this.[1]

When Sarah tries to amuse baby Alison, her mother says: "Sarah is good with babies." Jane takes it as part of her role as a mother—though she may not think of it as such—to encourage her daughter in a mothering role. (It is the women, not the men, who watch the children go into the house. The readiness of Jane's nurturant responses, so explicit in relation to her daughter, has already been suggested earlier, when she was quick to ask Bob if he was all right after he had dropped the match on his trousers.)

Steve Polsky understands his role as that of final authority (and his sons might experience a certain amount of anxiety if they eschewed this role as adults). He is ready to make the decision about what to serve; "the usual," he says—the family's ways should prevail. His wife may instruct, arbitrate, and negotiate, but his is the last word: "Go get dressed" or "Show Sean your toys." Yet his (unconscious) mapping of his role in family life should not be construed as insensitivity. Faced with a specific person, he is concerned about Bob Murphy's ability to walk round to the back of the house and is quick to offer him help with a chair or cigarette.

Much of Steve's reality is defined by the world of work. He feels comfortable talking with Bob Murphy about their jobs—discussion about work is the easiest way for strangers, particularly men, to get acquainted. Moreover, talk about work is an easy springboard to other topics, such as town politics and issues of wealth, status, and influence.

We can do no more than touch here on some of the factors associated with getting acquainted in America.[2] The mobility of Americans demands a quickly engaged, casual sociability of the sort that allows the Murphys and Polskys to get together for a picnic. The Polsky children learn from their parents' approach to sociability certain rules helpful in building ties in a highly mobile country where ties are often broken: be neighborly; a good way to get acquainted is to discuss work; don't reveal what makes you different all at once; look for formats, such as a church fair, which will give you a path to a sense of community.

Although it was not spelled out in our story, Jane's and Alice's contribution to the discussion might have as much to do with the activities and interests of Mr. Davies' and Ted Vernon's wives and children as with their work and political influence. This division of subject matter by sex is far from hard and fast, but in general Steve would tend to be less well informed than Jane about the families of the men he spoke about or, if he were well informed, choose not to talk about them (they occupy less significance in his map of the life of the town). Jane might be less well informed about aspects of the men's working lives or, if she were well informed, less inclined to give emphasis to their public roles. Overall, Steve would be inclined to think a certain family could be discussed in terms of the public role of the man who heads it, whereas Jane would require far more detail about the nature of its members and the structure of their private life together.

Children, listening to such a discussion, even if they do not understand or care much about it, pick up not only the generally economic and political emphases of the men's conversation, but the fact that this concern is an appropriate, even essential, part of talking like a man. Bit by bit, as they listen over the years, they are prepared (especially if they are boys, but increasingly if they are girls) to find it entirely appropriate to ask and to answer the quintessential American question: What do you do? They also become prepared—especially if they are girls—for another sort of discussion that might be put thus: "What do you care about and for whom do you care?"[3] But the chances are that in most families the latter question is made to seem secondary to "What do you do?" A child might pick up this subordinate quality from the fact that it is his mother, not his father, who discusses matters of care and caring—and in a tone that is less assertive, less emphatic, and less authoritative than his father uses. However, this norm is changing.

Familiar rituals such as a picnic make social life comfortable for new acquaintances. They also instruct the young who see certain social patterns in operation, in this case meeting and entertaining equals. Expressed in the behavior of the Murphy and Polsky parents during the ritual of the picnic are assertions about rules and roles appropriate to everyday life as well as to special occasions or special people in our society.[4]

The Polsky children's first clue that the picnic will be somewhat special comes early: Jane asks, "What shall we serve?" as she thinks about the coming picnic. In using the pronoun "we" rather than "I" she signals some departure from the usual. Ordinarily, she would use "I" to assert her power as cook and to make a cook's decisions. There are solemn explanations and warnings not to embarrass the guest—or shame the family—by taking an obvious interest in Bob Murphy's disability. Later the children hear their father welcome Bob in louder and more jovial tones than he usually welcomes a visitor. Some of this may have to do with the anxiety of meeting strangers for the first time, but some of it has to do with the anxiety of greeting a guest with a disability. Jane and Steve are a bit less sure of each other's lines, a little more forthcoming and jovial than usual in order to assure Bob (and themselves) that they are not put off by his handicap. Such changes in manner are notable to a child.

The messages that their parents convey to Dave, Sarah, and Toby about Bob are complex: they have to do with concern, anxiety, and stigma. In contrast, the Murphys prepare their children to understand the reactions of others toward their father.

A physical handicap is like a caste mark in the way it operates socially.[5] "We care about making this man feel at ease and we fear his disability will cause him to hurt himself," the Polskys' words and behavior suggest, "but we are threatened by him, too. His handicap threatens our sense of invulnerability." Concern and even anxiety for Bob's safety are socially acceptable feelings; anxiety over the taint or "contagiousness" of a handicap is not, and the emotion is likely to be veiled in socially mendacious behavior, the pretense that they have sufficient composure to be unaffected by Bob's disability. As suggested earlier, the child of six and over is willing to subscribe to a social lie, while the younger child barely tries. Toby, without his mother's preparation and prohibition, might have been curious at the sight of Bob's crutches or asked him if he had too much to drink. As it is, Toby recalls that Bob's behavior is like that of an intoxicated person he asked about a few weeks earlier—the similarity of movement catches his attention more than anything his mother has said. He does not, in fact, do anything his mother told him not to do, does not say anything about Bob until attacked by his brother, but he feels no compunctions about making a plastic soldier move like a drunk (after all, his mother didn't prohibit *that*). He is at the age where it is natural to try out and test the nature and limits of reality. And he learns that violating his mother's warning is serious—his brother and sister are ashamed of him.

Whatever their age, children take in not only the social lie, but the reality of their parents' reaction as expressed in gesture, tone, and glance, as well as words.[6] The older ones may wonder what more their parents know but will not tell. Sarah, not far from adolescence, has questions about Bob that go beyond anything her parents have said. She wants to know if his disability prevents sexual performance or fertility. She may be quite sensitive to the strain in her parents' voices when they discuss sexual matters with her, and she may assume a link when she hears a similar strain in their voices as they anticipate the visit.

The Polsky children's experience of the Murphy visit is shaped not only by temperament and development but by the spoken and unspoken messages they receive from their parents—messages that are influenced by their parents' temperaments and histories, and by the conventions and beliefs of their culture. The Murphy children, on the other hand, may be especially aware of what the visiting rituals represent because, with Bob as their father, they are part of an "out" group, a position that affords them—in addition to occasional inconvenience—a chance to learn how sure people are of themselves and each other, and on what grounds people accept or reject each other.

Chapter Three
The Intimate World of Family

> *If you haven't been happy very young, you can still be happy later on, but it's much harder. You need more luck, you have fewer resources within yourself and fewer possibilities of enjoying the world.*
>
> —Simone deBeauvoir "A Talk with Simone deBeauvoir"

In making sense of their own experience, children draw upon the patterns of predictability, protection, expression of feeling, and social relationships that characterize their family world. These patterns are set not only by the intimate relationships of parents and kin but by the place of the family in the public world and the experience of parents in that world.

In this chapter we consider first the intimate world of family and its particular, intense, and very private relationships. In the following chapter we look more closely at the public roles of parents, especially at their work. Our purpose in both chapters is the same: to spell out some of the structures of everyday life from which children construct not only an inner emotional life rooted in private relationships, but a map of social reality. Implicitly we suggest the limits—psychological, social, and economic—on the power of parents to make choices about what their children will learn of American life or to have a voice in public decisions that affect them.

In contemporary American society the partnership of a man and a woman that is the basis of a family implies sexual attraction, as well as an affinity of personality, interests, vision, lifestyle, and sometimes background. The meeting and merging of mind and self as well as body, referred to as romantic love, is the ideal underlying the modern companionate marriage. It is different from the partnership of earlier times when, despite whatever attraction and affinity existed, the prime purposes in marriage were meeting the economic necessities of the household, transmitting and maintaining property, and perpetuating a name. The couples depicted in this book married because they loved each other and wished to rear children together, not because either of them had a farm that needed an extra hand or because the man felt an obligation to father an heir to the family name.

The family is an intimate construction, not only because of the intimacy of the relationship, but also because when a man and a woman marry they reconstruct their social maps of the world to include each other, their experiences together, and everything the other means in terms of tastes, interests, prejudices, and personality.[1] In a modern marriage each partner is likely to be the most significant landmark on the other's map, or at least on the part of his map marked "private life"; and the private sphere for most people is one in which they count on feeling most themselves, on having the sharpest sense of identity. (In times past a spouse may not have been such a significant landmark, especially for a man; the community may have been a more important part of his social topography.)[2]

At the same time that partners redraw their maps to include each other, they must work out their roles in relation to each other and the world. In doing so, they are influenced not only by their experiences together, their perception of each other, and by the messages current in the society about what marriage should be, but by what they have seen and known of partnering in their parents' lives. Many marriages founder because partners cannot blend their discrepant early representations of adult roles and rules or their constructions of the everyday life of a marriage. Suppose a man from a low-income family who is making a good living marries a rich woman who has inherited her wealth. They must construct a joint reality that shares a perception of financial constraint and leeway. The wife will not necessarily be a big spender, nor the husband a pinchpenny. Perhaps she scrimps in small ways—uses every leftover, saves string, is restrained in her style of entertaining. Perhaps her husband likes to be a lavish host—feasts were rare when he was growing up and much looked forward to. He may hate leftovers, having eaten too many in his time. On the other hand, he may insist on carrying a large life insurance policy, which his wife thinks is unnecessary, given her assets, and have savings accounts in several banks, unable to put out of his head the memory of his father talking about banks failing in the Depression. Their effort to construct a joint reality may be complicated by her feelings about work. Perhaps she doesn't want to work, feeling that her unearned income is ample contribution to their household. Yet her husband may insist that at the very least she qualify herself for employment in case "the bottom drops out." Or she may want to work, finding home life not sufficiently fulfilling, and he may oppose her wish, determined to be the family's sole breadwinner.

A further, and perhaps even more critical, social reconstruction of reality takes place when the couple has a child. Sometimes this reconstruction is delayed until the birth of a second child when it must almost inevitably occur. (While there is still only one child in a family, it is possible for a couple to think of themselves as a couple accompanied by a child. When a second child is born, it is almost impossible for them not to think of themselves as a family.) But the birth of a child does more than force the redrawing of a person's cognitive representations of a social world and its possibilities. It awakens perhaps unexamined or until now unremembered elements of personal history which have a place in maps the individual parents began to assemble when *they* were children.

Just as a husband and wife draw on what they have seen and known of partnering in their parents' lives to forge their own scheme of marriage, so, as parents, they draw on their own personal histories in deciding how to raise their children and how to live as a family. They are not apt to reflect on this process or view it critically; rather they are more likely to gradually build a scheme based on pragmatic, piecemeal answers to questions like: How much should a baby be held and cuddled? How strongly should independence be fostered? Must a child finish everything on his plate? Is it right to slap a child? Should a child be allowed to talk back to his parents? When should a child be told about God or learn to pray? Should there be a special family dinner every Sunday? Should it be in the couple's house or should it be at one of their parents' house? When should children help with chores? Sometimes answers are sought within the current practices of their friends and neighbors or in magazines and books; but many times they derive from parents' childhood experiences, which are coded in gesture, habit, and remembered maxim or anecdote—a submerged, unexamined mass of beliefs and practices about human relationships, the nature of child rearing, and the choreography of family life.[3]

Deeply rooted conceptions of family life are among the hardest issues for a couple to examine or negotiate, first, because it is extremely difficult to see them for what they are and, second, because a strong emotional charge informs them. Bitter divorces between once deeply attached couples testify to the often unfocused rage that attends an unsuccessful effort to reconstruct a romantic partnership to include children and to accommodate each partner's assumptions about the nature of intimacy, childhood, and family. One of the difficulties of constructing an effective scheme of marriage or of family life is that in American society it is common for people of very different backgrounds to meet and marry, especially since the social changes that preceded World War II and that were accelerated by it. Differences in family background may flow from the personalities of family members or from ethnic affiliation, religion, income, class, or social status. Diversity of background often contributes to mutual attraction between two people and adds richness and vitality to family life in America, but it poses special problems for parents attempting to map a coherent and satisfying child-rearing style.

STRESSES ON THE PRIVATE WORLD OF THE FAMILY

The new social freedoms Americans enjoy have had several effects on how much nurture and intimacy the family can provide children. Parents may feel constrained and restricted by young children, held back by the demands of care from the development of their own potential. The fact that child rearing and the development of individual potential are often experienced as being in opposition is itself a sign of the changed times we live in. The freedom with few strings attached that many single adults and, to a lesser extent, couples without children enjoy can cause parents to feel they are caught in bondage, isolation, and stress, especially when their children are little.

At the same time, parents often look to each other and to their family as the only reliable sources of warmth and dependability, a fortress against a sense of isolation and uncertainty in the world beyond the home. In preindustrial times, Americans were much more able to blame their misfortunes on forces beyond their control—natural disasters, incurable diseases, the will of God—and thus were able to avoid a sense of crushing responsibility for their failures. Such rationales are not easy to adopt today. We Americans have been conditioned by immense technological and scientific advances to believe in the power of society to solve its problems through rational means and our own power as individuals to determine the course of our lives. While society will give us credit for our successes, we feel the brunt of blame for our failures. The father who cannot find a job to support his family feels his unemployment more as a mark of personal inadequacy than the work of changes in the economy beyond his control.

Parents in favorable circumstances may feel more personally empowered than if they were members of a society that believed talents or positions of influence are a gift from God. They may also feel more in command because they—or their society—have more control over nature than their forebears did. But most parents daily experience the unassailable power of others and of political and economic forces. They have little recourse when it is decided, for example, to mechanize agriculture and reduce farm jobs, to wipe out whole departments of skilled workers, to relocate or sell a plant, to close out a department, to make a craft obsolete overnight by having the work done more cheaply in another country, to deduct taxes or dues from pay envelopes, to run a road through a residential district, or to require a credential or a license for work that previously did not require one.

When bruised by the forces of God and nature, a person can complain but ultimately loses the struggle without losing face; but to lose a battle with a human force, or to resign oneself to the dictates of human institutions without a fight leaves a bitter taste, a sense of self bereft of respect, of helplessness, inadequacy, or impotent rage.

Helplessness, rage, or a more diffuse sense of diminished self occasioned by encounters in the world beyond the home encourages adults to look to the private world of the couple or the family for countervailing comfort and protection. These expectations can place unbearable stress on a marriage. Two individuals can hardly be expected to protect each other's self-esteem, sense of wholeness or significance, in a world whose public life can call them into question almost without notice. When children's needs, demands, and expectations are added, the strain can be even greater. Strain is often complicated by a sense of guilt; if parents fail to provide what is expected—or what they themselves expect—to spouse or children, they may blame themselves. After all, in a world where people have so much rational control, shouldn't individuals be able to solve their problems, to figure out a way to do better?

THE KNOWLEDGE EXPLOSION

Technological change has meant that for most purposes man's own muscles, the tools he has used as a direct extension of his muscles, and the beasts that have served him are supplanted by inanimate and often invisible sources of power: fossil fuels, electricity, and nuclear power.[4] Ships that once relied on the wind now run on gasoline and diesel; horses that once pulled a town's carts and carriages are replaced by the internal combustion engine. Technological changes and changes in the scale and nature of social institutions have made it much harder for children to gain an accurate sense of how the world works—and harder for parents to tell them about it. The technology of a sailing vessel (or how to wield an ax or a sledgehammer, or how to control a horse) can be described to a young child, partly because the workings are visible. Now, although it is relatively simple to explain the *principle* of jet propulsion, it is quite another matter for a parent—even the rare one who understands it—to explain the elaborate technology on which the functioning of a missile or a space vehicle depends. The books so loved by young children (such as those by Richard Scarry) that show how machines work and how buildings are built can now give only a very limited and somewhat dated picture of how work is done; they can be true only up to a point and not true about the direction in which technology carries us.

Furthermore, technological change has a progressive and cumulative effect so that each generation's childhood is lived in a world that differs more from the previous generation's than the previous generations did from its predecessor's world. The world of a man born in 1935 has changed more in comparison with his father's than his father's did in comparison with his grandfather's. At the turn of the century, a father had to explain electricity to his children; now a father has to account for modern transistorized equipment or a computer-controlled production sequence—if he can.

Even something that used to be simple, such as buying a bicycle, has become more difficult. Seventy-five years ago there might have been one or two national brands and a locally manufactured product with a few selected options. Many children made their own bikes out of parts; foreign imports were either not available or available only in large cities and to the rich. Now few bikes are homemade and few local manufacturers have survived. National markets, aided by quick transportation and mass-media advertising, have made the purchase of a bicycle a confusing choice with abundant possibilities. You can't just buy a kid a bike: you have to know what's in fashion in his town, how safe some of the new designs are, and whether a bike will endure both hard wear and a change in fashion. As so often in modern life, a parent who is out shopping for a bike is forced to rely on the advice of an expert.

Like technology, social organizations have become more complex and impersonal and their workings more invisible. The needs of a vastly increased and increasingly urbanized population have generated a series of bureaucracies like those administering voter registration, licenses to drive or work or build, the Internal Revenue code, Social Security, Medicare, and veteran's benefits, to name just a few. However, one does not have to think of federal, state, or local government bureaucracies to understand what has happened, but only of the supermarket, hospital, or school system in one's local town.

In most localities the one-room schoolhouse is a thing of the distant past, and the years since World War II have seen the growth of complex school organizations. In time, certainly by high school, most young people understand what they have to do to get by in school and what they can and cannot do with impunity, not only with respect to academic performance but also to social behavior. Yet a high school student might find it impossible to draw an accurate chart of the way the school bureaucracy works or to describe in words who holds the reins and why things happen the way they do. His teacher or parent might not do any better. It has become harder to understand the organization of social units just as it has become harder to understand technology, and for analogous reasons, size, scale, complexity, change. It takes longer before a young child and even a motivated adolescent can begin to understand how they work. Not only is it harder for children to comprehend what their father does in a financing company or in an aerospace complex than it was for children whose father worked on a fishing boat, but the whole society in which the aerospace organization and the financing company are embedded has become harder to explain in ways that are simple enough or concrete enough for a young child and still reasonably complete and accurate.

The challenge posed by the expansion of knowledge is particularly acute for parents with respect to information bearing on child rearing, especially in areas such as health practices, medicine, psychology, and the cognitive development of children. Television, magazines, and daily newspapers flood parents with information concerning every aspect of child care from breast-feeding to moral development. There are symposia on child care at schools, community centers, and churches. What are the advantages of breast-feeding? What are the consequences of bottle-feeding? Pamphlets at the pediatrician's office give answers, but maybe quite different answers. How can you develop your child's imagination? How can you develop his intellectual powers? Several paperbacks on the rack at your local drugstore may tell you to teach your toddler math, whereas others may suggest it is detrimental to your child to do so. Are you going to wreck your child's development if you are a full-time working mother? Most advisers say no, but some literature intimates that you may. Do you have trouble disciplining your children? A variety of experts stand ready to tell you how to do a better job. Moreover, commercial interests use scientific findings for their own purposes. The food industry exploits nutritional and health information; the toy industry exploits knowledge about the cognitive development of children. These and other industries play with the anxieties of parents and the susceptibilities of children to promote their products.

The popularization of information concerning child rearing has made every parent a potential expert, but at the same time parents of every socioeconomic level are asking if they are doing the right thing or enough of it.

The expansion of knowledge may affect the family's ability to provide care, protection, and intimacy in ways that go beyond the challenges posed by keeping abreast of new information. The provision of care is influenced to some extent by a sense of continuity, if not of permanence. This sense may be an illusion, but it is nevertheless important to parents' convictions about the value and feasibility of their child-rearing task. No one knows how much change people can sustain before they can no longer maintain a sufficient sense of continuity with their past to rear their children with conviction.

DOING THINGS TOGETHER AS A FAMILY

Many of the shared tasks once necessary to maintaining a household are no longer performed in the home: Most food, goods, services, recreation, and instruction are now provided by specialized organizations and institutions outside the home.[5] This, added to the separation of home from work and the fact that in one of every two families both parents work, sometimes at more than one job, has reduced the time (and the necessity) for a family to do things together. As a result, family members spend less time at home today than their counterparts did in earlier eras and, while there, are seldom engaged together in essential household activities.

Just as it is hard for a couple to maintain a relationship unless they share some interests, it may be hard for family members to be more than perfunctorily close unless they act in concert—at the very least eat together and talk about their day. Yet, according to one newspaper survey, few American families share more than three or four meals a week. Sharing becomes difficult if home life takes place in left-over time and if much of that time is devoted to vicarious encounters with television people.

This is not to imply support for an idealized version of family life—the sort of thing suggested by passages in *Little Women*, Dickens' novels, or Laura Ingalls Wilder's *Little House* books, or in nineteenth-century engravings of a family gathered around the fire or around a big table under a hanging lamp. The individuals playing cards and sewing by lamplight were as often imprisoned as supported by the family life of their day. Notions about sharing and caring may have been more an ideal than a reality for many, part of the glorification of the home as a bastion against the newly industrialized world outside; and those for whom it did approach reality were to be found mostly among the middle and upper-middle classes, whose members had some strength and leisure time left at the end of the day. In fact, shared family activities may have been as few in the past as they are today—perhaps fewer. But some sharing of household tasks was inevitable, among women and children in particular.

It is possible that for most people a sense of closeness is derived less from talking things over or from an overt demonstration of affection than from daily or seasonal undertakings to which each person makes a contribution and which have a constructive purpose. People are likely to feel their own worth confirmed and acknowledge that of others through the shared routines of daily life. In many families few shared rituals remain that offer occasions for reciprocal gestures of intimacy. Increasingly, family members must consciously invent activities to preserve ties with each other. Although these activities are not needed for physical survival, they may be a precious and vital part of the worth and meaning of their lives.[6]

WOMEN'S ROLES

Changes in women's lives in contemporary society have had far-reaching and as yet not wholly known effects on family life. The modernization of women's lives can be viewed as taking place in two stages. The first, which occurred as the result of industrialization, gradually relegated all women, except for the poor, to the home. Made increasingly nonproductive from an economic point of view, they became the defenders of all the humane values associated with the home and opposed the cut-throat world of industrial capitalism.[7] It was a role to which all women were expected to aspire. If a woman whose husband provided for the family became active outside the home, her activities—almost certainly not for wages—were in support of values compatible with nurturing and instructing the young: she may have worked for a church, a hospital, a missionary society, or, especially if she was upper class, the arts.

The second stage in the modernization of women's lives coincided with the technological revolution and, in part, was the result of it. This led many women to feel ambivalent about being exclusively a wife and homemaker. Economic changes have lessened the popularity of having large families: medical advances, especially in contraception, have made childbearing a matter of choice. The ideal that underpins women's new role is the same as that which has long provided a rationale for men: a conception of self-fulfillment through financial rewards, the realization of personal ambition, and the expression of talent. (It is important to keep in mind, however, that the goals of self-fulfillment and self-expression are attained by few workers of either sex, particularly in times of slow economic growth.) A broad range of women are only now adopting this new ideal. It is the antithesis of the earlier notion that self-fulfillment comes through homemaking, child care, and the pursuit of romantic love.

The unprecedented revolution of rising expectations in women's lives has complicated the family's task of providing nurture and intimacy. If both parents have roles outside the home and these roles develop to shape their lives toward different ends, it becomes much harder to maintain a marriage built on the premise of a common destiny. Two people who married under one set of circumstances may be required, as the woman moves into a new position in the world, to reconstruct their mental landscapes—the rules and roles that previously guided their life together—and the reconstruction may change beyond repair the terms on which the couple originally built their relationship. Some marriages may be happier because both partners find satisfaction in their work, but new opportunities for women can lead to marital instability. When they are less economically dependent on men, women may be less inclined to continue in an unsatisfactory marriage. Moreover, societal support for individual fulfillment outside the framework of homemaking and child care may also encourage them to end their marriage. Marital stability can be threatened, too, by men's response to women working outside the home and to their pursuit of self-development independent of traditional roles. As women work and make other commitments outside the home, they are often not as accessible to their children as their children or they themselves may wish to be. And just as they have less time, they often have less energy to nourish the emotional needs of their family.

There has been considerable rhetoric in recent years urging the greater participation of men in child care, but given the structure of most jobs even the most willing father has little flexibility.

The situation of women and men with respect to work—new for women and essentially unchanged for men—their conception of their domestic roles, and the vulnerability of the contemporary family raise questions about supplementary child care. In 1977 day care cost an average of $2000 and by 1984 was close to $4000 or more a year, putting it out of the reach of perhaps two-thirds of all families. In families such as the Polskys and the Murphys, where one income is already supporting the family, wives may be able to earn enough to pay the day-care fees for their children. (However, if what they want to do is go to school, they may not be in a position to pay for tuition, books, *and* day care out of their husbands' salaries.)

Good day-care centers are hard to plan, administer, and staff; moreover, there is still opposition to institutional child care, much of it stemming from nineteenth-century conceptions of family, home, and woman's place. Whatever the underlying reasons, the day-care situation only emphasizes how society is blatantly failing to respond to the serious needs of families. This is partly because women and children—the direct beneficiaries of day care—are relatively powerless in the public arena, and children, at least, are voiceless as well. It also happens because inadequate child care affects the private lives of individuals; the price the society is paying is not apparent or easily quantifiable and will perhaps only be revealed over time.

What direct messages does the situation of the modern family have for children? First, the changes in the lives of men and women have affected roles within the family, the concept of family itself, and thus children's conceptions of sex roles. Both domestic roles and work roles have become less sex specific.

Second, stresses on the family from a variety of quarters may mean that a majority of American children will face discontinuity in their intimate world sometime during childhood and will find it necessary to redraw their social map before it is even sketched. If their parents divorce, they may have to accommodate to life in more than one family. No one knows whether a young child is capable of feeling securely rooted in two (or more) places called home or with two casts of characters called family. For that matter, no one knows whether two adults need inevitably be the essential attributes of a child's concept of a protected, intimate family world that is faithful to him and offers him comfort and protection.

LINDA AND CLIFF

Cliff Fried and Linda Clancy had been going out together since they were fifteen. They were high school seniors now, but they seldom had the place and privacy to make love. One August evening they found out that they could have Linda's house all to themselves for three hours.

"Sure it's okay?" Cliff asked.

"Sure," Linda replied. She counted quickly in her head: she was sure she was still in the "safe" days. (Sometimes when they had intercourse Cliff used a condom; the infrequency of their sexual relations made it easy for Linda to rationalize not seeking contraception for herself. And besides, the premeditation involved in going to a clinic would make it harder for her to avoid her own confused feelings about sex before marriage.)

For about a year Linda and Cliff had been talking about getting married, maybe three years after their high school graduation. By then, if everything went as planned, Linda would graduate from nursing school and Cliff would have only one more year to go to college. Linda figured that she could support both of them by working as a nurse while Cliff finished school.

When Linda missed her period in late September she did not tell anyone, not even Cliff. At first she told herself she might just be irregular again as she had been when she first started menstruating. But when she had missed her period for nearly three months, she couldn't pretend any longer that things were normal.

If her outward life continued as before during these three months, her inner life had changed a great deal. She felt dominated by two conflicting inner voices. One, a scolding voice, kept asking her what her parents would think if she told them. The other said reassuringly, "Now you can get married. You didn't want to wait three years anyway. You can go to work as soon as the baby's a few months old. You can go to school later, maybe when Cliff's finished. Mother can help with the baby. It'll be hard, but you can manage."

A lot of the time the reassuring voice didn't really talk to Linda; it just sketched in happy pictures: Linda telling Cliff they were going to have a baby and how thrilled he would be; Linda and Cliff with an apartment of their own; Cliff studying in one room and Linda feeding the baby in the next.

When Linda told Cliff she was pregnant, his reactions were not what she had imagined.

It was New Year's Eve and they were driving to a party. They passed the high school. "Just think," Cliff said, "six months from now we'll be saying goodbye to that place for good. I'm really ready." That was the moment Linda chose to tell Cliff about the coming baby.

Cliff swerved to the side of the road and stopped short.

"What did you say?" he asked.

More haltingly than she had imagined, Linda explained.

"Have you told your folks?" he asked.

She told him no.

"You'd better tell them fast...." He was silent for a minute. "On second thought maybe you'd better not. Have you thought of having an abortion?"

"An abortion?" she cried out. "Maybe you forget I'm Catholic. It's bad enough getting pregnant." She stopped herself. This wasn't what she had planned to say or how she'd planned to sound. She started again. "Listen, Cliff, we could make it. Really, I mean if we get married. It would be hard but we could do it."

"Married?" Cliff responded. "Are you kidding?"

They began to shout at each other, and soon Linda said he should drive her home or she'd get out of the car and walk.

When she returned home her parents asked her what the matter was. Linda broke down and told them everything.

The following week was difficult. Linda's father was in a rage, first at Cliff, then at his wife, Linda, and himself, then at Cliff again. Her mother was angry too, although the word she used was "disappointed." (As her mother and father quarreled about the situation, Linda learned that she herself had been one month on the way when her parents got married.)

After they cooled down and considered the alternatives, Linda's parents called on Cliff's parents to talk things over. Neither family had money to spare. Linda's father was a fireman, and her mother worked part time as a dentist's receptionist. Cliff's father was a bookkeeper for several small businesses, and his wife took care of Cliff's younger brother and sister. However, Cliff's parents agreed to help Cliff pay the cost of the baby's delivery and to remind him of his responsibility to contribute to the baby's support. Linda's parents agreed to furnish the layette and crib and to provide a home for the baby.

To Linda's and Cliff's surprise—and relief (even Linda's relief)—neither pair of parents pressured them to marry. Hurt by his response to her pregnancy, Linda was much less sure now that she wanted to marry Cliff.

The months did nothing to revive Linda's hopes and dreams. By the end of January her pregnancy began to show. The principal said she could no longer attend school because of insurance regulations, but she knew he meant that she was a bad example. In accordance with the law, he furnished her with a home tutor. Linda didn't see Cliff any more, nor did she see much of her girl friends. They didn't seem to have much time for her, and to her surprise she didn't have much to say to them. She was lonely and hurt, alternately grateful that her parents tried to help her and furious that she had to fall back on them.

Her mother and father took good care of her although she often sensed a great deal that was unsaid behind her mother's pinched lips. Once they suggested putting the baby up for adoption. She reacted almost as strongly as she had to Cliff's suggestion of an abortion and ran crying to her room. An hour later, her mother came in and sat on her bed. "Linda," she said, "whatever you do, whatever happens, you and your baby will be welcome here. This is your home."

Linda embraced her mother; she felt grateful, relieved, and unexpectedly like a little girl again. Only later did it occur to her that it would have been easier on her conscience if her mother and father had thrown her out.

Linda went into labor three weeks before the baby was due. She was at home alone, and on impulse she called Cliff. He said he would be right over. In a few minutes he drove up with his father, and they took her to the hospital.

During the long wait that followed, Cliff asked his father: "Does this baby get my name . . . our name?"

"You mean on the birth certificate? Not unless you and Linda are married."

"I don't like that," said Cliff.

The day after Jennifer was born Cliff went in to see Linda.

"Have you seen Jennifer?" she asked.

"Jennifer?" Cliff said. "Our baby?" He felt emotion flood through him when he said these words. "She's fantastic."

He was thinking, "This is my wife; that's my kid out there in that bassinet."

When he got home Cliff got on his bike and went off for an hour. As he biked it seemed to him that the whirr of the tires whined wife-life, wife-life, words that seemed in opposition to each other. How could he ever build the life he wanted if he were married—and responsible for Jennifer? But how could he just go to college in the fall as if Jennifer and Linda didn't exist? A month later Linda and Cliff were married.

For the first year of their marriage they were together only on weekends, when Cliff stayed at Linda's house. During the week he lived in a rented room near college, fifty miles from their home town. Cliff enjoyed college and was making new friends. He decided to major in business.

Linda was housebound with Jennifer, but she was happy. She was glad to be married, and for the moment Jennifer was all the new experience she wanted.

By the end of Cliff's freshman year, however, Cliff and Linda very much wanted a place of their own. They rented two rooms on the top floor of a house owned by a widow. (They felt lucky that she had agreed to accept Jennifer.) The kitchen was a closet, "but at least it's ours," said Linda. Once there, they were brought up sharp against what it cost to live on their own. The apartment was furnished, but they still had to buy things such as a toaster and a reading lamp. Moreover, Linda had not realized how much she had relied on her mother's help with Jennifer—and the help of the rest of the family as babysitters. Now she could not leave the apartment unless Cliff came home—and it seemed as though he never did. He had taken a job working from 7 a.m. to 3 p.m. in a factory about a mile from school, and he was seldom home before 10 or 11 p.m. Linda was alone with Jennifer; her only adult companionship consisted of chats with the landlady and the checkers at the supermarket.

After Thanksgiving, as much to break her isolation as to supplement their income, Linda took a part-time waitressing job. Their landlady was glad to care for Jennifer: she seemed to genuinely like children and somehow to have the strength to keep up with a toddler. Linda didn't like the way she called Jennifer a "bad girl" when Jennifer acted up, but necessity kept Linda's mouth shut.

Linda enjoyed getting out of the house to go to work, but she still felt lonely. She could share very little of her experience with the two other waitresses. They were her age, but neither of them was married and neither had children. They did not go home to a toddler who spilled spaghetti on the floor but to easy evenings of drinking beer, listening to music, or smoking pot. Moreover, they were going to school part time.

As Cliff's courses began to require him to spend more time at the library—even Friday and Saturday nights—Linda grew increasingly resentful. They began to have frequent quarrels, which mounted in intensity, until one night Linda ordered Cliff out of the house. He went to spend the night with some of his fellow students.

"Linda and I had a fight," he said. "Can I stay here till we get it together?"

But they never did get it back together even though they spent some weeks seeing a marriage counselor at a nearby agency. It was a relief when they agreed after the long winter to get a divorce, but within a few days Linda's relief changed to panic. The support payments Cliff had suggested did not cover her costs with Jennifer. Her parents had offered to help if she returned to their house with

Jennifer, but that would be very humiliating. She worked longer hours but cleared very little once she had paid the landlady.

Six months later the divorce became final. Then, on one of his visits to Jennifer, Cliff told Linda that he had been laid off at the factory.

"I'm going to get a job," he said. "But I'm not going to get that kind of job again, not if I can help it. It took too much out of me. I'll give you what I can but I can't promise."

Linda felt angry, confused, and frightened. She knew that without Cliff's weekly check, she would have to ask for her parents' help.

Physically Linda had been dragging for weeks, and she finally went to the doctor. While she was waiting to take a blood test, she looked through the glass partition at the white-coated technicians moving about efficiently. Several of them were about her age, yet they seemed to belong to another world. They had been to school; they had good jobs; they probably had money for clothes and a good time.

A few minutes later, when one of these young women was putting a Band-Aid on Linda's arm, Linda voiced some of her feelings. "You're lucky to have the job you have. I'd give anything for a job like yours."

"It's a pretty easy course: two semesters at Community." That was the name of the local two-year college.

Linda sighed. "I couldn't even do that," she said. "I have a three-year-old and I'm divorced. My ex-husband's out of a job. He's not giving me anything."

"Why don't you go on welfare? That's what I did," said the young woman. "I have a kid too."

"Go on welfare?" said Linda and then stopped herself for fear of being insulting.

"What's wrong with welfare? They'll pay your tuition and your kid can go to whatever day care you choose as long as you're in school."

Linda walked out of the laboratory hopeful for the first time in months. When she reached home she called Community and asked for a catalogue, and then she called the social agency and made an appointment for an interview. She swallowed her pride, took the welfare payments, and enrolled Jennifer in a pleasant day-care center where she seemed happy. She studied hard but enjoyed it. Within eight months she had landed a job similar to the one held by the young woman she had met. It was a job that allowed her to support herself and Jennifer, if only very modestly.

* * *

Although Linda and Cliff are not necessarily typical of young parents, they are representative of many young women and men who become parents while still teenagers. Linda's occasional sexual intercourse with a boyfriend she loves, her reluctance to use contraceptives, her resistance to abortion, and her decision to keep her baby—with or without Cliff's help—are shared by a growing number of adolescent girls who are sexually mature at an earlier age than their mothers or grandmothers were and whose sexual explorations, however limited, begin much earlier.

The outcome of our story is more hopeful than many of Cliff's and Linda's counterparts in real life, but positive outcomes are more common than was once believed.[8] Although Linda's and Cliff's families were not affluent, they offered them more assistance than families of teenage parents sometimes do. Moreover, the fact that Linda and Cliff were from families who expected them to do well in life may have given them an added impetus to find ways to make their lives more satisfying.

A closer look at Linda and Cliff as child-parents and the Clancys and the Frieds, their parents, reveals some of the themes discussed in this chapter.

The conversation that followed the Clancys' initially explosive reaction to their daughter's pregnancy came rather quickly, considering the delicate and complicated issues involved. If we could have heard their words—or better still, read their thoughts—we would probably have discovered the major themes of their life together. They themselves had come to terms with getting married because Linda had already been conceived, and they had realigned their personal views and sense of themselves to accommodate Linda and the children that followed. They had become the Clancy family.

Implicit in their conception of family are two elements that are of great help to Linda. First, families stand by their own. Even though she is bitterly disappointed that Linda must put off going to college, Linda's mother tries to say supportive, comforting things because that is the way "we handle rough times." Second, the issue of paternal responsibility was settled for them long ago when they agreed they created Linda together, and they built a pretty good life after having accepted that fact. But sometimes, when they are alone, they may remind each other that although their marriage has worked out, they would not want to force a daughter or a son to marry too young.

The response of Cliff's parents to Linda's pregnancy may have been very different. His father may have offered reluctant support, while his mother may have withdrawn in pained silence. We imagine that Cliff's forthcoming fatherhood rekindles old issues between his parents that have never been ironed out—issues having to do with raising children. The unresolved nature of these issues encourages each to imagine that the other is to blame for Cliff's predicament. Cliff's father is Jewish, the son of a local merchant whose family fled from Europe when he was a baby. Cliff's grandparents were hurt and angry when their son married a Norwegian woman. But the couple's life together was idyllic for several years and even for a year or so after Cliff's older sister was born. Then they seemed to part ways over the proper balance of cuddling, discipline, between-meal snacks, freedom to roam the house, and how long to keep a baby in diapers. When Cliff was born, his parents' disagreements became more intense. They never quite succeeded in reconstructing a joint sense of family from an earlier view of themselves as a couple. Instead, without much conscious thought, they divided their lives and tasks into territories, assigning house and children to mother and job to father. But even this division was not a complete solution, for Cliff's father enjoyed playing with and indulging the children. As Cliff grew to manhood, he treated his mother as a somewhat distant friend and turned to his father for comfort and advice.

Linda and Cliff are several steps removed from being ready to reshape their ways of thinking in order to become a family. Neither has left home, physically or psychologically. Not expecting to share their lives completely for at least a few years, they feel no need to construct a mental landscape in which they see themselves as a couple. Not surprisingly, their honest efforts to be good parents to Jennifer sometimes seem immature; nor is it surprising that Linda, faced with full-time child care, seems to grow up more rapidly than Cliff. Like most young people his age, Cliff devotes his energies to establishing himself as a person on his own. Over time his view of the world leaves less and less space for Linda and Jennifer, until at last Linda feels he has pushed them past the edge of his life.

Linda's efforts to meet Jennifer's daily physical and emotional demands—to be her mother—add to her efforts to separate from her own family and become an adult in her own right. She struggles to make a life with Cliff, although their marriage may have potential for success more in fantasy than in fact. Finally she resolves to face a difficult set of facts and to find a way to assure her economic independence—even at the cost of the welfare stigma—so that she can be both Jennifer's mother and a person in her own right.

Linda's resolution to find a way to raise Jennifer on her own, and her implicit opening of the door to a better family life at some future time by ending an unsuccessful marriage, may draw its strength in part from her parents' marriage. Despite her wish to be different from them, she admires their closeness and the care they have taken of each other. Although the particulars of her life are different from what her mother's were at her age, and, in fact, would not have been imaginable for her mother, something deeper than surface events and circumstances suggests that mother and daughter may see life in quite similar ways. Linda's mental landscape includes places for faithful, satisfying relationships and has many possible paths for exploring solutions to her present circumstances. It allows her to endure disappointment and social stigma without foreclosing possibilities for new relationships or other experiences in the future. Moreover, Linda's view of her own life, and life in general, may be as important to Jennifer's construction of a life map as the facts of their turbulent life together. The strengths Linda exhibits, which are drawn from the same sort of map as that of her parents, may offer Jennifer stronger social and emotional nourishment to grow on than she might have had if Linda and Cliff had withdrawn behind civil masks and stuck it out for Jennifer's sake.

Linda, Cliff, and their parents make unexamined assumptions about the locus of responsibility for children in American society. No one in either family blames external forces when problems arise, nor do they expect much help, social or financial. When Linda is barred from school, neither she nor her parents question the principal's decision or the adequacy of a home tutor. They do not expect to have a voice in public decisions that affect their lives.

Although a variety of social agencies might help Linda and Cliff to think through their plans, each assumes that agencies only place babies for adoption or counsel married couples. After the divorce, Linda learns by chance that going on welfare will allow her to attend school, receive a small stipend, and place Jennifer in free day care. Because she has good basic skills, confidence in her abilities, and a high school diploma, she can enter a technical program, do well, and find a job when she finishes. The stigma she feels when she accepts welfare, if only for a year, is nearly inevitable in our society where dependence on the public dole is associated with failure. In fact, as in Linda's case, it may be quite the opposite.

When she starts her new job, Linda will face child-care problems that were temporarily solved while she was on welfare. Free day care will no longer be available, and the cost of sending Jennifer to the center she likes so much could take close to a third of Linda's take-home pay. Linda may use a variety of baby-sitters instead. If she is lucky, she may find a parent cooperative in her vicinity, although she may have trouble contributing her share of time and effort. Or there may be a partially subsidized child-care center at a hospital where she could work. But if she is like most mothers who raise children alone, she will have to make do until free care is provided by public schools and then arrange for after-school activities and a neighbor to look out for Jennifer until she gets home.

If she does find a subsidized child-care service, she is likely to consider it a "gift" (although she feels entitled to a public education for her child). Her attitude is shaped by the American belief that families take care of their own needs and should be in a position to take total care of their young children until they are of school age.

Cliff and Linda spent a lot of time together when they were in high school—going to the beach, studying, bowling, seeing friends, occasionally preparing a meal together. Once Jennifer was born, they had little opportunity to renew or restore the familiar rituals or gestures of intimacy that were once woven through their time together. They lived quite separate lives, together mostly in bed or with Jennifer, with whom each had developed some of the easy gestures and rituals that make doing-nothing-in-particular so nourishing to close relationships.

Perhaps Linda and Cliff had no time left for each other because they didn't really want to be with each other. But their situation differed little from the patterns of family life in Cliff's home or in many other American homes, where each member's work and social activities are shared with people who are near strangers to everyone else in the family and where the chores are commonly divided up in such a way that each family member does his share alone.

Linda and Cliff do not talk much about what is best for Jennifer—they have more basic problems to solve. But in her few spare moments Linda may seek and discover many articles in magazines or bits of information in television soap operas that alert her to the scientific view that a child's first few years are in some ways critical. She hears advice from her family, her landlady, and practically everyone she meets, yet it does not always strike her as adequate or applicable, and there are times when she wishes there were someone she could turn to when Jennifer has a bad night or when her own impatience and perhaps rage at her baby's irritability scare her. Nevertheless, she assumes that she should be able to manage on her own, that she is somehow inadequate if she feels the need for answers, for a break, for someone to keep her company.

Linda's conception of her own womanhood reflects elements of her mother's traditional devotion to home and children and elements of a contemporary woman's consciousness of her potential for a life outside the home. It is her participation in this consciousness that allows Linda to entertain the idea of going to school, finding a job, and if necessary supporting her household alone.

Linda decides to use a baby-sitter and then a day-care center, but she may often wonder if both she and Jennifer will one day regret these arrangements. Have they spent enough time together? Have her arrangements for child care been too makeshift? When she begins to wish "if only," Linda's thoughts may turn to what she has done wrong or what might have happened if only she were rich, or if only Cliff had "really" loved her. It would not occur to her to ask how different her situation and Jennifer's would be if adults took some collective responsibility for all children to assure them protective care no matter who happened to give them life or what the circumstances of their upbringing were. She thinks like an American in this respect. Young women in other parts of the industrialized world would find her assumptions backward in view of her country's leadership in so many areas.[9]

If we speculate about Jennifer's mapping of social reality and ask how she might make sense of what she has taken in of family life, we can suppose that she might, for example, be sensitive to adult moods and express in her choice of words and in her play such themes as "mommy cry," "dolly sad," or "daddy go away." Leaving and being left may enter her play and her dreams more often than they do for other three-year-olds, because her daddy did leave and doesn't live with her anymore. Her fear that she is to blame will almost inevitably show up somewhere. Because she's been to a day-care center she may have a broader sense of differences among adults who have little in common with her kin. She may have worked out some ways of meeting their expectations while getting them to pay attention to her needs and interests.

It is not really possible, however, to be certain just how Jennifer's play, dreams, or words will reflect the sense she's made of her experience. Like most children, what she makes of what she takes in will be tempered or sharpened by her biological predispositions and by how well her parents help her anticipate and respond actively to the changes and emotions she will witness in the life story of her parents.

Chapter Four
Seeing the World
Through Parents' Lives

> *I am a 12-year-old girl with seven sisters and three brothers. I hope that whoever gets this tree will write back to me. Dad got 80 cents for this tree. What did you pay?*
>
> —A note found on a $15 Christmas tree.
>   Jack Mabley's column, *Chicago Tribune*

> *They struggle to instill in their children some private sense of honor or dignity which will help the child to survive. This means, of course, that they must struggle stolidly, incessantly, to keep this sense alive in themselves, in spite of the insults, the indifference, and the cruelty they are certain to encounter in their working day.*
>
> —James Baldwin, *Nobody Knows My Name*

In contrast with the intimate life of the family, the public world of work, business, government, and even the comings and goings of people in their cars or on foot in shopping malls or on city streets is often highly impersonal.[1] Moreover, a distinction between public and private is basic to most people's conception of their lives. The contrast and distinction made between the two worlds lead people to forget the great extent to which the family is shaped by the role of its members in the wider society—that is, by their working lives.

The messages parents bring home from their work are a vital element in children's social education. They give form to their first hazy picture of their own place in society, where they can go, and what they can do. Messages about work and income are not children's only source of information about the society's economy, political system, or other social arrangements. But they are among messages so often repeated that children must inevitably take them in.

This is not to deny the isolation of the modern family from the world of work, but the physical separation of home and work does not screen from children's view their parents' economic and social position in the society. The inner maps children make of their world and their perception of roles and rules are influenced by their parents' income level, social status, and the nature and circumstances of their work, even if at first they have only an indirect and largely implicit knowledge of them.

Yet to some degree a belief exists that children are immune, at least as long as they stay within the sanctuary of the family. Although few people articulate this belief, it is a psychologically important rationale. Most public statements, and much that is written, assert that the family can set its own style, protect its children from outside influences, and provide a place of spiritual retreat, recovery, and pleasure for its adults. American parents are first of all Americans, imbued like their ancestors with a zeal to chart their lives free from outside interference. Implicit in the American dream of individual freedom and prosperity to each according to his efforts and talents is the assumption that parents shape their children's destinies through their strength of character, resourcefulness, and personal effort.

As much as parents—and other family members—are a child's first and usually best resource, modern parents have many competitors in the process of influencing their children's lives. Some of those influences, such as television and school, act directly on the child, while others, such as work, income, and social position, act indirectly by shaping parents' lives.

The child's very presence in his family may affect his parents' attitude toward work. The personal and social meanings of work vary considerably during adult life. It can be fun to be a waitress or dishwasher when you are young and footloose, or enjoyable to work as a cashier if you are growing older and like to keep active. But during the child-rearing years, the personal and social implications of work become enmeshed with a parent's determination to protect and provide for children and to offer them a model of adult life they can respect and perhaps emulate.

Once a couple become parents they look at their life in a new way. They take stock of their social worth and examine the heritage—material, social, spiritual—that they will pass to a new generation. The material and social composition of that heritage is profoundly related to income and social status, more often than not through the kind and profitability of their work.

Stocktaking at the birth of a first or second child may lead a man to look for a more secure job—or to seek the kind of work he has always wanted. Stocktaking for a woman is more complex; the birth of a child forces her to confront that part of her life as a grown-up that has to do with mothering and nurture. She may decide that this is the only work she will do for a number of years and put off involvement beyond the home. Or, as is increasingly likely, economic reasons, her own conception of herself, or the isolation of child care may lead her to look for a job—or keep the one she has. In any case, once a parent, a woman is apt to think more carefully and concretely than ever before about her roles and her relationship to the world.

WORK, WORKERS, AND FAMILY LIFE

A family's situation as a unit of society is largely determined by the work the parents do. There are several key elements to a parent's work, each of which affects his life and the life of his family. The most obvious and basic of these is income. It not only purchases the necessities of life—food, clothing, shelter—but it also limits or increases the options for satisfying other needs and preferences.

A second key element in a person's work is the nature of the work itself, and the conditions and constraints it imposes. In all societies people partly organize their lives according to the work they do and the people with whom they do it. In addition, work shapes a sense of social identity and self-esteem, which may be nourished or eroded by work and the conditions surrounding it. While income may be a powerful force in determining the boundaries of family life, the nature of work appears to have an even more profound effect on people's sense of themselves as effective and worthwhile.

A third element, only in part intrinsic to the job itself, is the meaning a person gives to it. For some people, the job is satisfying or not only in terms of its social context and the income it provides. Some workers get "work sick" on weekends and during vacations, not because they miss the job but because their fellow workers have become the mainstays of their social world. But for many people the work itself is important to their satisfaction with life, perhaps most important during the years when they are conscious of the example their lives set for their children.

The meaning that a person gives to his work is determined not only by personal inclinations, but also by the way in which society views it.[2] The way that others judge the value of our work influences our feeling about ourselves and what we do. The ministry and teaching, for instance, are professions in which people may find deep meaning and at the same time enjoy the esteem of others, factors that compensate for long hours and low pay. A corporate lawyer may find his work satisfying even when it is not deeply meaningful, because it offers him power and prestige.

Our society values intellectual work that involves the use of words and numbers. It also values the work of administrators who manage people and maintain the structures of complex technological and bureaucratic organizations. People who work with their hands are thought to do leftover work, for manual labor is often considered residual in a mechanized and technological society. It is hard for people who do such work—sometimes even when they are highly skilled craftsmen—to overcome its social stigma, to find meaning in it, and to feel they are valuable. Their attitudes in this respect may show up in their assessment of themselves as less smart than people who do paperwork—and they may caution their children not to follow in their footsteps.[3] (However, identification with the counterculture, which rejects society's attitudes toward manual and physical work, may for a few be a path to greater self-esteem.)

Perhaps the most subtle factor influencing the meaning a person finds in his work is the baggage he brings with him of self-expectations and the expectations of others. The son of a minister might go out and make a fortune running a chain of discount drugstores, thus satisfying a boyhood ambition to be rich, but he might be nagged by the belief that he has failed his father. The attitudes and values of society and of individual families combine in complex ways to sculpt the meaning a person will find in his job—and the messages he will pass on about work to his children. But perhaps most critical is his sense of whether or not his work "makes a difference."

A person's sense of well-being seems to derive in part from his experience of himself as an active, initiating, and effective agent. Satisfying work activities are not only those that result in financial rewards or social status, but those that leave a mark on the external order of things. Aimless, repetitive activities seldom engender a sense of well-being; often they do quite the opposite. A study sponsored by the U.S. Department of Health, Education, and Welfare revealed that in 1973

> what workers want most, as more than 100 studies in the past 20 years show, is to become masters of their immediate environments and to feel that their work and they themselves are important—the twin ingredients of self-esteem. Workers recognize that some of the dirty jobs can be transformed only into the merely tolerable, but the most oppressive features of work are felt to be avoidable: constant supervision and coercion, lack of variety, monotony, meaningless tasks, and isolation. An increasing number of workers want more autonomy in tackling their tasks, greater opportunity for increasing their skills, rewards that are directly connected to the intrinsic aspects of work, and greater participation in the design of work and the formulation of their tasks.[4]

A look at the work of Bob Murphy and Steve Polsky, the men portrayed in the picnic vignette in chapter two, suggests the interrelation of the social meaning of work, the intrinsic qualities of the job itself, and the income it earns—and the complex effect of these factors on the individual's status, sense of effectiveness, and self-esteem. Both men have roughly the same income—let's say $25,000 to $30,000 a year—but their work is vastly different. As a master plumber, Steve may feel the satisfaction of being reasonably independent in the way he moves about town from job to job and in the way he is on his own in handling his work. As a corporate employee, Bob spends his days in a large plant where he may be tied to rigid schedules and bureaucratic procedures and have less independence than Steve.

In our society where high-status work is increasingly technological, intellectual, and managerial, Bob's background as engineer and his job as assistant manager (and therefore part of the power structure of his company) may give him a sense of self-esteem that Steve may never have as a plumber. However, Steve has the direct, visible, tangible satisfaction of being able to see the immediate results of his work—say, installing plumbing in a new house. Bob may or may not see how his administrative skills make a difference in the way things are run at Newcom; he may have to infer from his bonus that someone believes his work benefits the company.

Their sense of "making a difference" will be affected by society's attitudes toward the jobs they have, how much they have internalized and interpreted society's attitudes, and the kind of life their jobs make possible for their families. For most Americans, being an assistant manager is more prestigious than being a plumber, yet many people may think of a plumber as someone solid, necessary, and identifiably useful to the community in a way that they may not about an assistant manager.

Self-expectations and the expectations of others they have known well, in addition to the attitudes of society in general toward their jobs, shape Steve's and Bob's feelings about their work. Imagine that Steve's father owned a small store that failed during the Depression. His uncle, however, was a plumber, and to Steve his uncle's work, even if dirty, was much more secure. The security of Steve's own work as a plumber might be deeply significant to him in relation to that childhood experience. Perhaps Bob's father was a farmer and Bob an only son. His father may have hoped Bob would take over the farm, but realizing that his handicap made this unlikely, urged him to accept a scholarship at a technical college. Bob's success may have represented the more-than-fulfillment of father and son's hope, built upon the ruin of another hope.

How—and to what degree—do children in a family absorb the adults' attitudes and feelings about work? We can begin to answer this question by taking a look at a particular family.

THE GIANNINIS

Joanne Giannini is eleven. She's in the sixth grade. Her brother Joe, twelve, is in the seventh. Their little sister Donna is only five, a kindergartener.

The Gianninis live in a small one-family house on a quiet street. There's no traffic on the street and the children often play there with their friends. Events on the street are a source of dinner-table conversation, but so is school.

One day Donna tells the family over dinner that her classroom was much too hot.

"What about it?" Frank Giannini asked.

"My teacher said she was going to melt from the heat and I said she wouldn't melt if you took care of our school."

Donna said what she did because her father is a school custodian—in fact, he is custodian of the school Joanne attends.

All three Giannini children have grown up knowing something

about schools that most children never think about—not only about the heating plant but about the painters who make the lowest bid and use cheap paint that peels off in a year; the kids who stuff so much paper in the toilets that they overflow; and the day Mrs. Ashcroft, the English teacher, called Dad to get a bumble bee out of her classroom.

Joanne likes having her father work in her school. Just knowing he is there makes her feel good although she does not see him more than once or twice a day, and sometimes not at all.

It is good, too, in another way to have her father at school. That was proven earlier in the winter when Joanne's skin ailment got so bad she couldn't sleep, and her father found a specialist who figured out what was wrong.

It happened this way. One day Mr. F., the principal of the school where Frank Giannini works, called him in to help him fix a broken venetian blind. Mr. F. noticed that Frank looked worn out and asked him what was the matter. Frank said he had been up night after night with his oldest daughter. She had a rash; she couldn't sleep. Mr. F. suggested taking her to his cousin, a dermatologist. And that's how the Gianninis found out that the chlorine in the pool at the Y was causing Joanne's trouble. The dermatologist instructed her to stay out of the water for two weeks and then put on a water resistant ointment when she went swimming.

Although her father's contact with the principal and *his* social network helped the family find a cure for her rash, Joanne is old enough to see that there are drawbacks to her father's work. For instance, if the school is open at night or on a Saturday he has to be there. She doesn't like it when he gets right up from supper and goes back to school. And there was the time she was a finalist in the swimming contest at the Y, and he wasn't able to come. That time she was angry and cried, but mostly she doesn't say too much because she knows from listening to her parents talk that her dad is paid overtime when he works nights and Saturdays and that her parents count on this money for a lot of things.

Joanne has a somewhat different impression of her mother's job. When Donna, Joanne's younger sister, Giannini started kindergarten, Rose went to work at the local hospital, where she prepares trays for patients.

Rose doesn't say much about her work. Once Joanne asked her whether she ever saw operations, and Rose laughed and said, "Not in the kind of work I do." And once when Dad complained about the meat sauce at dinner, Mom burst into tears and went into the bedroom. Dad went in to comfort her. "What's the matter?" Joe asked when he came out. "Her supervisor's been giving her a hard time. Seems a lot of patients got the wrong food on their trays, but your mother's sure she didn't do it."

The main thing that Joanne notices about her mother's work doesn't have anything directly to do with her work at all. It has to do with Saturdays. Saturdays are different now. It used to be that Mom would take the car and drive Joanne and Joe to their swimming classes at the Y. Or else they would all go together in the bus if Dad wanted to use the car. But now that she is working, she never comes with them, because she needs Saturdays to do her housework and her marketing.

(Rose is a fussy housekeeper, like all the other women in her family—her mother, her grandmother, her sisters. She can remember her grandmother polishing every piece of furniture every week and then placing on each piece a freshly laundered bureau scarf that she herself had embroidered as a girl in Poland.)

Joanne's mother always scrubs the kitchen floor last, after she has cleaned the rest of the house, gone marketing, and put the groceries away. She yells at the children if they come into the kitchen with dirty shoes after she has cleaned the floor. She says her work has to last at least twenty-four hours.

By five o'clock Saturday Rose is exhausted. The family doesn't have the money to go out to dinner or to the movies more than once or twice a winter; but even if they did she would be too tired to go. All she wants to do once she has served dinner is watch television, and it takes her last bit of strength to urge the kids to take their baths and see that their good clothes are in order for church the following morning.

(On the Saturdays she works, Rose cannot get her housework done. Once Frank said that he and Joanne and Joe would clean the house, but when Rose got home the kitchen floor looked streaky and she did it all over again. She dusted and vacuumed again, too. That was the last time Frank offered to clean the house; after that, if she worked on Saturdays she cleaned on Sundays.)

Joanne feels many things about her mother's job, and not all of them are consistent. It feels grown-up to go downtown on the bus alone with Joe; but she misses the talks she had with her mother. Although her mother has always been fussy about the house, it seems that she is even fussier since she started working. Yet Joanne knows her mother's paycheck has bought her the pretty coat she wears to church. She loves the coat and she is proud of her mother for buying it for her.

What Joanne hears at family gatherings at her paternal grandparents' house may add to her pride even if she is not aware of it: "How's the job?" her grandfather or one of her uncles asks her mother in a tone that is a shade different from the one they used with her in the past.

Joanne might have felt differently if she had listened in on her mother's conversations with her own family. Rose doesn't talk to her family often: they live two hundred miles away in Detroit and the tolls add up. When she does, her mother never fails to say something like, "You still with the hospital? How's Donna?"—which means, how could Donna possibly be all right with you working? Or Rose's mother may ask, "What are you going to do when summer comes?" That means, who is going to take care of Donna? "She'll go to her aunt Catherine's down the street," is the answer Rose always gives her mother, but it is not at all clear that this will be so. Catherine, Frank's sister, has two children under five and another on the way. She may not want to take on Donna full-time for the summer. In fact, Rose may not even ask her although she's pleased that Catherine is there, down the street, at the other end of the phone. But that means someone else has to take care of Donna.

"I'll take care of her," Joe volunteers when his mother and father discuss the problem at dinner. He likes little kids and he is good with them.

"Joanne will take care of her," Frank says, "and Catherine's down the street."

"I can't in the morning," says Joanne, "I'm going to swim every day."

"Joe could take care of Donna," says Rose.

"Joe's got to get out with other boys," Frank says.

"What if he stays home mornings while Joanne swims?"

"This swimming has gone far enough," says Frank. But in the end it is agreed that Joe will sit with Donna during the mornings while Joanne goes swimming. They can ask Aunt Catherine to mind Donna if there is something Joe really wants to do in the morning. Frank and Rose will put in for separate vacation time so that the children will not be alone so much, but that means no family outings.

Sunday usually means a visit to Frank's parents for dinner, but one Sunday the Gianninis decide to stay home. "We'll have Sunday dinner just ourselves," says Rose. And she makes dinner, which begins with spaghetti and clam sauce and finishes with a babka. She sets the table with a special cloth embroidered by her grandmother. Dinner is a great success; even Donna, who "never eats clams," likes the clam sauce. While they eat the family talks about buying a boat. "We'll have to wait and see," says Frank, but he doesn't say no. "Why don't we get a second-hand outboard?" says Joe. "I see ads for them all the time."

When the meal is over, the older children go out to play with friends, and Donna asks if she can go see her cousins. Frank and Rose do the dishes. As soon as they are done Frank goes into the living room and tunes in the ball game. Rose sits down at the kitchen table and a moment later finds herself crying. She doesn't know what she is crying about, but when Frank comes in during a commercial she says to him, "It's not the way it's supposed to be." They talk for a while and one thing they decide is to take at least one week of their vacations at the same time and do something together, even if it is only going to the beach for the day. "If we don't," Rose says, "pretty soon they won't want to do anything with us anymore. They're growing away from us so fast."

HOW WORK AFFECTS THE GIANNINIS AND THEIR CHILDREN

Frank Giannini makes $19,000 a year in salary and another $2000 to $3000 in overtime. He has the satisfaction of knowing that although his formal education stopped with high school, he can provide for his family and take care of the house because of his skills. Moreover, although Frank's income is not grand, he belongs to a union that has secured decent fringe benefits for its members—paid vacations and health insurance. His wife is not working to pay for absolute necessities—food on the table or a roof over their heads.

If Frank listens to a TV news commentator, he may hear about the national median income for a family of four. He can be comforted by the fact that although many have done better than he has, others have done worse.

Joe and Joanne perceive that their father's income provides them with the necessities of life and a degree of comfort and security.

(They are aware, however, that his salary buys no luxuries. Joe's suggestion that they buy a second-hand boat is an attempt to tailor his dreams to the reality of their financial situation.) Their perception of their family's situation based on what they see of their classmates' lives and of what they see on television may assure them that they are "somewhere in the middle." More concretely, their father's income has bought them a house (when interest rates were low) although Joe and Joanne are old enough to know that Frank makes mortgage payments every month and to know that the word "mortgage" means they don't exactly own their house—at least not completely. The house may give them a feeling of solidity and suggest that their family has realized a part of the American dream, presented to them again and again not only on television and in magazines, but in their school and library books: the little white house with the lawn around it or Mommy in her well-waxed kitchen looking out at Dick and Jane playing in their own backyard.

The Giannini children may feel themselves more substantially provided for than many of their classmates who live in apartments, whether in multiunit buildings or in the three-story frame houses that still exist in some of the older neighborhoods in their town. (Some of their feelings will derive from the privacy and space a house affords, some from the portrayal of house-owning families in the media, and much from what their parents say or imply about owning their own home.) But Donna may discover that one of her friends who lives on the top floor of an old three-story building considers living up high a sign of greater status than living on the ground floor.

Frank has a degree of personal control in his job as custodian. He may have a half-time helper whose work he supervises, and, more important, the comfort and safety of everyone in the building depends on his care of the building and its facilities. His work leaves a visible mark for people to respect. When painters or carpenters come to do a job he is their hour-to-hour supervisor, even though the chief custodian or the business manager of the school system may stop in to see how the job is going.

Frank has considerable autonomy—as much perhaps as the foreman of a small factory. He can use his judgement on how to get a job done; he may have a budget for repairs and maintenance that he can spend as he sees fit, only checking with the chief custodian if costs run higher. There are certain things he must do by certain times, such as regulate the heating system or incinerate the trash, but he is relatively free in the way he schedules the rest of his day or week.

Frank may choose to handle some minor repairs himself—installing new washers in taps, a new ball in a toilet, mending the sash cord in a window. If he tried he might have difficulty extracting extra payment for these services from the school bureaucracy, but he may "pay himself back" with a little extra time spent chatting with an old friend at the nearby hardware store or playing ball with kids at recess.

In general, Frank's job affords him a freedom of movement and choice that is far greater than that enjoyed by many workers in America, such as assembly-line workers, typists in a typing pool, or telephone operators—and even by many workers in higher-status jobs, such as teachers who must cover a specified curriculum and can leave their classroom only at scheduled times.

Frank's job puts him in touch with a variety of people, some of whom are better educated and better connected than he. Perhaps he feels that some of them are arrogant or presumptuous, or perhaps he feels inferior to them now and then, but occasionally he has the chance to give them advice about fixing things or buying tools—and often there are opportunities for interesting and informative conversations. They may also help him, as on the occasion when the principal referred him to a dermatologist. He has contacts with students that may be casual—perhaps only a "Hi, Frank,"—or warmer and more personal if he admires art work or a stage set, or, more serious, if he catches students defacing school property. Less frequently he comes into contact with parents; he may offer directions to a mother or father looking for a certain classroom, and he has to be present to open and close the building when parents come to an evening meeting. In all these encounters he is recognized as a person who plays a necessary role within the community of the school. Workmen who come to do repairs or renovations in the school are another source of social contact. If he gets to know some of them over a period of time, he may take his lunch break with them and talk about work or sports. Now and then one of them may offer Frank the chance to moonlight on one of their jobs.

Frank may feel that he has not met the expectations of his father—who encouraged Frank to do well in school and get a white-collar job—and that somehow his job as custodian makes him a failure. However, we can imagine that he has a background that allows him to feel more positively about his work. Perhaps his father was a laborer working on the city's road crew, and work as a custodian represented a considerably cleaner, more highly respected job and therefore one much easier for Frank to value. Custodian may have been a job that Frank's father aspired to, a job that a lucky uncle had managed to find. Frank values the skill and know-how it takes to care for a large modern building. Although he may complain when Mrs. Ashcroft asks him to get a bee out of her classroom and complain even more loudly when kids stop up the toilets, he finds it satisfying to be needed in a crisis as well as in the ordinary operation of the school (in fact, complaints can be a way of demonstrating how much one is needed). His work—and the meaning he attaches to it—contribute much to Frank's self-esteem.

Joe, Joanne, and Donna can conclude from what their father says and how he seems when he comes home from work that earning a living, although occasionally frustrating and often full of annoyances, has its rewards too. They know he is pleased when he has made a repair himself in an ingenious way or when he has managed to adjust the thermostat and air ducts in the school so that fuel is saved and one part of the building is not too hot and the other too cold. They believe he is the best school custodian there is, and that his work "makes a difference" not only to the mechanical running of the building but to the comfort of those who spend their day there.

Unlike most contemporary American children, the Gianninis' impression of what their father does is not based solely on what he says or his style of behavior when he comes home from work. They know what his world is like because the world of school is their world, too. The social map they are constructing and revising as school children has some of the same features as the map that gives form and direction to their father's daily life. Their acquaintance with their father's working world makes it easier for them to appreciate and understand what he does—and in a sense who he is. It is possible for them to imagine growing up to do work like this, although Joanne may wonder whether she would really want a job like her father's even if women are custodians when she grows up.

The Giannini children may perceive that their father does not have the same kind of social position their teachers have (and be surprised to learn he earns as much or more than some of them) or the power within the school and the community that the principal has. Yet he is not as powerless as a replaceable person in an assembly line. Although they give the matter no actual thought, in time they will know that in his job he had an effect on the world that no one can doubt. He is effective as a provider, effective in his management of the building, and now and then he has a more personal effect by providing some extra service—or gaining some piece of information useful to his family's well-being.

The messages Joanne, Joe, and Donna receive about work from their mother are very different from those they receive from their father. At the hospital where she works, she prepares regular and bland diet trays. Following written instructions, she scoops portions from the steam table, checking the portion-control instructions for the first few and judging the rest by eye. She may care about how she arranges the food on the first few plates, but after ten plates or so she fills plates by rote—mashed potato, turkey slice, jello, mashed potato, turkey slice, jello.

For this she earns close to the minimum wage and takes home almost $7000 a year after taxes. Her earnings do not put dinner on the table, although inflation has meant that they are beginning to buy some necessities.

Rose herself is glad of every penny she earns and wishes she had some skill that would bring her more income, but she thinks of her earnings as supplementary income. She is horrified every time she thinks of several of her coworkers who are trying to support families on what she makes.

The children think of their mother's income as "extra" money, much as she does herself. But they may be a little confused: Does it buy luxuries or necessities? What is their mother's role as earner? What does her going to work say about the family's economic position? These questions may be just as hard for the Giannini parents to answer as they are for the children. They are the sort of questions that inflation poses for many families today; a factor in women's changing conceptions of their role.

Rose Giannini has virtually no autonomy or chance to express her opinions or talents in her work. She is a good cook, but on the job she is not doing the cooking. At home she is accustomed to being complimented on her preparation of food, but in the hospital she never hears a patient's comment. Accustomed to seeing what gets eaten and what gets left on the plate, she never sees what gets sent back in the hospital. Her job is analogous to that of any assembly-line worker. She is involved with only one element of a whole process and has no opportunity to see or participate in the whole. Her case may be particularly frustrating, because her work involves something she knows how to do well. The nature of her work severely limits the meaning she can find in it. She cannot help but feel powerless, a replaceable part in the immense machine of the hospital's operation.

However, acquaintance with her coworkers provides some pleasure and relief. She enjoys chatting with them during lunch and coffee breaks, sharing with them complaints about the job, gossip about personalities in the kitchen, anecdotes about home and children. But her acquaintance is limited to them; the people in higher positions in the hospital are a world apart. This may be vividly borne home when she takes Joanne to see the dermatologist—and discovers that his office is only two floors above the kitchen where she works.

The Giannini children see their mother come home sighing with relief, often exhausted, and almost never enlivened by something that happened on the job. If she speaks positively about her day at the hospital, it is about her coworkers' lives outside the job, especially their children. On weekends they see her straining to do her housework, convinced she must do it as well as before. She is, as a result, often irritable, snapping at them if they forget and track dirt across her clean floors. They may conclude that "everything is harder for her now" and realize that it has something to do with her work, although they may not be able to formulate for themselves that the kind of work she does adds to the strain of working. It seems to exact a heavy toll, although it helps meet the family's economic needs. In general, her experience will suggest to them that work—or perhaps just women's work—is not satisfying, although the income it brings, however scanty, is welcome. Frank and Rose Giannini's combined gross income puts the family in an economically secure position. They are among the third of American families who can be called "comfortable," those with average incomes beginning somewhat above the median. However, the Gianninis achieve this position only through the efforts of two earners, and until a few years ago Frank's salary alone would have afforded them the same or nearly the same degree of comfort and security. It is taking more just to stand still, and the Giannini children perceive this fact and its consequences for family life through remarks about their father's overtime work and their mother's role as earner. They are taking in a perspective on economic reality—one they cannot articulate but one that will remain a point of reference for all their subsequent encounters with economic realities or economic theories.[5]

The Gianninis' combined income is not too far from Bob Murphy's or Steve Polsky's. But the status associated with the work they do is less—dramatically less in the case of Rose's work. The social contrast between Bob's position as assistant manager (and college-educated engineer) and Frank's job as custodian is marked.

The contrast with Steve Polsky's work as plumber is more subtle. Both are blue-collar jobs, but Steve's is a "dirtier" job, in fact and in myth. However, with energy and acumen, Steve can become something of an entrepreneur. The upper limit on the income he can make is not nearly as fixed as Frank's. He has a chance to achieve some of the status money can buy—membership in a golf club or a cruise to the Caribbean.

Most important, Steve and Bob are the sole earners in their families. It is their income alone that puts their families toward the upper end of the "comfortable" income category—and incidentally gives their wives the time and energy to participate, if they wish, in a number of activities that have a certain status attached to them—tennis, book clubs, or volunteer work.

While Alice Murphy and Jane Polsky can spend a pleasant, sociable morning planning the craft tables for a church fair, Rose works at an alienating, low-paying, low-status job. Alice and Jane, if they are so inclined, may become part of the volunteer power structure of their community; Rose will probably never have the time and energy for such a role, although she might have managed to work at the hospital as a volunteer before she got a job there.

The Giannini children know that they are "somewhere in the middle." By the time they are Joanne's and Joe's ages they will begin to be aware that this "middle" is not quite the same as that of their classmates whose parents' situation resembles the Polskys' or the Murphys'. In fact, it is a "lower", or less educated, form of the "middle" and often reaches an earlier economic plateau. It is unlikely that either Giannini parent will be able to find a very much better-paying job. Unless Rose seeks further training (which she cannot afford), she cannot advance very much. With only a high school education Frank probably cannot do much better than he has already done. The Giannini children, listening to their parents, will take in the message that "this is it," that there are no big rainbows over the horizon. They will grow up thinking of their parents as effective providers; and they will think of their father, if not their mother, as having and doing a "good job." But their image of what is possible for "people like us" in the future will probably be more limited than that of the Murphy children and the Polsky children.

It is probably fair to say that the less income there is, the more tangible a reality it is in a child's life. For children growing up in affluence, money can be about as unimportant to their consciousness of everyday life as eating or sleeping—they take for granted that most things they want or need will be there. They may never, in fact, understand the importance of income to the life they lead, unless they undergo a sudden reversal of circumstances.

For children whose families are struggling to keep food on the table, income is important, which is not to say they note how much a parent brings home or how money is spent. But they are aware that leftovers are not optional, that spilled milk is not just a breach of etiquette. Television has made children far more aware of the things money can buy and the places it will take one. It may be that today children assess their family's income level in the light of what they can and cannot have of the things they see on television.

PLACE, POWER, AND POSSIBILITIES

As children accumulate impressions of their parents' working lives, they gradually build a picture of their family's place in society, their power, and the possibilities that are open to them. Place has to do with the family's class and status in society. These terms are used to express a variety of meanings, but most generally they refer to income (or wealth), educational level, residence, and the prestige that attends one's work. In a consumer society, money can often buy class and status. But money is not the only way to status; an old and famous family name may assure one's prestige, as may a culturally important (but meagerly paid) profession such as art, music, writing, or the ministry. In general, "middle class" is the label to which almost every American aspires—even many who are rich but feel that it is elitist and undemocratic to think of themselves or present themselves as "upper class." In fact, "middle class" is a label used to describe a wide income range and a considerable range of life styles. It tells us very little indeed.

Power concerns the family's ability to act effectively, to influence their own lives and those of others, to make decisions, and to be able to carry them out. In contemporary society one of the meanings of power is access to an ever-growing body of knowledge. Is what is just discovered still pertinent or obsolete? How can you get to the person who knows how to get something done (find a lawyer, an accountant, a psychiatrist, a real estate agent, a learning-disabilities consultant, a repairman who can fix the oven, or a consumer advocate who can help you get action from a manufacturer)? High-income, high-status, educated people are in a far better position to obtain such expert advice and help than low-income, low-status, uneducated people; there is, as one commentator has put it, "a social distribution of privileged meanings."[6]

The Giannini children know that their father has a certain scope for personal effectiveness in his job, although he is hardly a power in the school system. They also know that his access to the principal gives him the power to obtain the name of the specialist who treated Joanne's rash. But consider what their sense of power would be if their father were a member of the faculty of the local medical school. Then the dermatologist might be a family friend or acquaintance, someone the children had seen in the house. At the very least they would know that their father had phoned the dermatologist as a peer or chatted with him about Joanne's problem in the faculty dining room.

Consider, on the one hand, what they would feel if they were dependent on their mother for information about a specialist. In this case, if Joanne had a bad night, they might end up in the emergency room "taking what they could get," powerless in relation to the leviathan of the hospital.

Perception of power and perception of possibilities are closely linked, although not identical. The Giannini children's sense of the possibilities open to them is probably somewhat greater than their sense of the power the family wields. One might imagine a family supported by a low-paying manual job where, despite the powerlessness inherent in the work and income situation, a parent is unusually resourceful and energetic and finds ways of getting what the family needs. It is also possible to imagine a rich family with all the power and opportunity money can buy whose children, nevertheless, are psychologically powerless to pursue the possibilities open to them.[7]

Children cannot articulate their sense of place, power, and possibilities in abstract terms. But they perceive where they stand in

Seeing the World Through Parents' Lives

relation to others in particular situations. Consider the common childhood experience of going to the zoo. Here are some of the questions children may gradually learn to ask—and to answer—about their visits. If we go to the zoo, can we go only once or twice a year because Dad and Mom are too busy or too tired most of the time? Do we go only when the school rents a bus? Or can we go frequently because we have the time, energy, and transportation to do so? When we go to the zoo, does it make a difference whether or not we go on the one or two free days? Can we have all the potato chips we want, or if we must limit ourselves to one bag, is the reason money or a prohibition on junk food? When we go to the zoo, do we flash special members' passes that distinguish us from the other people going through the turnstyle? Are we the sons or daughters or acquaintances of the man for whom the new aviary is named? Or do we visit the zoo as part of a group of children who are looked upon as potentially troublesome, made to wait, and lectured about behavior?

A child's sense of the place, power, and possibilities of his family and himself is of lasting influence in his life. It is an awareness that can be modified, but, like his early mapping of intimate life, it tends to be enduring and entrenched. For many, the possibility of finding ways to create a more satisfying way of life may seem remote, or the dreams of childhood may be erased prematurely because their realization is out of the reach of "people like us."

Chapter Five
Finding a Place on the Team

> *Neither the life of an individual nor the history of a society can be understood without understanding both.*
>
> —C. Wright Mills, *The Sociological Imagination*

Until children are six or seven, they are primarily "family children." Unless they go to day care or nursery school, they spend most of their time in a family setting, among people their parents know. Around the age of six or seven, cognitive developments help children take a place among strangers beyond the home while remaining identified with their family world. To their rudimentary map of social reality bearing the imprint of their family's values and ways of viewing and doing things, they add the topography of social worlds beyond the family as they move into peer groups, classrooms, games, or sports. At this age children are adept at learning how to adapt to the rules that govern relationships in each of the new worlds they enter. They can join a group of children on the street where they live, where ages and sometimes interests vary much more than they do in a group of classmates. They learn how a pecking order is established, how conflict is negotiated, who is in and who is out and on what basis; what you can do and what you cannot do; what are, for instance, the criteria for compassion, tolerance, or blame. They can recognize that the roles and rules that apply on one street may not hold on another, and they can accept that school and street are each worlds of their own.

Recollection may characterize the years from seven to twelve as a time when life was quite full of horseplay, adventure, discovery, friendship, frustration, broken bones, a measure of boredom, and a secret life separate from adults. But days of fun and games and friends—or their absence—set the stage for learning and rehearsing the lore, the skills, the values, the organizational styles, and the sanctions of the society one has inherited. The peer group is probably as powerful an influence as adults, perhaps more so.[1] But the peer culture (though our memories suggest otherwise) is never created from scratch nor passed on as dogma. It tends to accommodate important traditions to major social changes and to local events.

With peers children construct a child-world, yet this child-world exists within a social context established by adults or, more accurately, by the major institutions that define the society's mainstream. Children's experience—both their direct interaction with peers and their inward beliefs, self-expectations, and fantasies—is shaped by this adult context.

Although the context of their play with peers may be idiosyncratic to childhood, its social forms, especially those concerned with managing social encounters, parallel those of the adult world. In this chapter we shall examine how this process works in the game of baseball, but it is true for other activities as well and for the informal social negotiations of the school-age child—deciding whether to skateboard or play ball, whom to include and whom to exclude from a group, and when to assert a right to join or lead others who are not eager for one's company. In their relations with their peers, children have opportunities to test, extend, confirm, or reject the rules and roles that have become part of their social experience so far. Moreover, they have a chance to assess some of their fantasies in relation to the real possibilities of their lives.

In addition, the peer world offers children glimpses of other family worlds and a sense of how other families are like or unlike their own. It may offer them a chance to meet parents who assign meaning or importance to events that their own parents may neglect, avoid, or refuse to consider.

BASEBALL AS AN INITIATION INTO AMERICAN LIFE

At least for boys, and for increasing numbers of girls, sports are the most important activities through which six-to-twelve-year-olds step into an intermediate world beyond the family world but not yet the work world. Here is the story of three boys playing baseball, a game that embodies a typically American set of mind. In saying that baseball embodies this set of mind we are implying that sports are not to be thought of as mere entertainment—the frills of American culture—but as a profound expression of that culture, having elements of a civil religion, no less serious for being enjoyable.[2]

As ten-year-old Chris biked toward the park with his glove in the bike basket and his hat in one hand, he saw the Sanchez boys, Al and Tony, coming out of their house. He put on the brakes and urged them to come along.

When the three boys reached the field, the game was just beginning. Two of the biggest kids were acting as captains and choosing up sides. Chris saw that none of the boys was more than a couple of years older than he was.

"Hey, Chris," cried someone. "We're taking you."

Chris was agile for his age, and he had a strong throwing arm.

"Hey, Al. You're coming with us," others yelled. Al was older than Chris and had the makings of a good pitcher; he was also quite a hitter. No one welcomed Tony. Tony was a little overweight and not very well coordinated, but what he lacked in talent he made up for in enthusiasm.

At last everyone was chosen—even Tony. Al and Tony were on one team; Chris was on the other. Next, the boys had to decide which team would bat first. "Let's flip for it," said Joey, one of the bigger kids and one of the best ballplayers. Al and Tony's team ended up at bat, while Chris's team took the field.

The boys began to play. A short, dark boy was first up. He shot a grounder past the shortstop's outstretched glove and ran happily to first base.

The next batter was out on a routine fly ball.

The third batter was an older boy whom Chris knew as a good ballplayer. As the ball left the pitcher's hand, the boy shifted his stance and slid his right hand up the bat to bunt. Contact was made, and the ball rolled down the third-base line. The batter took off for first base as fast as he could go. He arrived in plenty of time. Meanwhile, the kid from first base rounded second and beat the return throw to third. There were excited shouts from everyone on the team.

The next batter was Al. The first pitch was a ball below the knees. Al let it go by. Then came a hard swing—and a miss—strike one. But Al connected with the third pitch and sent a towering fly ball over the centerfielder's head: a home run. "Three runs in," the kids shouted as they slapped Al's back when he crossed home plate.

Now it was Tony's turn to bat. Tony missed the first pitch. His brother watched him: Tony was holding the bat near the end and it was a bit heavy for him, Al thought. "Tony," Al yelled at him. "Choke up a little."

But Tony was too preoccupied to hear and still held the bat near the end when the pitcher delivered again. Strike two. Then, three. He was out.

"Too low!" Tony's teammates cried. "A bad ball to hit. Well, you'll get him next time."

"I blew it," Tony said, disconsolately. "I just didn't see it right."

One out later, Tony's team took the field. There was some discussion about the positions they would play; as a result, Al went to shortstop and Tony to right field. The pitcher was Joey, the best all-around player in the neighborhood. Lots of the boys believed that some day Joey would be a professional ballplayer. Teasingly, they called him "catfish" and they half believed what they said.

Chris watched Joey warm up with evident admiration and some dread for his own turn at bat. Joey could throw very hard for his age and had excellent control. He also made clever use of his change-up. Chris watched despairingly as batter after batter struck out. Maybe it was going to be a shutout. Then he remembered his dad telling him: "Don't panic. Just remember to keep your eye on the ball." It was his dad who taught him to throw and catch, even to bat, back in the days when he was just a little kid using only a plastic bat.

Just then one of his teammates hit a fair ball to the infield; seconds later an argument erupted. Who had reached the base first, the runner or the first baseman? Chris's team argued for the runner; Al and Tony's team for the fielder. For a moment Chris thought a fight would break out between two hot-tempered kids, but finally Joey said in a commanding voice, "Aw, let him have it. Maybe it was a tie anyway."

A minute or so later everyone had grumbled his way back to his position, the argument was over, and the game resumed.

Now it was Chris's turn to bat. He positioned his feet carefully. He kept his eye on the ball, still in Joey's hand. And then it was coming toward him. He was ready for a fastball, and Joey had given him a change of pace; fortunately it was low and wide, and Chris watched it go. He stepped out of the batter's box, rubbed his hands with dirt, and moved back in. He swung the bat a few times and tried hard to concentrate. He seemed to hear a voice inside his head, repeating his dad's words: "Don't try to second-guess; just keep your eye on the ball." He watched Joey's delivery and he swung. He didn't really know, minutes later when he thought about it, whether the ball was fast or slow, high or low; all he knew was that he heard the crack of the ball against the bat and started running.

But the excitement was not over yet. He had hit a grounder to Al, who, after fielding it, threw to second. The runner, Chris's teammate, dived for the base—and beat the throw. Chris himself arrived safely at first. Two on, two out: a chance to score some runs. But the next batter struck out and the inning was over.

It is not hard to imagine that Tony and Al's team won with Joey's pitching and Al's hitting. But it is not hard to imagine either that Chris said, "Great," when his father asked him what kind of time he had had later that evening.

What does playing baseball teach Chris, Al, and Tony about their world? What does it add to their social topography, their map of the world? What does it impart about rules and roles?

Let us begin by saying something about the game of baseball.

When Chris, Al, and Tony play baseball, they are not only having fun and testing, developing, and refining their physical skills; they are taking in key elements of American culture that will influence their sense of what is admirable and what is to be despised not only in play but in work and civic life. Baseball is the game of a society that places enormous emphasis on "individualism and personal honor, and the dignity of a man alone"[3] yet at the same time insists that the individual associate himself with the team. Playing baseball, a boy—less often a girl—absorbs and practices a certain set of mind that sees the individual as an actor in a reasonable, rational world.

Baseball is also the game of a society that believes that what matters in life can be counted. Every aspect of the game is measured and computed in the elaborate keeping of scores and records. The dimensions of the diamond, too, suggest the rationalism of a country that took shape during the Enlightenment: 90 feet to a side, 360 feet in all—the circle converted into a square. Physical prowess and even irrational or violent impulses will be acted out on the geometrical stage of a diamond and accounted for numerically.

Chris, Al, and Tony learn a great deal, too, about the complex rules that govern the role of star in our culture. The pitcher, for instance, is a key player in baseball and yet is also part of the team. Even if he is an exceptional player—a star—in a very American fashion he is expected not to make too much of his stardom. Chris, Al, and Tony know of Joey's special abilities—as does Joey—but they would criticize him if he treaded upon them too often or fell down in his role as a team player. The following quotation from a boy's guide to baseball suggests the complex demands made of the pitcher—and incidentally is a fine example of roles and rules presented to a child in explicit form.

A Pitcher's Duties

1. A pitcher must keep in good condition. He keeps well and strong by obeying training rules.
2. He must develop a strong arm so that he may be able to pitch a full game. He practices every day to keep his pitching arm strong and limber.
3. He must learn to have good control over his throws. He cannot afford to make "wild" throws. Good control comes with much practice.
4. He must be able to field balls that are hit to him. To "field" a ball means to be able to catch, throw, or stop a ball.
5. He must back up throws made to the infielders. He cooperates with the entire team at all times.
6. He must be able to cover first base when the first baseman fields a ball away from the first base area. To do this it is necessary to think quickly and move with speed.
7. He must learn the team signals. Since he is part of the team he should know the signals for the various plays.
8. He must learn the catcher's signals. This tells him what kind of pitch to use for the different batters.
9. He must try to strike out the batter or make him hit into an out.

Here is where strong, skillful pitching pays off.

Now you know why the pitcher is such a busy person. You can also see that the champions did not take their places on the mound in one easy lesson.

Most young boys like to start out by being pitchers. But as their muscles grow and become stronger, and as they learn more about the game, many change to positions that are more suitable to their ability and style of play.[4]

The pitcher must develop skills to their peak—ideally, he must be strong enough to pitch a full game. Yet baseball is not a game of brute force: in the third duty of the pitcher the authors stress "good control." But in addition to describing the skills he must develop, they also emphasize his role as a member of the team.

Try rereading the precepts quoted above, substituting for the baseball references terms instructing a young man how to succeed in business, in government, or as chairman of a community service organization, and you will see how baseball is a paradigm of American society—and how much Chris, Al, Tony, and Joey learn as they play about the "right" path to success, the relationship of skill and discipline to the pursuit of success, and the obligations of the successful individual to his team.

The way in which baseball reflects American society is amplified by Michael Novak in his book *The Joy of Sports* as follows:

> [Baseball] is to games what the *Federalist Papers* are to books: orderly, reasoned, judiciously balanced, incorporated segments of violence and collision in a larger plan of rationality, absolutely dependent on an interiorization of public rules.[5]

In another comparison Novak suggests:

> Baseball is designed like the federal system of checks and balances. This is a conceit, to be sure, but the umpires provide a kind of judiciary; the offensive players, stepping to the plate one by one, learn like our executive that "the buck stops here"; the defense attempts to play in concert, a congress checking the power of the hitters. The parallel is far from exact. But the balance of the game mirrors an intellectual psychic love of equilibrium that is also exemplified in our form of government.[6]

Two important caveats should be added to our consideration of how baseball involves and influences young players today. First, in many locations in recent years it has become harder to put together the sort of informal pick-up game that we describe. Such a game depends on having an adequate and safe place to play and on living in a neighborhood where children know one another and can travel on their own with impunity. Such conditions have all but disappeared in some urban and suburban communities. In addition, a homeowner may be held responsible for injuries incurred on his property, or a school board for playground injuries that occur when school is not in session, leading both to bow to the conditions set by the insurance industry and by court decisions.

Second, baseball for young people is increasingly dominated by bureaucratic organizations like Little League. If sandlot baseball is characteristic of a less densely populated, more individualistic, and entrepreneurial America, Little League is characteristic of corporate America and contemporary urban or suburban life. Adults manage Little League, and their tendency is to slot players in certain positions according to ability and competence. Management is in control, and management decides who plays when and in what position. There is far less chance in Little League for a boy to play a variety of positions or to try a position because a player whom he admires and identifies with plays it, and far less chance for someone of limited talent like Tony to play at all. The game we describe is much closer than a Little League game to being a model of democracy in which all are given a chance to contribute. Chris, Al, and Tony learn that the talented Joey can emerge from an open contest among peers, but there is still a place for Tony. If they played Little League, they might pay lip service to this ideal, but the reality they would be learning would be that of a contest regulated largely by adults.

Little League has brought other changes to the game as well. There is less opportunity for children to learn from one another, to negotiate and resolve conflicts among themselves. When it is not clear who tagged first base, the runner or the baseman, an argument and near-fight erupt which are finally resolved by Joey's assertion of the rules. We have suggested that Joey is the acknowledged leader in this umpireless game. However, it is conceivable that another boy without Joey's athletic talent, but with some of his skills as a leader, might be the one to settle disputes and make decisions. In a Little League game the majority of decisions are likely to be made by an adult manager. Thus Little League encourages children to accept the authority of the informed instructor—the "because I say so" of boss or expert.*

In a Little League game, moreover, there is less opportunity to be

---

*Little League may, for some adults, offer opportunities for taking charge which may not be available at work. It may also offer an opportunity to take the role of the boss and dominate children, thus reversing the powerlessness they may feel at work.

teammates one day and on opposing sides the next. Little League players are generally assigned permanently to a team and are therefore in permanent opposition to other teams. This encourages a belief in more or less permanently drawn social lines, thus narrowing the opportunity for broad social identification.

In sum, the transformations wrought by Little League exemplify the bureaucratization of our society, its increasingly tightly defined if not narrower opportunities, its emphasis on specialization and the acceptance of authority based on expert knowledge at the expense of individual experiment. The forms and style of life of the Little Leaguer prepare him for life in modern corporate America; this new America grew out of the older entrepreneurial and largely rural world and was grafted upon it just as Little League grew out of and was grafted upon the old style sandlot game.

Games that have traditionally been played by boys, particularly team sports, provide practice in skills that will be needed in the public world of work. In these games children learn to act according to mutually agreed upon rules, to settle disputes, and to coordinate the activities of a diverse group of people.

Games that have traditionally been associated with girls, on the other hand, are preparation for the private world of home, family, and courtship. Traditional girls' games have fewer rules than boys' games and fewer areas of ambiguity that might require adjudication or the tolerance of a conflict situation. Girls' games are apt to break up faster than boys' in part because girls have developed, or been encouraged to develop, less skill and persistence in resolving conflicts and in part because, at least in athletic games, they have not been encouraged to develop their physical abilities to the same degree and are hence more easily bored or frustrated.

Janet Lever provides the following description of girls' games and the qualities they encourage:

> Girls' games may provide a training ground for the development of delicate socio-emotional skills. We have seen that girls' play occurs in small, intimate groups, most often the dyad. It occurs in private places and often involves mimicking primary human relationships instead of playing formal games. Their age-mixed play is the type that helps girls to develop nurturing skills. Finally, girls' play, to a large extent, is spontaneous and free of structure and rules; its organization is cooperative more often than competitive.[7]

However, times are changing. More girls are playing boys' games and often playing them with boys. Not surprisingly, given opportunity and freedom from censure, they develop high levels of skills and the capacity to negotiate disputes. It should be pointed out that games reflect changes already under way in adult social arrangements and do not *cause* such changes. Nonetheless, the freedom for boys and girls to play at the same game enriches and enlarges the experience of both sexes.

Something analogous might be said in relation to the handicapped. Implicit in advocacy efforts to assure access to normal social situations for handicapped children has been an awareness that it is primarily through observation and participation in the events and institutions of the everyday life world of their peers that handicapped children learn about the paths to mastery and fulfillment. These lessons are very difficult to learn from books or television, in part because the very act of social exclusion gives a message louder than any teacher's, author's, or film narrator's. A child does not have to be able to play baseball in order to learn about the social realities of peers. What is learned through discussions and observations of peers whom one knows on a face-to-face basis teaches many lessons about the world.

We do not suggest that all children should play baseball or any particular sport, nor that they should all participate in any one activity. Rather, we suggest that children's sense of their own possibilities is shaped by social messages implicit in social rules that govern, for example, inclusion or exclusion based on sex, race, or handicap, even when they have no relevance to a specific social situation. Those of us who are physically and psychologically able have been slow to acknowledge that our eagerness "to protect" the handicapped by caring for them in socially isolated circumstances protects us from feeling uncomfortable or vulnerable as we must when we first accept them in our midst, as the Polskys did when they invited the Murphys for a picnic. The benefits of social inclusion are still limited for the handicapped, but their inclusion can benefit others: The nonhandicapped child whose social constructions of reality make room for the full range of his peers' constructions has a richer and more accurate view of the world he is growing up in.[8]

Chapter Six
Stepping Into a World Beyond Family

> *Whereas members of relatively nonmodernized societies teach their children roughly what their children need to know for their adult lives, we teach our children what we needed to know for our lives rather than what they will need to know for theirs.*
>
> —Marion J. Levy, *Modernization and the Structure of Societies*

Traditionally, neighborhood, church, and school have been the institutions the child is most likely to encounter when he ventures beyond the intimate circle of his family. These may be called the intermediate institutions of the society in contrast to the primary institution of family and the major economic and government institutions that define how the society will be maintained or changed.[1]

Intermediate institutions offer families education, solace, spiritual fellowship, a sense of community, support, and occasionally entertainment. Parents think of school, church, or neighborhood as institutions that extend what they themselves offer their children, preparing them for life in American society. The intermediate institutions are to some degree a buffer zone between the family and the forces of society at large.[2] Often they offer networks of contacts and sources of information to enrich a family's life, help it solve problems, or find resources. Typically children are among their explicit concerns.

In recent years a new institution has taken shape—television. As an advertising arm of competitive economic institutions, American commercial television often serves its sponsors more faithfully than its viewers. At the same time it can be considered an intermediate institution, offering as it does education, entertainment, and a sense of community—in this case, a nearly global community. No one yet understands television's impact, but in its function as an intermediate institution, its effects are profound. It may be an even more powerful force for shaping society than we now realize.[3] In fact, if television is viewed as part of the economy's tool box and as an intermediate institution, it may be the one institution that is simultaneously part of society's major, intermediate, and familiar institutions. In some sense television is both a stranger and a familiar in the family, linking the family to world events and new knowledge in unprecedented ways, and quite possibly reinforcing formulas for social behavior at least as forcefully as they have ever been reinforced in a face-to-face community.

As society has modernized, intermediate institutions have changed, and these changes have affected their links with families and the experience of children growing up. It is not easy to define or measure these changes, but it is clear that the influence of some institutions relative to others has diminished. Neighborhoods, churches, and voluntary associations have declined in influence relative to schools, hospitals, and, most of all, television. This shift reflects the thrust of social change in contemporary society in the direction of increasing human knowledge of and control over the material and social world.

CHURCH AND NEIGHBORHOOD

In late twentieth-century society churches and neighborhoods, historically the carriers and guardians of tradition, have to compete for the loyalty and attention of their members with other institutions, ranging from schools and television to professionalized social services.[4] Although many, perhaps most, Americans remain very much involved with neighborhood networks, church congregations, and voluntary associations, many neither expect nor seek their help in raising children. When professional resources such as hospitals and social agencies are available, more and more families turn to them for the help that in earlier times they might have sought from neighbors or from their church. Although these modern institutions provide far more expert help than was ever available to families in the past, their functions tend to be specialized. As a result, they are apt to respond only to specific problems rather than to a family's overall situation or to the individual as a whole. In addition, they are a resource only when a problem arises—their personnel are seldom part of the daily or weekly social rituals of a community. In an analogous way, commercial television, while it provides more accurate and extensive information about what is going on in the world than any local informant, nevertheless does so in a totally impersonal manner.

Moreover, professionalized institutions are relatively lacking in the social ties that are part of the life of organizations such as churches or neighborhoods. Often the full range of what a neighborhood or a church offers depends on the people who have been there for some time and on their particular social bonds, sensitivities, connections, or skills. Services and support to neighbors or churchgoers may be good, bad, or indifferent, but chances are that, more than most modern institutions, church congregations and neighborhood networks give their members a sense of belonging, of being protected as a group vis-à-vis the major institutions of government and economic life.

Although there are thousands of neighborhoods today where families know each other and children get together in games on the street or in backyards, there are many in which residents have little contact and share little except sidewalks and a common street address. Many adults are content with such a neighborhood; they enjoy the privacy it affords and the liberty to build their own social networks out of friendships formed at work, through their church affiliation, and their leisure or political activities. Children who live in such a neighborhood—even very young children—learn to form social and cultural ties that are outside their immediate physical environs. We do not know that this is a less desirable introduction to the world than growing up in a traditional neighborhood, but it is a different and, for the preadolescent child, a more difficult social world to map without considerable help from adults. Choosing friends and activities according to criteria other than geographic proximity emphasizes individual self-fulfillment at the expense of living in a community filled with familiar faces. Some have speculated that one consequence of growing up in such a manner may be that children do not feel any responsibility for the people, spaces, and structures in their neighborhood, seeing them only as something one drives past on the way to somewhere else.[5]

SCHOOL

Whereas neighborhoods and churches have lost ground to other institutions in modern times, schools have gained tremendously in influence. There are two reasons. First, as the one institution that has an unquestioned link with children and parents, the school potentially draws families together by providing a common meeting ground and purpose. Often parents look to the school for the help with child rearing they may find missing in neighborhoods and churches. Or they may expect schools to provide *all* the buffering and bridging functions between the family and the wider society.

Second, the explosion of knowledge and the removal of work from homes and farms have led the school to serve a wider gamut of the population for a longer portion of their day and for a greater number of years. Movement in this direction began in the early nineteenth century with the establishment of the public school system. At that time, however, formal education was not needed for most of the society's work, and school did not bulk large in the lives of many children. Once education became a requirement for all but the least desirable jobs and was both free and compulsory, schools grew in size and complexity until they became a billion-dollar enterprise and a dominant force in children's lives. The large size of schools, the large scale of school systems, the range of specialized experts, the proliferation of laws, and the multiple sources of funding for special programs require a far greater degree of bureaucratic organization than schools ever required in the past, exposing young children for long periods of the day to life in a complex organization.

One of the primary functions of schools at the elementary level is the inculcation of symbol skills, both verbal and numerical, which will make the child competent in the world of everyday affairs, as well as providing him with a ticket of entry to specialized schools or the working world. Facility with symbols is of vital importance in the modern world. Some competence with verbal and numerical codes is demanded by all but dead-end jobs and in the decisions and paperwork of everyday life. Encounters with all modern institutions—hospitals, banks, the Internal Revenue Service, the Bureau of Motor Vehicles, unemployment compensation, social security, welfare, and even the supermarket—require the ability to read and write and often to make numerical calculations.

Equally important, skills make it possible for a person to develop a "public voice," that is, to speak, read, and write with the syntax of power and influence, the only sort of voice that will assure him a hearing in public places. If a child does not master symbolic codes efficiently and at the prescribed time, chances are that he will be denied not only rewarding work but also a public, and finally, a political voice.

A more subtle, but no less real, function of schools is the inculcation of behaviors and attitudes that express the central values of American culture. These include efficiency, tenacity, a delicate balance between individual initiative and team play, and strategies for resolving conflict smoothly.

The public school system was founded in part to pass on American values to a heterogeneous population. One of its missions was the social transformation of the children of immigrants before their presumed backwardness and waywardness could jeopardize the social order of the core Anglo-Saxon culture. Schools were also to be the vehicle for children to develop their talents, regardless of their origins, and to acquire skills that would allow them to take advantage of America's opportunities. A child who could not—or would not—absorb the normative social values was to a greater or lesser degree rejected. "This is the way to do things," has always been the social message taught by school and implicitly, "This is the way to do things if you want to get ahead." Children's reactions in the face of this teaching may vary all the way from "This is the way to do things, and it's easy for me" to "This is the way to do things, and there's no way I can win."

Rather than thinking of schools as moving all children in the same direction and in the same way, it is more appropriate to think of schools as exerting forces and pressures to which children react in a variety of ways: some children succumb; others eagerly embrace them; still others actively rebel against them; and many are caught up by them in an ambivalent, tense, and potentially destructive relationship. Typically, the school reinforces the values a child has learned at home, but for some children it contradicts them. When this happens, it is soon clear to children that, as far as society's purposes are concerned, school is right and home is wrong; they learn that if they resist the efforts of the school to shape them, they will pay a heavy price. Most children fall into line.[6]

Children's entrance into first grade is a major rite of passage from the family world to the world of school—a significant passage even for children who have been to kindergarten, nursery school, or day care. Although children meet the public world through friendship with their peers, on their street, in their neighborhood, or at church, their encounter with the world of school is probably the most important to their sense of the paths they can take and who they can be in the society. This is so because school is virtually the only institution that provides preparation and credentials for work and for an eventual social and political niche. It is the only institution, except for television, that gives every child an extensive introduction to the norms of the society.

School is a serious experience for children—as well as one that takes a substantial number of the days and years of their youth. They will be made to feel that it is serious by their parents, their teachers, their peers, and by the messages that reach them through television. The amount of time they spend in school and the seriousness with which it is viewed mean that they will have many inducements to accept the culture of the school—even if they hate it. If they succeed in school, their feelings of success may be a model for future success. If they fail or just get by—whatever the reasons—their hopes and self-expectations will very likely be low.[7]

"Doing well in school" has always been a promise of doing well in the particular world for which school prepares the pupil, not necessarily a promise that is fulfilled in later life, but still a promise. In past times doing well in school or even "getting through" at least meant access to a career as a minister, a lawyer, a teacher, or a civil servant even if it did not guarantee eventual success in one's profession. But there were many other walks of life to which school was not the key.

What success in school did not promise, in the past any more than it does now, was a good income. Clergymen, teachers, and even the majority of lawyers and civil servants were not rich men, and lack of schooling did not mean that an individual was unable to make money. A good income was a matter of owning land and working it well or of entrepreneurial ability. The skills required to be a successful farmer or entrepreneur involved only a very modest amount of book learning—and this could be learned at home or on the job. Most important, experience, not school, was the credential that gave access to the job.

How to give every child a genuine opportunity for success in school has been a topic of passionate debate, particularly in the last twenty years. For some, it involves valuing each child for what he or she is and equipping him or her with the skills that are essential to survival in society. For others, it involves changing the inequities in major social institutions, whose norms the school can only reflect.[8]

The following vignette illustrates some of the issues involved in the debate over educational opportunity.

TWO DAYS IN THE LIFE OF FLORENCE MOSBY

Late Tuesday afternoon in the week before Thanksgiving, Florence Mosby inched her car along in the rush-hour traffic heading west out of Chicago. She drove automatically, her mind elsewhere. She was thinking about a conversation she had had earlier in the day with Vivian Winters and trying to work out what she wished she'd said.

Vivian was a reading specialist. She had spent the last two days observing in the first-grade classroom of the inner-city school where Florence taught.

Like Florence, Vivian was black, and like Florence she was a graduate of the local teacher's college, where she had also received her advanced degree in reading. Like Florence, too, Vivian had been raised in Chicago.

Maybe it was everything they shared that made Florence listen carefully to what Vivian had to say—and maybe it was their similarities that made Florence wish she had succeeded in getting Vivian to understand her point of view.

As in most classrooms, there was a wide range of abilities among Florence's first graders and an even bigger range of readiness for learning to read. Some children had learned all their letters and some words—many from watching "Sesame Street" and "The Electric Company." Others could not name many letters and were only beginning to match appropriate sounds with letters and letter combinations. Some children took to language naturally, while others talked little, and Florence wasn't sure they always understood what she said. The class was no different from other first grades she had taught. What was different was Vivian's visit, which reflected the school district's new emphasis on basic skills and the school board's funding of a part-time reading specialist for each school in response to this new emphasis.

Florence had been teaching first grade for five years, and if she had to put a name to her approach she would have called it "combined." "Combined" meant a lot of things. She tried to be both tough and tender, firm and yet responsive to the children as individuals (as much as one can be with twenty-eight six-year-olds). And she used a variety of methods and materials. Most of all, "combined" meant that she did not break children into groups by ability.

Without regard to ability, each day Florence gathered a group and got each child to dictate a story that she recorded in the child's notebook. She then inscribed the words from the story on cards, which she slipped into a folder. These words became the child's words—to learn by sight, to copy, and eventually to combine in sentences. One recent story read: "I hate my baby. He shit his diaper." Florence had dutifully included a card that read "shit" in the child's folder, along with "baby," "diaper," and "hate."

At least once a week she helped a group improvise a collective story to which each child made a contribution. She wrote the stories in big letters on newsprint for everyone to see and collected them in an enormous binder that held stories written by previous classes—often older brothers and sisters of her current pupils.

This was the way beginning reading had been taught at Fairview, the primary school where Florence had done her practice teaching. It still seemed to her the best approach. (Florence's supervisor at Fairview had admired Sylvia Ashton-Warner, whose book *Teacher* Florence herself had read and been much influenced by.)

Vivian had criticized just about every aspect of Florence's "combined" approach.

"It's nice, Florence," she had said, "but it's a luxury you can't afford, and neither can these kids; I don't need to tell you that. What are you doing teaching kids to write 'shit'? That's not what they need to know. You're never going to get the slow ones into the first reader by spring at this rate. You're only human and the day's only so long. You've got to break them up into ability groups so that you can work with them more efficiently."

"But Vivian," Florence had said, "that's tracking."

"You don't need to call it that. You don't need to call the reading groups fast and slow. You can call them Tigers and Lions—anything you please."

Vivian had gone on to say that even if they did know, it was something that Florence had to do for their own good. Didn't she realize it was a waste of that bright little Mario's time to sit listening to three slow kids dictating stories when he really needed some pretty systematic drills with phonics? Florence had said that she did know Mario was ready for work with phonics and that she was trying to find the time to give him what he needed, but . . .

"That's just it," Vivian had said. "You can't give him what he needs unless you break up the class into groups and give the slow ones much more structured drill with component skills or they'll never make it."

Vivian had interrupted before Florence could give voice to the idea that even if Mario was ready for more phonics than she was able to give him, there was something to be gained, particularly for the slower kids, in sitting down together and telling or retelling stories—writing as well as reading them. The spark of excitement she could see when they got hooked on writing down their own thoughts seemed the bedrock of true literacy—what learning to read was all about.

She waited for a light to change, turning the matter over in her mind. Wasn't six just too early to track children, to let a child know that he wasn't as good as the next one, particularly in something as basic as reading? Why was efficiency so important? Wasn't there something more important, something that lasted all your life, in learning that you could write and read about your own experience in your own words, even if it meant that it took you longer before you knew how to decode "ought" or got "was" and "saw" straight? And did the two processes necessarily exclude each other? Couldn't they—if only she had the skill and the strength—somehow be combined?

But as she came to a stop at the next traffic light, Vivian's words came back to her: "These kids can't afford it; I don't have to tell you that." She knew what Vivian meant: poor black kids could not afford to waste their time in school or in the kind of classroom she was running. At least if you were Vivian (or the principal or the school board), you could argue this way. Even at six they had to make up for lost time. What did that mean? Did the stories they dictated, and their words in their folders, have to go? What about the interest areas she had set up for them or the reading and writing corners that she had stocked with books from the school library as well as booklets written by former first graders?

Once again the light changed and Florence accelerated. She was within two blocks of the turn for the day-care center that her four-year-old son Brian attended. She felt a surge of anger. She thought of Darlene and Jackie, two of the slowest children in her class. There had been scores of children like them in the housing project where she had been raised. Without knowing the specifics of their family life she could guess what things were like for them at home. You could saturate them with Vivian's component skills and all it would do would be to turn them off. All the fancy new methods in the world and they might still not be reading by third grade if no one helped them give voice to their views of things or cared enough to listen.

Or was she, Florence, all wrong? Was she taking a gamble with the future of her own people, a gamble that would not pay off?

As she approached the day-care center, she began to think about her son. Where would he go to first grade? She wished he could go to a school like Fairview, but she knew that the primary school in her neighborhood was much closer to Vivian's ideal.

Florence stopped the car and got out. The Sunshine Day Care and Nursery Center was the creation of two sisters, Jane Kresge and Dora Kresge Moffat. Dora was a widow; Jane had once trained as a nursery school teacher, had never married, and had cared for her father until his death. When he died several months after Dora's husband, the two women decided to start Sunshine. That way they could afford to keep the house that had been their girlhood home, living upstairs and converting the rooms downstairs for the children's use.

The house was larger and older than most of the houses in the neighborhood, a relic of an earlier time, its upright primness balanced by generous porches around two sides. The sight of it always conjured mixed feelings in Florence. Dora and Jane offered good care, but in style with their prim house they emphasized manners to a degree that made Florence feel uncomfortable. Yet basically they treated children sympathetically and did not force early academics on them. They had their faults, but at least they respected children's play and didn't denigrate it in favor of "work" or, worse yet, organized "learning" activities. The sisters loved music, painting, and sculpting, and, in exchange for a few good manners, tolerated a lot of messiness and exuberance. They didn't work on reading readiness, but one of them was nearly always available to read an extra story, and they had set aside a large area of the room for story reading and dramatization. There were crowns and capes and firefighters' hats and grown-up shoes. Perhaps they didn't have soul, but they were undeniably warm and caring in their way. Being in their day-care center felt more like being in a home than being in a school. She had been lucky to find such a program for Brian. Yet it was all so . . . white and old-fashioned—the house, Dora, Jane, and their program. True, there were black children (plenty of black families had moved into Glendale in recent years as she and Dan had), but the atmosphere, the music, the manners, the lunches, the way things were done were rooted in white European customs and did not reflect black cultural styles.

As she walked up the steps, her thoughts flashed back to the children she had taught all day, their faces, their voices, their words—another world, a black urban world, one she had known all her life. But was it Brian's world?

She opened the door. There was Brian among the other children, his snowsuit on but not zipped and only one boot on. Florence knelt down and helped him with his boot. He stood up and she zipped his snowsuit. They said their goodbyes and went out the door.

"Have fun today, Brian?" Florence asked as they walked down the path to the street.

"They made me go out and I didn't want to," Brian said.

"Don't you always go out?"

"I don't want to go out. It makes my nose hurt and there are no blocks outside and we have to stand in line 'cause some kids are so slow."

"Why does your nose hurt?"

"The wind makes my nose hurt."

The day had been the first really cold day of the year, with Chicago's famous wind blowing from the north.

"Tomorrow you can take a scarf and Miss Kresge or Mrs. Moffat can tie it around your face."

"I'm not going out tomorrow."

By now they were sitting in the car.

"The scarf will make it better," said Florence, turning the key in the ignition.

"I want to play airport."

"Which airport?"

"The block airport me and Joel made."

"You can play with it when you're inside."

"I don't want to go outside."

Florence sidestepped. "What do you do when you're outside?" she asked.

"I want to ride the trikes, but Jamie and Rick won't let me."

"Ask them for a turn. They'll give you a turn."

"Miss Kresge told Jamie to give me a turn, and he kicked her."

"Then did he give you a turn?"

Florence glanced at Brian and saw that he was nodding. Then she concentrated on a swift turn before the light changed. A moment later Brian surprised her by saying: "Tell Miss Kresge I don't want to go out."

"Maybe I could tell Miss Kresge that the cold bothers you, but I don't think I could tell her what to do when she is taking care of you."

"Why?"

Florence was spared the necessity of answering the question by their arrival home.

The Mosbys lived in a neighborhood of small, nearly identical row houses built in the late fifties. They had bought their house four years ago, Dan's best year at work, when he had made $21,000 in his job as an insurance salesman. Dan worked for a small agency owned and managed by Ted Robbins, a black businessman and an old friend of Dan's father. Dan had been a junior at teacher's college—planning to follow in his father's footsteps as a teacher—when Ted offered him the job. He left school and accepted the offer. There was something much more attractive about working in a black-owned and managed business. For a while the agency prospered, but in the last year or two small operations like Ted's were hit hard, losing business to big agencies.

Florence saw Dan's car and pulled up behind it. She knew he was home early because he had been to a real estate workshop. She felt a twinge of worry as she did these days whenever she thought of Dan's work.

On the steps of the house she straightened her shoulders and gave a little tug to the skirt of her coat. If she had been aware of her gestures, she might have remembered that she had seen her mother do the same a thousand times.

Florence was the oldest of six children; her father had died when she was fourteen, and her mother had raised the family. Florence often thought of her mother standing at the ironing board ironing damask tablecloths and lace napkins for a hand laundry to make extra money after a full day's domestic work. Florence wondered again and again how her mother had managed to listen to all the kids while she ironed, often giving them a piece of her mind, telling them to clean up the kitchen or shine their shoes before going to school.

Florence opened the door and walked in. Brian ran ahead to greet his father who was folding the laundry Florence had put in the dryer in the morning. Sitting at the kitchen table with Dan was

Lester, Florence's youngest brother. Just this autumn Lester had come to live with Dan and Florence so that he could attend junior high in Glendale, a much better school than the one near the housing project where their mother still lived.

As Florence greeted Dan and Lester, she noticed that her brother's eyes did not meet hers. The thought flickered through her mind that something had gone wrong in school, and she felt a stab of responsibility and worry. Glendale Junior High was seventy-five percent white and twenty-five percent black: Lester was getting to know the white world as he never had before. What was happening? What had happened today?

"Momma, I'm hungry," Brian said. "When are we going to have dinner?"

"Give Momma a chance," Dan said, folding the last piece of laundry. "She doesn't even have her coat off. Maybe you and I could start dinner."

Florence went upstairs to change her clothes. She continued to think of Lester. She reviewed what little she and Dan knew of his life in school since he had come to Glendale. He was lucky; he had a sympathetic black homeroom teacher, Mr. Edwards, who was also his history teacher. Right now Mr. Edwards was teaching what seemed like a good unit on black history. But his understanding had not prevented Lester from being tracked in the lowest math group in the school. Luckily, after a few weeks, Dan and Florence had picked up on the fact that Lester was doing almost no math homework. "What's going on?" Dan had said. "It's too easy," said Lester, who was good at math. Florence had obtained transcripts of his test scores and requested that Lester be reassigned to a higher ability group. For once, she thought, a test score did something useful for a black boy.

Things had gone smoothly for several weeks after that. Then one day Lester came home with a black eye. "What've you been doing?" Dan asked. "Don't you know to pick on people you can beat?"

Lester threw himself down sullenly on his bed, and Dan waited for the story to come out.

It had started in the boys' locker room. A white boy had said to another white boy: "You smell like you had a monkey in your family tree. Get in the shower before your hair turns to steel wool."

"Who's calling who a monkey?" the biggest black boy in the school had asked.

"I'm not calling anyone a monkey," the first white boy said. "I'm telling Jock to take a shower. Can't I tell somebody to take a shower when he stinks?"

"Cut the shit."

A fight started and ended only when a teacher walked in and broke it up.

Dan was caught off guard when at the end of his story Lester asked: "Do they really think we smell?"

"Yeah, some do," Dan said. "What about it?"

"I didn't know," said Lester.

"There's a lot you don't know," said Dan. "There's a lot you'll learn. But you can't let it get you—keep cool."

Lester did not always talk to Dan and Florence about what he learned. For instance, he never said that he learned he could be good friends with a white boy at school, play ball with him after school, and never get invited to his house. But Lester learned other things at school. He enjoyed the classes, discussions, equipment, and library. Tracking and a departmentalized program meant that the few friends he had were not in all his classes. He learned to handle himself more independently and to take the initiative in making and keeping friends.

Florence knew as she entered the kitchen again that something had happened to Lester that day that he was not talking about. She realized she hadn't had a good talk with him for weeks. Maybe a lot more had been going on than she knew. Had she been busier or more preoccupied than usual? She thought all at once of her mother and of the conversations they had had while her mother worked. Her mother's life had been a lot harder than her own and still was. Why was it that Momma always found the time to talk? Was it something lacking in Florence, some strength Momma had and she didn't, or was it something in the helter-skelter way people lived now? But then maybe it was neither; ironing and cooking were different from correcting papers and reading professional journals. They kept your hands busy but didn't stop you from talking to your family.

When Florence took Brian to day care the next morning she asked if she could have a word with Miss Kresge.

"He's complaining about going out," she said. "I think the cold is bothering him. I'm sensitive to cold, and he may be like me. How long are the children out?"

"Half an hour in the morning and half an hour in the afternoon," said Miss Kresge.

Florence thought quickly to herself. That's one more time than anyone in our family would go out in cold weather. "Do you think he could stay in one of those times?" she asked. "He seems to be crazy about block play. Do you have any provisions?"

Miss Kresge frowned. "I'm sorry, Mrs. Mosby," she said. "I'm afraid we can't make any exceptions. We use the children's first outdoor period for staff meetings when student teachers are here, or as a break for teachers. Our staff are on duty for lunch, you know. The janitor cleans when the children go out in the afternoon. He has to be at his other job by four."

"Well then, would you be sure Brian wears a scarf over his mouth and nose if it's really windy?"

"I'll be glad to, Mrs. Mosby," said Miss Kresge.

As Florence drove to work, she felt torn between being angry and being resigned. She knew what Miss Kresge was up against. That's what it was like running a day-care center, and it was worse in a school. Certain things had to get done. You were dealing with groups of people, and that set a lot of ground rules right there. But then she wondered, did it really have to be that way? It hadn't been that way at Fairview, but then Fairview had operated with an ample budget and was in large measure the creation of a very special individual. If Fairview had been a day-care center and not a school, there would have been someone on duty in the classroom as well as in the playground so that Brian could have stayed indoors and worked on his airport. There would have been space for a separate staff meeting room and money to pay for after-hours cleaning service. But then only privileged children could afford a school like that. Miss Kresge and Mrs. Moffat barely managed, and Florence knew that some of their slender profits went into one or two scholarships for children whose families could not afford the full tariff of $65 a week.

But where did that leave Brian? Did he have to learn at four years of age that you had to go out and stay out for a prescribed length of time even if you were cold and were absorbed in something else just because that was what the group was doing? Did he have to learn about standing in line? What was the experience teaching him? What wasn't it teaching him? Wasn't it the very opposite of what she was trying to teach her first-graders? Her mind turned to the day ahead of her.

She had been planning to spend the whole reading period on what Vivian had called "component skills"—even slow Jackie and

Darlene would have to do their best to sit still and blend sounds like b-all, b-at, b-ack. But something inside of her suddenly rebelled, and as she approached the school she changed her lesson plan. She was not enthusiastic about the primary reader she was using, even though it showed a mixture of white and black faces. It told a Pollyanna story about a black and a white family meeting at the beach. There was a merry-go-round nearby and somehow the white father ended up paying for rides for all the kids, and the black kids lost the games they played with the white kids unless the white kids helped them out. She thought it was patronizing and phony.[9]

As she parked in the school lot, she remembered a book she'd glanced at in the school library, a brightly colored picture book about the daily life of two black children, including some of the more down-to-earth details of daily life such as Darlene had mentioned in the story about her little brother.

With a few minutes to spare before she had to be in her classroom, she went to the library and found the book. She'd give Vivian and the principal their component skills, but she was going to devote some of the day to reading a story that might mean something to the class, echo their real lives.

That evening at home Florence overheard a conversation between Dan and Lester below. The night before, after Lester had gone to bed, she had said to Dan: "Something's on Lester's mind. I wish you'd talk to him."

"School's okay," Lester was saying. "History is cool. But I don't like what's happening."

"What is happening?" she heard Dan ask.

Florence heard a silence as Lester seemed to search for words.

"There's been a lot of stealing out of lockers. And a girl left her bag on a chair in the library while she went to the can, and it was gone. And everybody knows it's black kids doing it. I mean *I* know it's black kids doing it. I think I know which kids."

Now it was Dan's turn to be silent.

"Lester," he said at last. "It's not going to be any easier for you than it was for the rest of us. There are no simple answers after two hundred years of American history. You don't need Mr. Edwards to teach you that."

Florence felt that for the moment the conversation was complete. Involuntarily straightening her shoulders she went downstairs to join them.

THE PRESCHOOL CHILD

At the Sunshine Day Care and Nursery Center, Brian Mosby learns how to accommodate to the needs of an institutionalized order, dictated in part by considerations such as efficiency and in part by the licensing codes of municipal departments of health and fire protection, the state child-welfare office, agreements between the Kresge sisters and their employees, and arrangements with the college whose students are available for certain days and hours over the semester.

Whatever facts or symbols Brian takes in from his years in day care, he will learn how to behave in an American social organization, one where strangers come together for a common purpose. He will become something of an organization child and, in the words of one sociologist, will be asked "to accept organizational reality as given, adjust to routine, take on a limited rather than a diffuse obligation to the organization and guide his behavior by impersonal universalistic principles."[10]

"Why can't we have a real Christmas tree?" Brian may ask and be told that fire laws forbid any but flameproof synthetic trees in public places. "Why does Miss Kraus have to go? I don't want her to go. I like her," he may say on another occasion, speaking of one of the student teachers. He may be told that her practice teaching term is ended. He will not thoroughly understand the explanations, but they will indicate to him that Sunshine is a different kind of place from home. For all its homey, low-key style and atmosphere, it is to some degree part of the public world that he is entering for the first time.

Much of what Brian learns is derived from the messages conveyed by adults in their moods, tones, gestures, and facial expressions, as well as their more overt actions. In addition, he learns from the way time is scheduled, the way space is used, and the degree of noise and disorder that is tolerated. When he is told that he must go outdoors with the rest of his group although it is cold and although he would rather play with his airport made of blocks, he learns that he must tailor his needs and interests to the demands of an organization where time and resources set certain limits.

Moreover, he will learn that although his mother may be sympathetic to his needs and interests, she and his father are powerless to help him satisfy them in the face of their contract with an organization that assumes responsibility for Brian in their absence, one whose public license obliges them to meet certain conditions. At home his parents might let him come in if his nose gets cold or not even suggest that he go out on such a day; they might allow him to play with a block construction "just a little bit longer."

But school—even the Kresges' day-care center—is not governed by individual responses and decisions as is the home. A day-care center of forty or fifty children has administrative—and, in a small way, bureaucratic—problems. The solutions to such problems, expressed concretely in the way time and space are allotted, usually do not put individual needs first, but the needs of an organization to carry out its work efficiently.

The lessons Brian learns prepare him for life in contemporary American society, a world where rules and procedures related to the bureaucratic organizations of the society govern the social relations of its members. If he refuses these lessons—if he cannot tolerate leaving his block airport on schedule and cannot accommodate to standing in line and bracing for the cold—he will be subtly or not so subtly judged, marked as a "difficult" or "sensitive" child—or as one whose "meddlesome" parent is a lot of trouble for the staff to deal with. These categories are only a jump away from a category that sounds something like this: "This child probably will not respond well to the school experience." Brian already carries one social mark—he is a black American—and Florence and Dan know they must try to steer him clear of additional marks that will increase the burden of prejudice he must overcome as he goes through school.

What Brian learns about behavior appropriate in an institutional setting is intertwined with what he learns about behavior the Kresge sisters as individuals consider appropriate to school. They are kind but prim and place a high priority on good manners and restraint. They are in no way likely to depart from the bureaucratic "rules" which make their school function smoothly, except perhaps on special occasions. For instance, Mrs. Moffat may allow children to roll on the grass during an outing to a park. Miss Kresge, who is something of a sculptor in her free time and appreciates the way in which art can be a medium for learning, may on a visit to a zoo allow children to crawl on a sculpture group. Such departures from usual rules may signal to children the specialness of grass, sculpture, or the outing itself, although the personalities, style, and educational approach of personnel in day-care centers and nursery schools vary. However, although the style, personality, and convictions of individuals involved color a school, they cannot eliminate the demands they make on the child to begin to learn to accommodate his behavior to an institutional setting.

The emphasis of the preschool staff may be in agreement with the child's family world, or it may be quite different. In Brian's case it was somewhat different, and his mother, who was well aware of this difference, was not entirely happy about it. This sense of congruence or discrepancy will contribute to the picture the child forms of his own success or failure in the world beyond the home. But it is not a simple matter of "These-people-are-like-people-at-home-and-I-can-do-fine-with-them" or "These-people-are-different-from-people-at-home-and-they-make-me-feel-terrible." Brian might complete his years at Sunshine feeling (although he would not necessarily articulate it): "Miss Kresge and Mrs. Moffat are not like Momma, they ask me to do things Momma would never ask me to do, but I can do them if I have to." In this case he will have developed a sense of mastery, as well as an increased awareness that he and his family have certain ways of acting that differ from the way people act in the public world, at least in the form he first encountered it.

Although preschool programs vary considerably, the Sunshine Day Care and Nursery Center is in many respects typical and, with the exception of its primness, representative of dominant American values.

A casual yet impersonal civility is one of these values. It is promoted in the style of greetings and goodbyes, in reassurances that an outing will be "fun for everyone" although individual children may have anxieties about it. It may also be promoted when a story that has been read aloud is discussed by a group of children. Perhaps each child is given an opportunity to say what he thinks of the story and discouraged from interrupting others when it is their turn. If the children disagee about the story, the Kresges may try to negotiate a consensus. Moreover, they may not accept the reaction of a child who rejects the story out of hand, especially if his language is strong. ("Stories about ducklings are dumb," may be acceptable, but not "Duck stories make me barf," let alone "Fuck the ducks.")

Another value involves the control of impulses in the service of fair play. The Kresges or their assistants restrain a child who takes a tricycle away from Brian and urge the child to wait for his turn. On the other hand, they urge Brian to give the other child a turn when he is finished with his turn, to share. The impulse to hog the tricycle is inhibited, as well as the impulse to grab it.

However, the control of impulses does not mean that the child cannot assert his right to a turn. He is encouraged to be assertive in a civil way but not to be irrationally or impulsively demanding.

The Kresge sisters discourage shouting and loud voices in general. A soft or low voice is the acceptable public tone of our culture (especially for women, but one has only to think of the strong, silent types who are the heroes of American films to realize that a low but confident voice is ideal for men, too). At juice and cracker time a student teacher might remind the children to lower their voices.

Although the Kresges encourage Brian and the other children to share toys and take turns, they do not often encourage them to work together on group projects or copy each other's drawings, block constructions, or sand structures. "Build your own," is the message, and it is a message that fosters individual achievement and competition over cooperation. The Kresge sisters and their staff would be much more likely to give each child a piece of paper and ask him to draw his own picture of Thanksgiving than to unroll a thirty-foot sheet of brown wrapping paper and ask all the children to participate in the creation of a Thanksgiving mural. Although they might occasionally do such a "special" project, it would not be everyday fare.

In all their procedures, the Kresges encourage cleanliness, orderliness, and efficiency—cardinal virtues of the dominant American culture. Children line up before going outdoors or back indoors and wash their hands before their snack and before lunch. They learn to clean their paint brushes at the end of the morning and to wipe the table at the end of snack time. They are urged not to dawdle while they eat: speed—without the appearance of haste—is an element in efficiency. Different sorts of small toys—Lego blocks, beans, bits of styrofoam for construction—are to be put in labeled baskets when the children finish using them. At the end of the day block constructions must be taken apart and blocks returned to the shelves where they are stored. The idea is that the way to do things—even creative things—is to do them according to rational, efficient procedures and within fixed time limits.

Now and then the Kresges promote less obvious themes of our culture. They implicitly discourage painting in somber colors, setting out only red, yellow, and blue most of the time. Once when children are making up stories and telling them to one another, one little girl tells a story involving the death of a little boy's mother. Mrs. Moffat suggests, "Susan, that's an awfully sad story. Don't you think you could change it so that the mother was ill for a little while and then got better?" Americans have difficulty accepting a tragic interpretation of experience, and they pass on even to preschoolers a "bright side" or "happy ending" mentality. Sometimes even a happy ending is not enough: the Kresge sisters may have considered Maurice Sendak's *Where the Wild Things Are* too frightening to put on the book rack until they discovered that children themselves had been drawn to it in their public libraries.[11]

When children and staff discuss a story, an outing to the zoo, or the experience of children at home, other themes of American culture may be touched on and reinforced. Hierarchy, relative power, and age are important aspects of self-definition and the identification of others. "Are you the oldest or the youngest in your family?" a teacher may ask a child. Or a child may ask: "Could a tiger beat a lion, I mean if a lion is the king of the beasts?"

As in primary school, then, American values color the way in which preschool teachers carry out their function of imparting knowledge and giving children the opportunity to practice skills they will need in mastering reading, writing, and arithmetic.

Most of the preschooler's learning takes place in the context of play or play-like activities—puzzles, blocks, small model-building sets; cutting and pasting, drawing and painting; listening to stories, playing games, and going on trips. In their play with blocks and trucks or in the housekeeping corner, it is easy to see how the values of society may be imparted, not only by teachers to children but by children to other children on the basis of what they have seen on television and learned in their families. But there are other, more subtle ways to foster certain social formulas. Take, for instance, the cloth book that contains a number of different pockets, some with zippers, some with buttons, some with snaps, or the soft doll with buttons, snaps, and laces to do and undo. The materials are visually attractive and amusing for a young child to manipulate. They provide useful practice in coordination and in skills necessary for him to dress himself. At the same time, however, they stress the importance of independence and individual achievement at an early age: "See, I can dress myself." In another culture, one in which there were larger families, or more time, or less of a premium placed on productivity, initiative, and efficiency, there might be less reason to learn to dress oneself at an early age and pleasure to be gained in the grooming of one another. Moreover, these instructional toys take a technological approach to teaching skills, for each task—buttoning, lacing, snapping—is treated as an isolated problem to be solved. Finally, although the book may be charming and the doll may be, too, they are things, not people. They encourage learning to take place with less human mediation than it might if mothers, other adults, older children, or siblings helped and waited it out while toddlers buttoned and laced and snapped their own clothes. Such toys are not bad, but they are part of a society that often believes it can define its problems as a series of technical tasks and where the work the child grows up to do may involve competence with a narrowly defined task that is performed alone.

THE YOUNG SCHOOLCHILD

Vivian, the reading specialist, urges Florence to divide her first graders into ability groups so that she can work with them more efficiently, a common rationale for sorting children into homogeneous groups.[12] She urges "systematic work on phonics" and attention to "component skills."

The model underlying Vivian's educational conception is technological. Reading and writing skills are broken down into discrete bits, like segments of computer-coded information which the child, like the technical specialist, can in time learn to "reassemble" as a whole. The child is thought of as a technician: his time must be spent in the most efficient way to achieve the desired end product—in the case of primary students the acquisition of language skills. His quota is so many pink, yellow, blue, or red basal readers. Among other results, this technological approach to education inclines children to be goal oriented and competitive (how many pages have you read this week?) and to view the acquisition of knowledge as something impersonal and abstract.

Vivian suggests to Florence that she is running a real risk in departing from this model. Her message is clear: primary school is short; there is not much time to inculcate the skills basic to living and working in modern society.

Before assessing Vivian's approach, we must understand the critical importance of language skills and why so many children find them difficult to master. It is obvious that the more fluent a person's use of language, the better equipped he or she is to find meaningful work. But the significance of reading, writing, and speaking goes well beyond success in an occupation. Peter Brooks, in his article "Towards a Critical Reading of Reality," puts it this way:

> "Reading" covers the ability to decipher and interpret the messages transmitted through linguistic codes, from, on the most basic level, simple English sentences, to all the symbolic systems that man has invented. To be deprived of the ability to read is to be deprived of the primary leverage of human consciousness on the world around it, hence condemned to a position of frustration and exploitation. Our movement into a world where media of communication and propaganda other than the printed word become dominant only makes reading in the largest sense more important. The question of who controls and manipulates whom is more than ever a question of who owns and most effectively uses the word and the sign. The ability to read, interpret, and evaluate words, signs, and symbolic patterns—all based on the structure of language—is the very precondition of freedom. Only through the capacity to read the messages, benign or corrupt, proposed by the ambient society can one be in the position to judge and to choose in freedom. Only through the mastery of language, and understanding of the code and the messages formed from it, can the individual mind assert its resistance to the oppressive weight of "reality" and its transformative role in the world.[13]

Jobs that depend on communication of facts or concepts demand the extensive rendering of experience into speech, and often into writing. The salesman, manager, teacher, or lawyer must use words and concepts that capture the meaning of a transaction. Interchanges among doctors, nurses, technicians, and patients demand efficient exchange of information that, in few words, communicates precisely the essence of diagnosis, treatment, the results of tests, or the prognosis of an illness. Work in occupations such as these allows people to practice saying what they mean and making sure they understand—and are understood by—their coworkers. It provides practice using a public language, one that has commonly agreed-upon meanings, connotations, and denotations.

It also provides practice with the use of language as a tool for talking about spheres of experience that extend beyond the concerns of everyday life, beyond going to the store or having the car repaired. It makes it more likely that a person will reflect on and analyze his experience, that he will extend his knowledge of the world through books, what he learns on television, and what he is told of the experience of others.

By contrast, workers in jobs where verbal communication plays a relatively small role—such as much semiskilled and unskilled labor—may talk about the job during lunch or breaks, but their discourse will be more likely to center on subjects such as sports, vacation, and their children.[14] Talk of this kind will not necessarily act as a tool to extend their experience beyond the personal, the immediate, or the practical, leading them to generalize or analyze.[15]

What parents talk about at home and how they talk about it reflects their work and their position in society and thus contributes to the child's gradually forming a sense of his place in society. Children whose families are in the upper-income categories are much more likely to master the culturally dominant forms of language than children who are poor, especially if they are from a dark-skinned, non-English-speaking or foreign-sounding minority. Whatever their individual talents or shortcomings, middle- and upper-middle-class children will have a credibility based on fluency with the syntax and semantics of the public language of commerce, schools, government, and the major media. What they hear discussed is apt to be important in the world's eyes because of the nature of their parents' work lives and social positions, but *how* it is discussed is of at least equal importance, with the result that they absorb an ability to use language precisely and logically, a sense of denotation and connotation, a capacity to generalize, and a capacity for discourse—the rendering of experience into speech. Thus they will be far better prepared for the demands of primary school.

The guiding mythology of American schools says that Darlene and Jackie are starting out as the equals of every first-grader. But one from a poor white rural family and the other from a poor Puerto Rican family, they will not have as easy access to reading and writing as Florence and Dan's son, Brian, when they go to first grade. (Both Florence and Dan's professions call for extensive and sensitively applied communication skills—skills they developed not only within their families but extended through years of schooling and working.) Darlene and Jackie may be the equals of other children in cognitive and perceptual capacity, but unless they are exceptional individuals or have exceptional parents, their already established ways of rendering experience into words and their more limited repertoire of verbal concepts will almost inevitably impede their progress in learning to read and write.

One can hardly overestimate the seriousness of Darlene and Jackie's position, whether from the point of view of the judgment the school makes of them or the judgment they form of themselves. If they do not learn to read and write by the end of third grade, they will be branded as failures by the school and may consider themselves failures. Their "failure" will have consequences for their career in school and their eventual place in society, not only with respect to work and the demands of everyday life but also with respect to their capacity to speak with a public voice.

In the light of the foregoing, the deepest flaw of the technological approach to the inculcation of symbolic skills advocated by Vivian is its tendency to disregard the relationship of language to personal experience, or more accurately, the relation of formal language training to lived experience. The technological approach can disregard this relationship without much harm as long as it is applied to children who are already able to use language as a reasonably efficient tool for organizing and expressing their experience.

But if a child has not developed this language facility, teaching him to read according to the technological approach may result at best in rote skill. Thus one might teach a child all the component skills so that he can, in fact, read, but the words he reads will mean little to him, and he will not be able to use them to speak or write about his experience. In order to learn to read with comprehension and to work effectively, he needs to learn to express himself more extensively than he has learned to do in his preschool years and to use words and concepts that are part of the common language of the dominant society. The technological approach helps him very little in this process.

The Fairview approach is based on a very different philosophy. This philosophy holds that symbol skills, however sophisticated and abstract their eventual development may be, must be rooted in the experience of the child and, that if they are not, they will be neither useful nor permanent.[16] These convictions are the basis for all the teaching devices Florence employs in her classroom—recording individual and group stories, creating personal vocabulary lists, giving children a chance to be heard, and encouraging them to listen to one another. They may gradually be encouraged to extend the terms with which they encompass their reality, but they are not forced to turn their backs on that reality even if it is expressed in words like "diaper," "shit," "baby," and "hate."

If children are to be categorized as competent or incompetent by the end of third grade—judged on the basis of their symbolic skills—then Vivian's argument that there is not enough time for Florence's approach is a persuasive one. This is all the more true if purely technical decoding competence is the primary basis for deciding whether a student has passed or failed. But if both comprehension and decoding facility are expected, and if more time—perhaps an extra year—could be offered to children who come to school without skills in the language of the dominant culture, then Vivian's argument is less powerful.

Through primary school it is probably far more important to go slowly if all children are to be assured of the chance to become lifelong readers. Seymour Sarason put this very well when he recommended that teachers be forbidden to "teach" reading until third grade. Such an approach might encourage in children a sense of confidence in the validity of their experience and develop in them capacities to listen carefully and to speak out thoughtfully about their experiences and fantasies.

SCHOOL AND THE MARKINGS OF SUBORDINATE STATUS

In addition to classifying children by ability and performance, the school judges them according to their behavior. A certain standard of civility, acting independently yet controlling the expression of strong emotion, being punctual, and acquiescing to authority are virtues that may or may not be stressed at home, but they are esteemed in school and affect the way children are evaluated. Like the academic demands made on the child in primary school, rules for social behavior valued at school closely match those followed by middle- and upper-middle-income parents and are least congruent with nonurban, non–Western European, and lower-class life styles.

Behavior that does not conform to the social conventions of school—particularly if displayed by a child who has dark skin, speaks a language different from the dominant standard, or has a handicap—brands the child.

For many children from minority groups, school is the first protracted, day-to-day, inescapable encounter with the dominant culture. A dark-skinned, Spanish-speaking child like Jackie may be acquainted with the white, English-speaking world on television or in the person of his parents' employers, but he has never been immersed in it to the degree that he is in school; nor has he been forced to comply with it to as great an extent.

Like other children, minority children are sorted by the school, but they are marked as well—a social process that is an important factor in the way children are sorted but is somewhat distinct from it. Throughout history, societies have categorized individuals according to caste-like groups—"fit" and "less fit" groups—on the basis of a distinguishing physical or social characteristic. These are seen as the signs of a range of characteristics that justify assignment to a particular group. Thus, for example, dark skin is presumed by many to indicate lower academic ability, just as earlier in this century immigrants of Jewish heritage were judged to be genetically inferior.[17] These judgments, made by a society as a whole, are reflected in schools.[18]

Jackie bears a double mark: his skin is brown and his first language is Spanish. Jackie's command of English is limited; it has little place in his family world. If he is given psychological tests, he may be labeled as "retarded" by examiners and educators who see no injustice in the fact that they are judging the level of his intelligence on the basis of how well he understands directions in English or how accurately he uses English words to answer questions.

Darlene is white, and at first glance she appears to be free of marks that designate her as socially inferior. Yet her rural Southern roots, her dialect, and her parents' difficulties in coping with urban life may consign her to subordinate status, although in time she may be able to rise above it by modifying her speech and learning the ways of the city.

Children learn to interpret other children according to perceptible characteristics that have social meaning. Their learning is reinforced directly or indirectly through texts and storybooks, although these are far from being principal influences.[19] In the community children learn from explicit remarks but mostly from the patterns of social behavior of those around them. Within school they are socialized more subtly and pervasively to accept the subordinate status of minority children. They see dark-skinned children or those whose speech deviates from the English of the dominant culture or those who fail to learn to read by spring sorted into the "dumber" track, whether it is called "tortoises" or "hares." "Dumb" becomes one of the characteristics associated with minority children. Disruptive behavior (or at least behavior that is far more emotionally expressive than that tolerated by the schools) may, in turn, become another. The child called "dummy" in kindergarten may be the habitual truant in the seventh grade or the child who would rather fight than run, or the one who looks for a fight—who lights the fuse when he says, "Who's calling my people monkeys?"

The cognitive development of the school-age child inclines him to abide by the social roles and rules he has learned more rigidly as he grows older. A white four-year-old getting to know Brian at the Kresge sisters' day-care center may parrot a prejudiced remark he has heard his older brothers and sisters say, but his remark would not interfere with his friendship and would not yet become a shorthand tag for an entrenched set of rules. By seven this would no longer be so; social rules would mediate his reactions to Brian in such a way that he could no longer respond to him free of the judgement he has learned about superior and subordinate social groups. He would begin to expect that Brian would be put into a lower-ability group. If he had a black classmate who excelled in math, he would think of him as an unusual individual, an exception to the rules governing his group.

While school teaches the white, English-speaking child to mark unfavorably the dark-skinned, non–English-speaking, foreign-sounding, or handicapped child, this latter child learns to be marked. Frequently he internalizes the role school casts him in and lives according to the rules it sets. There could be no more acute or pernicious cause of self-blame than learning to be so categorized. A sense of failure derived from a visible or audible characteristic is so intrinsic, so visceral, that it is very hard for the individual to exempt even part of his or her identity from the consequences of subordinate status and to triumph over them. A child who does not surrender to society's demands is indeed an exceptional individual.

Even if minority children are academically competent and can function sufficiently well in school, and even if they have the strength not to give in to the label society has given them, they cannot escape from the schools'—society's—picture of their people. They must constantly separate themselves from this picture, prove to themselves and the world that they are exceptions to its rule. At the same time they are part of their people; they cannot repudiate their origins unless they are willing to pay an immense inner price.

The situation of the minority child will be clearer if we consider Lester, Florence's younger brother.

The mix of school time devoted to the acquisition of information and to the acquisition of symbol skills is somewhat different for the older child from what it is for the primary-grade child. Unlike the younger child, the adolescent can mentally manipulate symbols without reference to a particular concrete context. In the upper grades most of the school day is devoted, officially at least, to amassing information and to developing skills for organizing and evaluating that information. Once the student has learned the basic codes of reading, writing, and computation, he goes on to learn the codes of foreign languages or the special codes of algebra, physics, or computers.

However, if Lester had stayed in the city where his mother lived and continued going to school there, many of his classmates would have already rejected the school's offerings. For them information and new codes would be too loaded with implicit social messages that said: "These aren't for you." The evidence all around them would have suggested to them that getting somewhere depended on being street wise and shrewd and having contacts, and that playing the school's game was an almost sure road to nowhere.[20]

Lester's family has drawn on different evidence to give him the encouragement and the hope that school will lead somewhere rather than nowhere. Although she is no doubt well aware of the messages of his peer culture, Lester's mother may have cited the example of Florence and Dan's lives to make her own deep faith in the power of education persuasive in Lester's eyes. She may have insisted that times have changed and that today the law supports a black boy's determination to broaden his horizons. In this way an adult who is close to a minority child—most often a relative, usually a parent—can enable the child to become aware of broader and more differentiated possibilities, to chart paths to achievements that surpass those his position in society may otherwise lead him to consider.[21] Such an adult may have a sense of how to get things done and how to go after what he needs. Or he may have a less definable quality that may be called a spiritual determination to prevail.[22]

The decision to send Lester to the high school in Glendale is based on the assumption that Lester will do better in a school attended by many white children whose families expect them to go to college. Florence, Dan, and Lester's mother believe that such a school will set high standards and demand that students work hard. Moreover, daily life in a predominantly white school will teach Lester certain formulas that will prepare him for the competitive yet socially restrained white world he will have to negotiate as an adult. The more experience he has with the white world now, the more practiced he will be in interpreting new situations and switching automatically to the dominant culture's verbal and social codes when he needs to.

Florence, Dan, and Lester (and Lester and Florence's mother) are responding to the fact that school, in effect, sorts children into categories that become functional in the reward systems of society, at least with respect to the allocation of manpower to jobs. It *is* possible to become rich and powerful without an education, and some skilled workers earn more than some professionals, but the probability of gaining affluence, influence, and access to the "privileged meanings" and public platforms of society is strongly related to educational attainment.

The student learns not only to assess his abilities in relation to his contemporaries but to assess them in terms of the kind of work his skills will allow him to do. This latter assessment may not be very specific—Lester may not have thought about the various professions his mathematical skills will open to him; but in general school performance contributes to a student's sense of which doors are already closed to him, as well as those that are potentially open. The way in which academic subjects are taught to the older child sharpens this assessment and shapes his picture of where he can go and what he can do. Grades, tests, and other competitions reinforced by teacher instructions, comments, and attitudes indicate to the child how he is valued by the adult society for which the teacher and other school officials stand as proxy.

In addition to the social formulas implicit in the way academic subjects are taught, the school world imposes formulas for acceptable behavior on the older child just as it does on the younger child. The messages of the institution may be compatible with the messages of peers—which are more important for the older child than for the younger child—or they may be somewhat in opposition, so that the child may to a certain extent live in "two cultures"—the culture of school and the culture of his peers, both coexisting for part of the day.

In his new school Lester encounters a social organization that is familiar and yet quite strange to him. He likes the fact that more advanced science and math courses are offered as well as electives, that more challenging textbooks are used (everyone in his class reads with ease), and that many of his classmates ask tough questions. He soon learns that having a different teacher for each course leaves him with the responsibility of organizing his work and making connections across course lines. The scale of the school, the brisk pace of changing classrooms, and the departmentalization by subject give him a chance to find his way in a modern bureaucratic maze and to enjoy certain of its liberties while coping with its restrictions and absurdities, such as a ten-thirty lunchtime.

However, peer relations in his new school are both confusing and uncomfortable. Surrounded by boys and girls he does not know, he feels lonely and vulnerable. He is particularly conscious of his blackness and of the gulf that separates black students and white students at lunch, on the playground, and in friendship groups. He knows he is being sized up. At times he is afraid of the looks he gets, at other times he resents being judged in the same category as the smart-ass black kids whom he watched writing on the bathroom walls, jeering at teachers, or sashaying into class late. He soon learns that some of the black students strike a note of fear in everyone, and he does not want one of them to "initiate" him. On the other hand, he cannot help but be angry—at a school that automatically sorts him into the lowest math track; at classmates who do not invite him to parties at their homes although they are friendly enough in school; at a white boy who makes an obvious racial slur even if he is bouncing it off another white boy; at the presumption that it is black kids who are stealing from lockers. But he cannot help but be angry, too, at the black kids who steal.

More generally he must feel strain if not anger at having to distinguish himself as an exception to the social rules.

In some ways the trials and tribulations of Lester's first months in his new school and neighborhood resemble the pains any student faces in a new peer culture. But Lester is black and for the first time attending a school that enrolls white students. Although the school is officially integrated, it is clear that segregation persists in social groups and in the ways people think about things.

Mr. Edwards, his history and homeroom teacher, is a help, but Lester knows that no adult can solve his problem. He alone will have to find friends and discover the passwords that will ease his entry to the new peer culture. He alone will have to pay the price if he joins a group that he later learns is a liability.

In his new school Lester does indeed have a better chance of gaining the skills, knowledge, and credentials that will allow him to go where he wants in the society—and where his mother, his older sister, and his brother-in-law hope and dream he can. However, his social learning is more stressful than it would have been if he had stayed in his old school and neighborhood. Over time, as he becomes more at ease, he will recognize and sort out the distinct yet overlapping messages of peer group and school staff and use this awareness as the basis from which to begin questioning and comparing the values of peers, teachers, and parents, that is, to become a critic of the perspectives of others.

Chapter Seven
Messages From the Modern World

> *The central issue is that values, motivations and feelings are the expression in inner life of the institutions of which one is a member. If this were not true there would be no relation between the two and a culture could not function.*
>
> —Jules Henry, *On Sham, Vulnerability and Other Forms of Self-Destruction*

In a modern society like ours the institutions that shape the major outlines of the social order tend to be the major institutions of the economy (major corporations and banks, the Federal Reserve Board, major unions, etc.), government (the three branches of the federal government, the regulatory and service bureaucracies, and comparable mechanisms of states and major cities), communications (major print and visual media), and education (major universities and research centers whose faculties train future leaders, generate and publish new knowledge, set standards for professions, and consult with government, business, and the media). Regularly recurring patterns of thought and action characterize public life not only because the people involved in each of these sectors overlap to some degree or tend to share similar outlooks and life experiences, but because high technology, the possibilities it releases, and the ways of thinking it encourages tend to characterize and link these major institutions. Their common ways of planning, organizing, and going about their business lead to the sharpening of certain patterns in public life and to their regular recurrence.[1]

As described earlier, children learn to be people of their society from the regularly recurring patterns of their daily lives including the patterns of public life.[2]

An important factor affecting the child's learning about the patterns of public life today is the profound change of scale in the individual's and the family's relation to what we might call the known world, in part an effect of communications technology, especially television. Until not so very long ago, the known world for most people was largely that of their direct experience. For the great majority its geographic boundaries seldom, if ever, ranged beyond a distance they could travel by horse or on foot in a single day. Relatively few people depended on the manipulation of symbols found in books to get through their daily lives, and most people, when they sought to expand their world with the symbols or images found in books, chose the Bible. The traditional channels of oral transmission—tales, proverbs, anecdotes, etc.—conveyed to children as much or more information about their worlds as primers or chapbooks. The world that influenced them tended likewise to be close at hand, overlapping if not completely coinciding with the known world of everyday experience. The weather mattered (as evidenced by our rich cultural stock of weather lore and weather proverbs); the local strong man or rich man mattered (though his power did not necessarily extend very far geographically).

As the known world has grown wider for each individual and the scale and interrelatedness of its institutions increased, the influences it brought to bear on the individual or the family no longer coincides with everyday experience. The known world has become as wide as jet travel, and more importantly for most people, as wide as television can make it. But the world television brings into the home is one known through images rather than direct experience.

It is practically impossible to estimate at this time what the full consequences for children are of the changed balance between the individual and the worlds that influence his life, or the changed balance between direct experience and the flood of information and images with which he is inundated. But some things can be said.

Most families, no longer linked firmly as social entities in the neighborhood, church, community, or common work, find it difficult to fulfill their socializing task of building for their children strong yet resilient bridges between private and public worlds. Yet this link has never been more necessary.

The lives of families have always been affected by events beyond their thresholds, but today the institutions influencing families are more apt to be geographically distant, complex, and their operating principles invisible to the observer—that is, they are more apt to be large-scale corporate and bureaucratic organizations than they were a century ago.

It is not always clear who does what, why it is done, or where the buck stops. Such institutions have no less impact on the lives of families than the churches, the bosses, the neighbors, or the elders of a community a century ago, but they are much harder for an adult to understand in any kind of comprehensive way and much harder for him to explain to a child. It is harder to explain how Social Security works than the "poor farm" for the elderly that might have existed on the outskirts of a New England town; harder to explain the organization and influence of General Electric or General Motors than the influence wielded by a ship owner in a small port town. It is harder to explain the management of a conglomerate that bought out a family shrimp-packing business than it was to understand the management of the original business. It is harder for a child to understand a computerized bookkeeping system than a handwritten ledger, harder for him to understand about the preparation of a hamburger that is handed to him over the counter in a styrofoam package than the preparation of a hamburger on a griddle in a local luncheonette.

The changed balance between direct experience and knowledge of the world conveyed through printed and televised information and images means that on one hand a child (or his parents) may see on television events in Egypt or South Africa which, however biased and limited their presentation, may be fuller, more immediate, more intense and vivid, and available to a wider audience than was news of the next town in an earlier generation. On the other hand, what a child experiences of the institutions that affect his life from his vantage point within the family tends to be insufficient to give him an accurate picture of how these institutions work. In one sense he knows more of how the world works than ever before; in another sense he knows less because there is so much more to grasp and it is becoming increasingly invisible. Moreover, his daily experience is not necessarily a path to understanding what he doesn't know. It is not that daily experience doesn't tell him something, even something important, about the way the big world works, but that the way it works is seldom fully obvious. Books such as those by Richard Scarry showing how work is done suggest the limits adults face in explaining the modern world to children (or themselves) and, for the child himself, the limited application of his direct experience.³

Moreover, the word "explain" somewhat falsifies since it suggests an overt and conscious process, whereas the building of an inner map of reality is not a conscious process, although it represents each individual's sense of how things are and what one can or must do about them. The child's construction of reality proceeds with more information than ever before, but both information and experience are frequently insufficient in relation to the scale and complexity of the institutions and technologies that have an impact on his life.

A further consequence of the remoteness and invisibility of modern institutions and technologies is the increased significance of a new kind of privileged status noted often in the course of this book: access to privileged meanings. "Being in a position to know" matters more today than ever before, whether it is a matter of special knowledge about how a computer works or being privy to the decision-making process at the corporation that uses the computer. This becomes all the more so as the way things work—technologically and bureaucratically—becomes more interrelated and more remote from everyday experience.

Take the example of a child's experience of a fast-food chain (call it McBurger) in contrast with his experience of the usual small-town or neighborhood luncheonette. Parents enjoy McBurger for its convenience, reliability, the quality of its food, and its cheerful, if plastic, atmosphere. It's pleasant and easy to take children to eat to a place they're enthusiastic about. (Further on we'll discuss the way in which their enthusiasm is reinforced by the ads for McBurger they've seen on television.) But while they're eating their French fries, hamburgers, and shakes, children are learning from McBurger about the way the institutions of the society work, the nature of the work itself, and the relationship of the individual to those institutions. What they learn over lunch is consistent with what they will gradually learn about the bureaucratic, technological society they will live in as adults. However, although it is very much in line with the American ideal of technological progress and efficiency, what they learn at McBurger is at variance with the equally American ideal of the individual's ability to make choices and to control his own life.

Children can spot a McBurger easily and frequently as they drive with their parents or schoolmates, whereas they know few luncheonettes owned and operated by neighborhood enterprises. What children take in from the repeated sights of McBurger restaurants is an important fact of contemporary life: centralized management and technology make it possible to replicate sandwiches, fries, and even restaurants on a vast scale. Uniformity may be the result, but also predictability and even reliability—qualities that may be particularly appealing to children of seven to twelve years of age who are fascinated by rules.

Entering a McBurger restaurant, the child finds the same predictability and reliability in the decor, menu, and in the preparation of the food that he found in the external appearance of the building. He also finds a degree of impersonality. Where at a local luncheonette Mr. Q prepares the food and the child watches him work at the grill, the food at McBurger has been prepared at a distant plant and brought to the restaurant prepackaged by a refrigerated trailer truck. Mr. Q may or may not take the trouble to make a special order, but if he refuses, the child may be irritated with a person who could please him if he chose to do so. At the chain, there is no *person* to get mad at if a special request is denied—waiters and waitresses are just "following orders," "doing their job." There simply is no one in sight from whom one might try to wangle an exception. The customer has little way of voicing opinions about the choices or the quality of food to anyone in a position to make a decision. The remoteness and invisibility of the command of large organizations can give customers and employees an emotional and practical sense of impotence.

However, most of a child's visits to McBurger will seem far more personal because he is with family or friends, he recognizes a clerk, or he likes the spirit of the teenagers who hang around there. But the way things are done at McBurger is part of a recurring pattern which he will meet again and again in encounters with the public world.

Yet it is hard for the child to understand the difference between employment by a large corporation and a job working for a neighborhood restaurant or business. Here and there at McBurger he may glimpse signs of what a large, centralized organization is like: the waitresses wear little pins that read "140 hours" and "crew trainer," suggesting a competitive and hierarchic organization. A sign advertises that the chain offers opportunities for advancement, careers in management, and fringe benefits. (A local shop owner can seldom offer anything comparable.) But it is unlikely that the child will be able to interpret the significance of the sign or the pins the waitress wears, or, if he thinks to ask them, that his parents will give him an accurate interpretation. At most he takes in a pattern of commercial activity that will recur in many other commercial encounters. His direct experience, and often that of his parents, is a relatively inadequate guide to understanding how McBurger prepares him to accept the products and services of institutions he will *not* fully understand. However, once he learns how to behave in a McBurger, in a super food market, in an automat, he will have learned a way to cope with the highly managed market systems of modern life. This way of coping will seem natural—the way things are supposed to be.

A child's visit to McBurger is reinforced by ads for McBurger, which he has seen on television. The McBurger he eats at and the burger he eats there are joined in his consciousness to McBurger puppets or animated figures he has seen on television, to McBurger jingles and slogans—and to the whole of the information and image system that television offers him. Jingles, images, and slogans add to the lived experience a potency that it might not otherwise have. It is not the potency of personal association that might be linked in memory to the local luncheonette. It is probably closest to the potency of myth. Advertising speaks to that stratum of his personality from which both fantasy and belief spring, and which in a traditional society might not entirely separate the corn eaten from the corn god, the name from the named, the symbol from the thing symbolized.

Much of our modern rationalistic culture is built upon the usually unspoken but pervasive point of view that corn and the corn god, symbol and symbolized, are separate; but advertising, especially on television, touches that part of our consciousness that does not make these separations and that is not so modern. This may be all the more true for children, especially those under the age of six or seven, whose cognitive development leads them to see things whole. They may take in Mac the Burger along with their hamburger and hurry to finish before the evil Burger Snitchers grab their food away. If this is so, then modern communications media not only purvey to children an unprecedented array of information, they manipulate a deep part of human nature in an unprecedentedly calculated and sophisticated fashion and almost entirely to serve the economic purposes of large corporations.

Novelty, ease, and fun are themes used to trigger the advertising audience's impulse to improve life through consumption. Novelty has a basic attraction for all human begins, but it is particularly appealing to Americans if it is made synonymous, as it is in much of advertising, with progress. Most ads introduce what is new in a product line, even if the real choices have changed very little. Convenience appeals most to busy adults, and fun speaks most emphatically to children, although in a society affluent enough to have plenty of leisure, "fun foods" can be marketed to people of all ages. Advertising "fun foods" like those sold at McBurger manipulates an intrinsic aspect of the consciousness of children—their capacity for playfulness. Their tastes are shaped and their imagination and capacity for delight are heavily enlisted in the process. Every culture shapes its children's tastes and enlists their imagination. What is new here is the degree of conscious manipulation by craftsmen skilled at writing, drawing, photography, and animation who at the same time possess some knowledge about child development and cognitive processes and are living at the growing edge of popular culture. What is also relatively new is that the shaping of taste hinges on a definition of self-worth based on consumption, and that it serves the profit-making interests of large corporations.

To summarize, neither parents' nor children's direct experience or knowledge may be adequate in interpreting the major institutions that children encounter, although in a complex society interpretation is more than ever necessary because the patterns recur under many guises. Meanwhile, television not only offers answers to questions never asked before but speaks to that part of the child—imagination—that myths, folklore, fairy tales, or religious rituals spoke to in the past.

Nevertheless, although parents' interpretation cannot always provide children with a complete understanding of the world beyond the home, children do learn from their parents' encounters with the institutions of the larger society. In the rest of this chapter we extend some of our vignettes to suggest what they learn. Although the difficulties and frustrations of dealing with large institutions are often stressed, the benefits families derive from our economic, social, and governmental institutions are obvious. We do not want to minimize the benefits of life in our society. Our purpose is to focus on the problems a complex society presents to children's learning and sense of mastery.

HOUSING AND TRANSPORTATION

Suppose, for instance, that the school where Frank Giannini works as a janitor is closed because the student population is shrinking in the area. He is offered a job in a more suburban location, much further from the center of the city. Frank wants to take the job, and the new location promises many advantages for his family. The schools in the new area are good. Houses have larger yards than the Gianninis are accustomed to. Within easy biking distance there is a park with a baseball diamond and public tennis courts. At first glance the move looks like a very positive one for the whole family, but there are problems.

When Frank and Rose Giannini go house hunting they find that there is nothing in the area they can afford comfortably. Their present house is two-thirds paid for. They hope to sell it at a modest profit, but they will be lucky to do so: their neighborhood of old houses is barely holding its own.

Housing, however, is just one of their problems. Every house they look at in the vicinity of the school where Frank Giannini will work is at least a twenty-minute walk from a bus stop, and buses run infrequently. Now they are five minutes from a bus stop, and Rose's bus trip to the hospital where she works takes only fifteen minutes. Whereas now Rose is away from her family for an eight-hour shift plus a maximum of forty minutes' travel time, if they move and she continues to work at the same job, she will be away at least an hour longer than she is at present. Dinner and housework, which cannot be put off until the weekend, will come later in the evening when she is more tired. She will have less time to spend with her children and probably less energy too.

She considers quitting and staying home. Her upbringing urges her to do so, as well as explicit advice from her relatives. It is going to be even harder to justify being away from home for a longer day. But with higher mortgage payments, the family will need her income more in the new location.

What if, Frank and Rose wonder, they could sell their house for a large enough profit to be able to afford a down payment on a second car? But when they calculate the annual cost of running a car it takes close to a fifth of Rose's take-home pay.

In the end Frank takes the job, but the family does not move to the new location. Frank commutes forty-five minutes each way by car and Rose continues working at the hospital. They might have been able, just barely, to swing payments on a larger house, and if they had been lucky enough to make a profit on their old house, they might even have had the money to buy Rose a second-hand car. But they decided not to take the risk of higher monthly expenses and long-range indebtedness. It was not only inflation that made them wary, but also the prospect of college for the kids looming just a few years ahead. Nevertheless, although they are relieved at having made a decision, they are not without regrets. What if values in their neighborhood slip further? Later on, when the children are grown, they may not be able to get their money out. They feel as if they have missed a chance to improve their situation. They are convinced that under the circumstances they made the right decision, but in their hearts they blame themselves for being unable to afford the move.

What do the Giannini children learn about the position of their family in the larger society? They learn that their parents manage and cope: their father finds a new job when the school is closed down, and family life goes on much the same as before. But they learn, too, that their parents have limited room for coping and managing. Their hopes were raised initially about the move. They drove around the neighborhood where their father's new school was located, saw for themselves, and heard their parents comment on the advantages of the area. They may have visited specific houses and overheard conversations—what the asking price was, what the mortgage payments would be. They may have participated in discussions about their mother's transportation problems. In the tone of their parents' conversations, in accompanying gestures and facial expressions, as well as in the context of what was said, they will pick up messages of hopes raised and then frustrated.

Their interpretation of their parents' frustration will very likely be "if only we had more money then it would be easy," and their parents may feel much the same. This interpretation is correct as far as it goes, but it is the characteristically American response in which the individual takes responsibility for a situation that in some measure (in this case a very great measure) originates not with him but in the way the larger society works. To assume this responsibility means that if things go wrong the individual will tend to blame himself. "If only" might be focused equally well on a housing industry that has promoted private dwellings rather than apartments, local tax policies that permit lower property tax rates in suburbs which depend on central cities, the interlocking hegemony of the auto and highway construction industries which have created suburbs with no public transportation, or the tax advantages for businesses that relocate to the suburbs. These institutions—and the people who run them—are largely invisible to the Giannini children and their parents, although the results of their decisions have a considerable impact on the life of the family. This invisibility (and the complexity of the interests involved) means that the Giannini children can learn very little about the true sources of their parents' frustrations.

In fact, the relative invisibility, complexity, and interrelatedness of modern institutions mystify even parents who have jobs where they participate in decisions about tax rates, zoning, roads, and trucking expansion, or decisions to lure industries and population to underdeveloped subdivisions near major cities. The Gianninis have less chance than a city alderman, the owner of a trucking firm, a lobbyist for the construction equipment industry, or an officer in a national real estate brokers' association to understand why they cannot afford to move or why Frank's school was closed and the students sent to a school in the next district. But each of these individuals may ignore the relationship between the decision he or she makes or knows about first hand at work, a number of related issues he reads about in the newspaper or sees discussed on television, and the problems facing families on his block.

Perhaps the Gianninis wish out loud for better public transportation, and perhaps they say that "money cost less" back when they bought their house (and then they may be forced to explain what they mean to the children which leads to a discussion of mortgages and loans). It is very unlikely, however, that they will be able to explain how highway and automotive interests operate or that they will even think of doing so. Nor is it likely that they will be able to explain the factors contributing to the fluctuation of the mortgage rate. They may know that five years earlier several developers bought property in the area where Frank's new school is located and built on it. But unless there has been an exposé of the subject in the newspapers or on a local television station they do not know the legal and financial regulations from which the developers benefited. They may have read in the local paper that development of this particular area was used to justify the building of a connector between a local highway and a nearby interstate throughway, but it is unlikely that they fully understand—though they may have some inklings about—either the "deals" involved in this construction, the central importance of profit motives and repayment of old political debts, or the fact that the funds spent on the connector and other similar projects in the state could have gone into public transportation—that there was a policy change and that the choice made favored highway construction and the automotive and trucking industries.

The complexity and invisibility of the factors influencing the family's situation may make it easier for the Gianninis to fall back on explanations that put the blame on themselves.

GOVERNMENT INSTITUTIONS

Government agencies are notorious for their bureaucratic complexity. Without repeating in detail what is well known, we would like to suggest a scenario in which children might learn of their parents' vulnerability, powerlessness, and intense frustration in dealing with a government agency. Suppose Lester and Florence from our vignette in chapter six have a cousin, Ruby, who is the mother of four children. Ruby is forced to go to work when her husband leaves her and disappears. She lands a job in a state-funded neighborhood health-care center. She works for five months and then the funds are suddenly cancelled. She is out of a job. She does not qualify for welfare because she and her husband—she is still technically married—own a car and he is considered able to support his family. Nor does she qualify for standard unemployment because she worked less than six months. However, she does qualify for "special" unemployment, based on different criteria of eligibility, but after waiting for two months it still has not come through. On one occasion, when she goes to the unemployment office in desperation, she is informed that the computer "lost" her file and that she should come back the following week. The bureaucracy made the error, but she must pay the penalty by waiting.

At a time of crisis in her family's life she fails to qualify for help from two out of three sources and is powerless to speed up help from the one source to which she can legally appeal. She feels strain, frustration, powerlessness, and the near impossibility of making any of her encounters with the institutions she turns to comprehensible to her children. She may say to them, "Well, welfare won't help us because we own a car." Her words may make some sense if her children are old enough to understand the concept of rules, but it will be hard for them to accept the idea that helping agencies somehow do not help them when they are in such need. Their mother's experience will teach them about the defenselessness of their parent in the face of institutions on which, for the time being, they are dependent.

Florence and Dan may help Ruby out, but this sort of solution presumes that individuals take it upon themselves to solve problems that bureaucracies were designed to solve, not to confound. Think of a Ruby with no one to help—and there are many—for whom a public institution's failure to give the help to which she is entitled is that last straw in an already difficult situation.

* * * *

Although television, the housing industry, corporations that provide goods and services, and government agencies and hospitals are among the most important and obviously large institutions with which a family may come in contact, paying a gasoline credit card bill or a department store bill can involve them with bureaucratic and legal procedures, some of which were designed to protect their interests, however short they fall of that goal. In an effort to protect and inform consumers, federal regulations require companies to inform customers of the true annual finance charges and the procedures for challenging unjustified billing. But the instructions included with many utility and business bills suggests how helpless a customer may feel if forced to follow them.

Suppose Dan, Florence's husband, follows the procedures outlined, when he finds they are billed for an item they never ordered. Reading hastily he skips one item which states that "regardless of questions concerning a certain item, you are obligated to pay the parts of your bill not in dispute" and does not pay the undisputed amount while waiting for his claim to be settled. He is then confronted with higher finance charges and possibly a lower credit rating. A failure to read carefully could cost him an appreciable sum of money.

Dealing with these procedures exemplifies many aspects of the individual's encounters with modern institutions. First, it suggests the way in which law has proliferated—in this case law intended to protect the consumer as well as the company. Second, the institution with which one deals remains remote and invisible. Dan may never know even the name of the clerk assigned to his case and may discover no clerk is actually involved. Recourse is handled via the written word—or the punched card—not face to face, and it requires a high degree of reading comprehension and the ability to write a letter. Moreover, if the customer does not have the skills necessary to read the form and follow the procedures outlined, he may not succeed in establishing his rights. The financial consequences may be more extensive than what he owes or doesn't owe of the disputed amount: he may lose his credit rating and find himself unable to borrow money or to charge purchases.

If Dan fails to follow the correct procedure, or follows the correct procedure but his letter is lost in the mail or lost by the company so that the sixty-day time limit runs out, his credit card may be cancelled. "Can't you tell them it was a mistake?" Lester may say if Dan explains the situation to him. Dan may say that is precisely what he has been trying to do but that in trying to establish his first mistake, he has made things considerably worse rather than better. It may take the hiring of a lawyer to sort the whole business out, and that will cost more money than paying for the unordered goods. In any case Lester will see clearly the impersonality and intractability of a large corporation's machinery for doing business—for all that it has provided well-publicized procedures for protecting the customer.

If four-year-old Brian asks, "Why are you paying the man with money and not with your card like you used to?" it will be close to impossible to make sense of what has happened in terms that he can understand. If Dan tries, he may find Brian countering with the question, "Were they bad or were you bad?" A question difficult to answer. In any case all the proceedings will be totally invisible to Brian.

The episode can be contrasted with an episode a four-year-old can understand. Suppose the family lived in an earlier period and Dan was a farmer. If Dan went to town for supplies and returned home missing some items that he had unaccountably loaded into another farmer's wagon, the situation could be remedied through contacts that were personal and face-to-face. Brian could go along and see how it worked—and what he saw, experienced himself, would be close to being how it was.

FAMILIES AS INADVERTENT VICTIMS OF CORPORATE AND GOVERNMENT DECISIONS

From time to time families may be affected by the decisions of large corporations or by government regulations in ways that completely change their lives. Suppose that the plastics company that employs

Mr. Murphy, the handicapped engineer in our earlier vignette, has been dumping polluting wastes into the lake on which the plant is located. For some years before the Murphys moved to the town, local environmental groups had been publicizing the hazards to fish created by these wastes, but these groups had not had a noticeable effect. (Long-time residents know that twenty years ago there were plenty of edible fish in the lake and now there are scarcely any, but fish are not a sufficiently vital issue to rally public support when many of the townsfolk make a living directly or indirectly from plastics.)

However, federal regulations have grown tighter in the last several years, public consciousness has been raised—and then it is discovered that one of the chemicals being dumped into the lake is linked to a high incidence of cancer in laboratory animals. A year after the Murphys move to town the company is ordered to stop dumping its wastes into the lake and instead pump them into trucks and bury them in the ground in a location where it is hoped they will not contaminate drinking water or farmland. The company agrees to truck them as far as the town dump, but since this dump is within several hundred yards of a river that drains into the lake, the solution is not acceptable. The company refuses to truck them further, claiming that the costs are too high. It demands that the government subsidize trucking costs; if not, the plant will be shut down. The company is the town's chief employer. If the plant is closed it will mean a loss of 1500 jobs at the plant itself and at least as many more in the town. (For instance, the prosperity of Steve Polsky, a plumber, is derived from the housing boom the plant has brought to the town in the last ten years.)

If the plant closes will the Murphys have to move again when they have only just become accustomed to their new location? Will the Polskys have to face a shrinking income as the economy of the town declines? But after all, Steve Polsky and Bob Murphy are in relatively secure positions—one has a trade and the other a profession, both of which guarantee employment somewhere. There are many hundreds of workers in town who are not so highly skilled or trained, or who are older; these men (and women) may face months or even years of unemployment, and they may find a move fruitless or very hard to make, or both. Their children will ask themselves, "Can my parents take care of me?" and sometimes learn that the answer is "No." Some will become victims of their parents' frustrations. In time, too, if the plant shuts down, they will learn that their parents have been made powerless to take care of them by institutions far beyond their control: the government regulatory agency that decreed that the plant should stop polluting the lake, the company headquarters that closed the plant, and the other branches of the state or federal government that failed to subsidize the company's adequate disposal of waste.

"Will we have to move?" the Murphy children might ask or, "Why do we have to move?" The Polsky children might ask: "You said maybe we could go to Disneyland next year and now you say maybe we can't. Why not?"

Answering these questions will call for explanations of decisions made by men the children and even their parents have never seen, even though these decisions have had a tremendous impact on the lives of these families.

Jobs are only part of what is at stake. Sarah and Dave Polsky, aged eleven and nine, may ask: "Are we going to get cancer?" The best answer their parents can give is: "Probably not, at least not from Delta's chemicals. We're lucky here in town. We don't get our drinking water out of the lake. But the people in Cedar Spring twenty miles along the shore may be running a risk. They get their drinking water from the lake."

"Why didn't anybody stop it in time?" Sarah may ask. Her parents may be forced to answer: "Because no one knew." The children cannot help but feel anxiety both at the threat of illness and at the impossibility of comprehending—of knowing in time—the dangers implicit in technology. They will feel without protection from illness, and without even the "protection" of understanding. (If adults didn't see the threat to health involved in the wastes from the plant, how can they as children hope for protection and, in time, for comprehension of their world?)

Sarah may be old enough to decide that she will boycott all products made by Delta (in her personal campaign against the company she tries to allay some of her anxiety and feelings of helplessness by taking some kind of action). Her mother may encourage her, but her father may say: "I'm not giving up using plastic pipe. It's pretty damn handy." She may persuade him, however, to buy a different brand of gasoline than the one marketed by Delta, and for a while she may think she has accomplished something. But she begins to notice labels: a face cream of her mother's has a label on the jar that reads "Beauty-True, a Division of Delta Industries"; a few days later she notices that her favorite brand of peanut butter is also made by a division of Delta; and a few days after she notices that her favorite shirt is made by another Delta subsidiary. She is learning a lesson about the reach of giant corporations that touch her life and the lives of the rest of us. The discovery does nothing to help her build her sense of personal effectiveness. She may be just old enough to remark to her mother and father that if Delta is making so much money with plastics, gasoline, face cream, fabrics, and food, they could afford to dispose safely of the wastes they are dumping down the lake or take care of the people in the town if they shut down the plant. And they may say nothing, sigh that the rich get richer while the poor get poorer, or even that entrepreneurs will not invest capital unless they are assured a high rate of return.

THE FOOD INDUSTRY

Suppose Lester, Florence's younger brother, is encouraged by his biology teacher to write a term report on nutrition. Lester begins reading, and pretty soon he has learned facts that he never knew before. He learns that many foods are colored with red coal tar dye and that many red dyes are carcinogenic; he finds that sugar, salt, and starch are routinely added to baby food; that even "pure orange juice" is often diluted with water and frequently colored to increase its appeal; that many of his favorite baked goods and snacks contain preservatives which have unknown and uncertain consequences for health. He finds that certain substances included to stabilize or enhance flavor in convenience foods may disturb the central nervous system and be implicated among the causes of hyperactivity in children. He finds that many of the luncheon meats and hot dogs that are among his favorite foods contain nitrites which may be carcinogenic.

Lester goes to the supermarket with Florence. With his new awareness he sees that the array of processed foods, especially snack foods, convenience foods, sweets, and soft drinks, seems to surpass the basic items in many shopping carts. Many of these foods are of limited nutritional value and have a high proportion of salt or sugar, two substances that can be detrimental to health when taken in large quantities over many years. He examines the juices, the juice drinks, and the "ades," searching the fine print of the cans and bottles for the proportion of actual fruit juice in them. He looks at the breakfast cereals—fully occupying half an aisle in a big supermarket—and sees that some old-time favorites are almost invisible in an array of vividly printed boxes which he recognizes from television. He listens as Florence requests sliced turkey, not turkey roll, at the delicatessen counter. He asks her why she does so. She tells him that turkey roll is reconstituted, that water and preservatives have been added to it, and that the process of reconstitution may change the chemistry of the food and therefore its nutritional value, a bit of information she learned from a program on public television.

When they get home from the supermarket Lester helps Florence unpack the groceries. He pauses to read the print on a package of frozen jelly doughnuts. "6 Yeast-Raised Donuts," he reads. "Hey," he says. "These are made with yeast. Does that mean they're natural?"

"There wasn't a doughnut ever made without yeast," his sister tells him.

Somewhat more skeptically, Lester keeps reading. "Made from real fruit; 100% natural flavor," he reads. The words are printed in a splashy yellow star on the front of the box. That sounds pretty good. Then he reads the ingredients listed in fine print on the back and sees that the "real fruit" is a remote presence in a list of substances some of which he can hardly pronounce, let alone identify: "enriched wheat flour, grape jelly, water, shortening, sugar, yeast, dextrose, nonfat dry milk, salt, lecithin, mono and diglycerides, leavening, dough conditioners, sodium stearyl-2-lactylate, vegetable gum and cellulose gum, artificial colors, BHA and BHT." "If you buy sliced turkey, not turkey roll," Lester says to Florence, "then why do you buy these? They're full of junk."

Florence hesitates before she answers. She is aware of what constitutes good nutrition and increasingly aware through magazine articles as well as TV programs of the health hazards created by too many convenience foods, snack foods, and preservatives.

"It's hard to find anything else in the supermarket," she says, "and I'm too busy to fuss. It takes a lot longer if you make everything from scratch, and you guys are always looking for sweets."

But before Florence goes marketing again Lester decides that the whole family should cut out food that includes artificial flavoring, colorings, and preservatives. "Well then," Florence says. "You come along and pick them out."

They pick out fresh fruit and vegetables, whole grain bread (more expensive that the soft white stuff), fish, chicken, and meat.

But when their shopping cart is half full, they pause and confront each other. "What am I going to eat when I get home from school?" Lester asks. "A glass of milk and a couple of pieces of toast, an apple," Florence tells him. "You gotta be kidding," Lester says. Potato chips or a candy bar and a soda have been his preferred after-school snack for several years, a pattern she and Dan decided not to challenge. Disgruntled but resolute, he passes by the frozen doughnuts and the shelves of chips and sodas. Then he pauses: "I've got an idea," he says. "You make a cake and a couple of pies. You know, healthy pies out of good ingredients." Florence tells him that now he's the one who's kidding; has he forgotten she has a full-time job? "*You* make a cake and some cookies," she tells him, and reluctantly he agrees. Lester doesn't mention the sugar or fat content of the baked goods, and Florence leaves well enough alone, thinking he can face just so much in one day.

"Meat and fruit and vegetables are still real," Lester says as they are driving home, "even if there's still a lot of junk in the stores."

But that night at the dinner table Florence says: "I don't know how real these tomatoes are. They don't taste the way tomatoes used to, at least not the way they used to in summer time."

"They're just not very ripe, that's all," Dan says.

The following day, however, Lester's biology teacher draws his attention to an article that describes the development of the "new tomato"—bred firmer and tougher-skinned to withstand mechanical picking, to travel better, and to have longer "shelf life" in the supermarket. But as he reads further Lester learns that this new tomato is different in ways that affect its nutritional value as well; it is reddened by exposure to ethylene gas in special gassing chambers, but this does not mean that it is ripe. It just looks ripe; the chemical balance of acids and sugars characteristic of the naturally ripe tomato has not had an opportunity to occur. He also learns that there is less vitamin C in one new breed of tomato, although he isn't sure whether that is a result of breeding for tough skins or the gas-ripening process—but he knows vitamin C is fragile. He wonders whether he was right when he said vegetables were still real—or at least what kind of "real" they were.

In the course of completing his biology project, Lester becomes aware of what the great majority of children—and adults—accept without question: the changes technology has made in the food we eat. Some of these changes, such as freezing processes and refrigerated trucking, have brought fruits and vegetables to families in every corner of the country at all seasons of the year and given Americans with enough money to buy fresh or frozen produce an opportunity for the best and most varied diet in the world.

Other changes have spread to our tables with an unprecedented "chemical feast" which, as a book of that title documents, the Food and Drug Administration has been unable or unwilling to regulate adequately, in part because the agency has been unable to combat the lobbying and delaying tactics of food industry corporations.[4] A few large corporations produce a very large proportion of the basic food we eat. The decision making and the vast reach of these corporations are invisible to the public. Unless the public brings to bear great pressure, it is almost impossible to influence these decisions. Moreover, putting pressure is not only a matter of political organization, gaining a platform and a voice, but—as too often in modern times—of mastering a body of quite technical information.

Lester, for instance, may be pleased to learn, soon after the completion of his biology project, that the PTA at his school is looking into the adequacy of the lunches served to students. But several months later the project is only just getting under way. PTA members have had to learn about different sorts of nutritional assay procedures and the methodological problems associated with them. They have discovered that their frozen school lunch is mass-produced, so that any inquiry or pressure from a single PTA can be safely ignored. To their dismay, they have found that an investigation of their own school's lunches leads them to explore a maze of major corporations. Their school lunch is produced by a division of a TV-dinner company, itself a wholly owned subsidiary of an international communications conglomerate.

In addition to all that he learns in his biology project, Lester may learn through what he overhears of his school PTA project something about the control major corporations have over the food industry. It is less likely that he will become aware of the way in which his tastes and those of other young people are being influenced by advertising.

Of the institutions of the larger society we have glanced at, the food industry is the one with perhaps the most direct and encompassing impact on children's lives not only because of the basic importance of nutrition but because so much food advertising on television is aimed specifically at children, or else is conceived in such a way that it charms children.

It may be, too, that foods that are suitable for mass marketing, have a long shelf life, and measure up to the photographic image of them have a particular appeal for children, especially children in the six-to-twelve-year age range who seek predictability and rules about what is stable and controllable. For this reason, regardless of their taste, absolutely uniform frozen doughnuts, conforming each to the other and to the photo on the box, may be more attractive to children than the less than perfectly shaped doughnuts which their mothers may deep-fry at home.

The food industry confronts the family with a dilemma which Lester and Florence faced in the supermarket: if you do not choose from what is readily available, can you choose otherwise? The answers may lie in the time, energy, money, knowledge, and imagination you have available—scarce commodities in many lives. But the dilemma is complicated further: how free is choice, or is choosing really choosing if it is only within a narrow range of alternatives and if the tastes that in part govern your choices have been manipulated by those who are out to sell you? Essentially these are the questions posed by many of the bureaucratic and corporate institutions of our society.

LEARNED HELPLESSNESS

Understanding the large institutions of the society and influencing them are much harder for ordinary Americans than for the rich and well informed, although even the latter have no easy time. They may have great difficulty getting the facts and understanding what is really at stake concerning issues in any of the areas we have touched on, but they will have access to fuller information, more facility in interpreting information, and more options for action than the average parent.

The poor are the most obvious victims of a phenomenon that has been called "learned helplessness," which may be a pervasive response to personal powerlessness at every social and economic level. It is often the result of the remoteness and intractability of large institutions or confusion about the advantages of one course of action compared with another. If your personal skills and attitudes seem to have little effect on the choices available to you or on the institutions that, for all their remoteness, have an important impact on your life, the only way you may be able to accept your situation is to decide you are helpless in the face of your situation.[5]

One peculiar aspect of modern life is that choices expand and narrow almost at the same time. In either case, we feel that we should be able to understand and take effective action because so much more knowledge is available and so many social forces are in human hands and therefore, we reason, amenable to rational consideration. But the interwoven nature of modern government, commerce, media, etc., often creates incredible barriers to understanding or alteration. Or to put it another way, a change in one thread often has little effect on the fabric—unless one pulls a critical thread.

If you have no choice but to buy the food in the supermarket (no place to plant and no farmers to buy from); no choice but the houses or apartments available (no possibility of building with the help of family and friends); no choice but to buy a second car if you are going to take a certain job; no choice but a polluted water supply; no choice but to deal with the intractable bureaucracy of government agencies, even if you leave the city, you will take the choice offered unless you are a person of rare ingenuity and courage. But if you make the obvious choice, you are resigning a little of your own sense of personal effectiveness which, however subjective, is vital to self-worth. Most insidious of all is the fact that you may not know—indeed often don't know—that what you choose is not the only possible reality, that things may be otherwise. This ignorance may be protective—it is often too painful to think of what might be but, for one reason or another, is not available to you. Ignorance may also be the result of immersion in the culture so that your map of how things are conforms to the choices it offers, stifling your own inner voice of dissatisfaction telling you that your needs are not being met, your powers not being used, that things are not as "they" say. The danger is that large institutions are so encompassing, so persuasive, that the inner voices of individuals become stiller and smaller; peaks and valleys of their early representations of reality are leveled or closed; what should be heard as anger, assertion, or a creative variety of individual expression and alternatives becomes an echo of the institution's messages, or else a passive silence.

We could end this chapter on this pessimistic note, but it would be false to do so.

In a closing vignette about a child's visit to a hospital we will try to suggest the complex interplay of individuals and institutions, stressing not only the power of large bureaucratic organizations relying heavily on technology to function in ways that suit their own purposes, but the capacity of individuals to bring about change in these institutions.

One day when Julie was visiting her friend, Rachel, both little girls decided to climb a big tree at the back of Rachel's yard. They went higher and higher. For a while they played happily, but then Julie lost her footing and tumbled to the ground. Indoors Rachel's mother heard Julie's screams and came running out.

By the time Julie's mother had arrived, Julie was not screaming from shock but from the pain in her leg. Her mother decided to take her to the emergency room, but she called her husband first.

"Don't take her to University," he said, "not after what we went through two years ago. Take her to St. Clare's and I'll meet you there."

Two years earlier, when Jerry had cut his forehead, they had been kept waiting for treatment for more than two hours at University Hospital, and the nurse who had cleaned Jerry's wound had responded to his tears by saying: "Don't you think you're a big cry baby? Better save those tears for when you really need them." Neither of his parents was allowed to be with him while the stitches were put in, and no one had explained to him when they put him in a restraining jacket that he would not have to remain in it for more than a few minutes.

At St. Clare's Julie and her parents were not kept waiting for more than half an hour, but when Julie was admitted to the examining room, procedures were not very much more humane than they had been at University Hospital. Her parents were not allowed to accompany her while her leg was X-rayed. After the resident on duty had examined the X ray, he said to her parents within earshot of Julie: "It's broken in two places. An orthopedist is going to have to look at it. I'm sure he's going to want to put a pin in."

Julie started to cry again. "I don't want a pin in me," she screamed. "Pins hurt."

It was her mother, not the resident, who explained that this would be a different kind of pin, not a safety pin or the straight pins Julie had seen her mother use when she hemmed a dress.

It was another hour before the orthopedist appeared, and during that hour Julie's parents sat with her. She was still in pain, but she had plenty of strength to bombard her parents with questions, many of which they could not answer: What's going to happen?

What kind of pin are they going to put in? When will my leg stop hurting? When can I go home?

When the orthopedist looked at the X ray, he did decide to put a pin in Julie's leg. "And she'll have to be in traction," he said to Julie's parents.

"In the hospital?" they asked.

"For four weeks," he said.

"Isn't . . .?" they said. "Can't . . .?"

"No, this is the best procedure." He was already moving out of the door. As far as he was concerned the conversation was over.

A few minutes later a nurse brought in a form for Julie's parents to sign authorizing the necessary procedures to put in the pin.

An orderly appeared to take Julie to the treatment room.

"Can't you come with me?" Julie asked.

"No, they can't" a nurse replied. "They'll see you later."

While Julie's parents sat in the waiting room, they asked each other many questions. Just how high up in the tree had Julie been? Had Rachel's mother been negligent? Was traction necessary? Then they heard a scream and Julie's desperate call for "Mommy." After her cries subsided, they continued asking each other the questions they wanted to ask the doctor. Couldn't the doctor have put Julie's leg in a cast? How would she ever endure being in traction? How would they arrange their lives to be with her as much as possible?

At last a nurse summoned Julie's parents. "She's ready to go upstairs," she said. "You can go with her."

Julie looked very pale when her parents saw her and she was strapped down. "My leg doesn't feel," she said. "The doctor stuck a needle in my leg and it doesn't feel any more."

Her mother explained that the doctor had injected an anaesthetic so that he could insert the pin painlessly and that in a little while she would recover the feeling in her leg. She hoped she was right and that the numbness didn't herald something more serious.

Upstairs in the hospital Julie was settled in a four-bed room. Within a few minutes an orthopedic resident came to attach the traction equipment. He asked Julie's parents to wait in the hall while he did so.

Anxiety and waiting were beginning to get to Julie's father. "This place is no better than University Hospital," he said, but at that moment a woman in her forties approached and introduced herself as Mrs. S., a staff person from the Child Life department of the hospital. She explained that it was her job to serve children's psychological needs while hospitalized and at the same time to ease the anxieties of parents. She answered many questions Julie's parents had, reassuring them that once Julie's leg was in traction it would no longer be painful and telling them that although Julie would not be able to get out of bed for four weeks she would have many activities to keep her busy. She urged Julie's mother to spend the first few nights in the hospital with her. She said that for some years now the hospital had made it a policy to encourage parents to do so.

During the next few days Julie's parents came to appreciate Mrs. S.'s services: she talked with Julie about her accident and showed her the X rays of her leg. She explained to Julie's parents that young children have very little understanding of the inside of the body or what a broken bone means. (In fact, Julie's mother discovered that Julie believed that since her leg was broken, it would never be whole again.) When Julie was frightened at the appearance of six strange young men, two young women, and an older man who all stood around her bed and looked at her leg and talked as if she wasn't there, Mrs. S. explained that the older man was teaching the younger people to fix broken bones like hers.

One day Julie's father arrived to find that Julie was painting in bed. Mrs. S. had covered her with a plastic sheet and supplied her with paints and paper. Another day she participated in a cooking project with other children. Her whole bed was wheeled into the playroom and a portable oven brought in. One child sifted dry ingredients, Julie chopped nuts, another melted butter and chocolate, and eventually brownies were baked.

When Julie had a bad spell of nightmares Mrs. S. urged Julie's mother and father to alternate staying with her until she had fallen asleep. One day Julie's mother had no one to leave Jerry with when she came to see Julie. She called Mrs. S. who said: "Bring him along." "But children his age are not allowed . . ." Julie's mother said. "That's all right. I'll take care of him," Mrs. S. said.

Impressed and grateful for Mrs. S.'s skill, Julie's mother asked just how she had chosen the Child Life field. Mrs. S. told her that fifteen years earlier one of her own children had been hospitalized for an extended period, and she had been horrified by the way the hospital staff had failed to meet any but his physical needs, at the same time restricting her to limited visiting hours so that she could not care for him herself. "It was that experience as much as anything that made me jump when I saw an ad two years later for a recreation staff worker in this hospital," Mrs. S. told Julie's mother. "Once I got involved I studied for a master's degree in child development part-time. I've been on the job nine years, and the Child Life program has grown and grown. There are six of us now; there were two when I began, and I hope we are not eliminated in the next round of budget cuts.*. You should have seen the way things were when I started. Parents couldn't spend the night. The recreation program was minimal. And maybe worst of all was that most of the star staff were insensitive to kids as people. They thought of them as bones to be set or hernias to be stitched up. And parents were just annoying distractions! We spent a lot of time educating doctors and nurses and bit by bit we are beginning to have an impact."

Hospitals are intermediate institutions, but in recent years their frequently large size, complex organization, and use of technology have given them much of the character of specialized commercial and technological institutions of the society. Moreover, in the case of the university-affiliated hospitals, the emphasis on research and teaching means that the advancement of knowledge is as much a concern of the medical staff as patient care. The contemporary evolution of hospitals has meant that patients—including children—receive care and cures that could not have even been imagined in the past. However, the psychological needs of the individual may be lost sight of. In fact, the scale of the hospital and its emphasis on technology and specialization which are essential aspects of modern medicine may in themselves add to the stress of an already stressful experience, in particular because they encourage impersonal dealings with people and because they favor an attitude of mind that does not think of the whole person but of his separate symptoms or ailments. To remedy some of the ill effects of the evolution of modern hospitals, new departments such as the Child Life department are being created, staffed by a new category of professionals. Sometimes a pediatric ward is reorganized so that parents can spend the night. Sometimes a major innovation is attempted which requires a variety of changes. An example of this might be the Care-by-Parent Unit, an inpatient facility of the Uni-

---

*As this book goes to press, many hospitals have reduced their Child Life staff because of cuts in hospital budgets.

versity of Kentucky Medical Center where parents from rural areas care for their children under the supervision of the nursing staff.

Most of all, remedying the dehumanizing effects of hospitals as large-scale modern institutions requires a long-term commitment to sensitizing and educating the entire medical staff. The task is a difficult one precisely because the forces shaping the hospital and its personnel, like those shaping other modern institutions, favor specialization, not attention to the individual as a whole person.

Pressure to keep the whole person in view may come from concerned professionals within the institutions—and indeed must come from them to be effective—but it may also come from concerned outsiders, including, in the case of pediatric care, parents. Julie's mother, after her experience with Julie's hospitalization may be interested in becoming a hospital volunteer and working with Mrs. S. or she may join a parent advocacy group working on behalf of hospitalized children.

Our vignette illustrates the interplay between individuals and institutions. A large modern institution, in fulfilling what most of its staff would perceive as its functions—and doing so, most of its staff would say, to the best of its ability—nevertheless fails to respond to one of its clients—Julie—as a whole person. To name only one instance out of many, in the vignette Julie might have had a much less stressful time (and so might her parents) if procedures had been explained to her and her questions anticipated and answered during her long wait for the orthopedist.

At the same time, our vignette suggests the way in which a large organization can be rendered more humane through the efforts of individuals not only through their direct human responsiveness but their attempts to alter the structure of the institution. When they have an impact, the efforts of a Mrs. S. mean that Julie's experience in the hospital is different and better than it would have been at St. Clare's ten years ago—or what it still might be today in many hospitals. They may make a difference, too, to the contribution the hospital experience may have on Julie's map of social reality.

The experience of mastery, especially in directing events that are physically or emotionally painful, marks a personal map with competence and confidence. Whether children encounter accidents, family tragedies, or just the complex maze of modern life, they can grow and thrive if we help them talk about their experiences, assist them in constructing strategies to improve circumstances, teach them to evaluate the effectiveness of their actions, and encourage them to teach their skills to others. A far greater burden than personal stress or the complexity of modern institutions is the belief that one must submit, that one has no leeway to act or change circumstances.[6]

Postscript

The argument of this book, with its emphasis on the changed balance of power among modern institutions and on the influence of economic and social circumstances on family life, may suggest a deterministic view that one vignette about a hospital Child Life program does not sufficiently allay. In closing, therefore, we want to point to the enormous variability, diversity, resilience, and resourcefulness of human beings. These qualities allow people to resist and to mold their institutions, as well as to be shaped by them. People, not faceless forces, chart the course of social and economic history by acting and reacting, or sitting undecided. Individuals act in and affect the routine and major events of public as well as private life. There is a complicated interplay between individuals and the institutions they invent and reinvent and the way they shape one another.

In terms of this book, the family is not only molded by its economic and social position and the encounters of its members with the institutions of the society, but it is capable of fighting back. Moreover, increasing numbers of parents are active on their own and their children's behalf. One can imagine Jane Polsky and Alice Murphy working for an environmental group fighting the pollution of the lake where they live; Rose or Frank Giannini, once they have discovered they can't move, using what little spare time they have to organize people to fight redlining in their neighborhood; Florence and her cousin Ruby joining a welfare reform coalition through a church group; Linda and Cliff, at the mercy of a bad landlord, discovering that there is a great deal they can do working with their local rent control board.

In emphasizing parents' capacity to act on their own and their children's behalf, however, we do not want to lay a new burden on individual parents, to say, in effect, it's up to you to change the way things work, nothing's going to change unless you, the brave individual, a contemporary Saint George, go forth, become a citizen advocate, and challenge the dragons of the society's institutions. Spotlighting the influence of the larger institutions on the family, this book has tried to put in perspective each parent's sense of responsibility for the course of his child's development, a common side effect of the American faith in the ability of the individual to chart his own life and guide the life of his child. We want to point out the interplay and balance between the force of institutions and the capacity of individuals, but we don't want to give the impression that we are leaving yet another major responsibility to individual parents alone. Collective action and pressure by private individuals can be potent forces for change, but ultimately pressure for change must come from within as well as from outside institutions. Most of all, those who belong to institutions must take responsibility for the values on which their livelihood is based, whether they act in the interests of their own children or in the best American tradition of concern for the public.

In a complex society effective action must be based on a critical understanding of the institutions whose policies and procedures one seeks to change. An example of effective action initiated by parents and based on a critical understanding of the problems it addressed is Action for Children's Television, which began in a Newton, Massachusetts, living room in 1968. A group of women began to discuss the effects of television on their children, particularly the advertising. They did not act until a year after they first began meeting, not until they had thoroughly understood the varied and highly complex economic, governmental, and psychological problems that were relevant, and not until they had worked out strategies that they believed would be effective. The media demeaned them as "those ladies from Newton." But the "ladies from Newton" gradually made an impact on American children's television by informing the public, pressuring broadcasters, and speaking out loudly and persistently enough to be heard by the Federal Communications Commission and by citizens groups across the nation.

Surely the "ladies from Newton" were informed by a firm sense of their entitlements as citizens—and a firm belief that they could make themselves heard, that is, that they had a public voice.

We can imagine that the work of our fictional characters on behalf of the environment, welfare reform, or some other cause is shaped by similar convictions. We can imagine, too, that their children are likely to take in these convictions, thus increasing the likelihood that they will grow up with the belief that they can have a choice and voice in society. Through their actions and convictions, Jane Polsky, Alice Murphy, Rose and Frank Giannini, Florence and Ruby, Linda and Cliff will enhance their children's map of social reality, marking it with the road signs of possibility.

It would be wrong, however, to suggest that only parents who are activists can give their children a sense that they can make themselves heard and chart a course full of possibilities. Personal resources on the part of parents, which may or may not be expressed as activism in the public arena, may make a great difference to children's understanding of their world and their place and possibilities within it. By personal resources we mean intelligence, determination, social competence, faithful friendships, and resiliency in the face of life's traumas and setbacks. Florence's mother is an excellent example of a woman whose personal resources remained strong despite economic and social privations, and these made a difference to her children's lives. She was able to see the choices that could be made, to teach her children that their voices could and should be heard, and that they were entitled not only to take action to improve their circumstances, but could do so and be effective.

There are hundreds of parents like Florence's mother for every one who joins a welfare reform coalition or works with a local rent control board—let alone launches a campaign such as Action for Children's Television. Unsung, they help their children chart a hopeful course, not merely by speaking of dreams, but by pointing out how they can be made to come true, one step at a time.

Nevertheless, it is also true that every parent's sense of his resources is to some extent shaped by his economic and social circumstances. And, as we have made abundantly clear, particularly in our discussion of the Giannini family, these circumstances shape the ways parents understand and filter the messages of the society to their children—and to the meaning their children take from them in terms of what they themselves will be entitled to strive for in life.

A focus on the economic and social influences on the family raises the question of what should be done to increase parents' sense of their powers and resourcefulness and at the same time to upgrade the raw material from which children construct a sense of the world they are growing up in. We believe that two streams of social reform must come together to accomplish these purposes. America has a long tradition of celebrating exceptional individuals whose personal resources and those of their parents have permitted them to prevail against the odds laid down by economic or social constraints, handicaps, national origin, or gender. In many social programs we have tried to teach ways that have worked for the few. We need more, not less, of these strategies. But a second path of reform is important, too, one that emphasizes changing the odds by altering economic and social opportunity structures so that the deck is not stacked so heavily in favor of some groups and against others.

It is easier to see how such structural changes work to encourage parents' sense of their own resources and choices—and less easy to see how they influence children's sense of their world and their possibilities within it. As we have shown, the growing child seeks and finds meaning for his life in a variety of socially defined circumstances. If these circumstances—many of which are governed by public agreements, most often by law—favor him and his family, he will take in their favorable message directly, through his experience at school, on the playground, or when watching television, and indirectly as family members and neighbors bring home the social messages of the larger world, along with the stains on their work clothes or the paper in their briefcases. Although it is impossible to predict the life course of any one child, one can predict outcomes for significant proportions of groups, knowing their demographic characteristics. In changing the social and economic structures that underlie the demographics, the likelihood that individual outcomes will be more favorable is increased. At the same time it becomes more likely that more children will grow up with a sense that their voices can be heard, that they have choices, and that they can take effective action on their own behalf and on behalf of those they care for.

Notes

Introduction

1. For an excellent discussion of the shaping of modern consciousness, see Peter L. Berger, Brigitte Berger, and Hansfried Kellner, *The Homeless Mind: Modernization and Consciousness*. New York: Random House, 1973. Also Alfred Schutz, *Phenomenology and Social Relations: Selected Writings,* Helmut R. Wagner, ed. Chicago: University of Chicago Press, 1970.

A society is modernized to the extent that it exploits potentials inherent in technological innovations, but only to the degree that its political system favors economic progress and its cultural traditions disfavor neither the goals nor the means of change. The power of technology lies in its capacity to release new means to control and direct nature's scourges and bounties and to create new approaches to old problems and unfulfilled dreams. In nonmodernized societies, the sources of power at man's command are most often animate, e.g., manpower or horsepower. When inanimate machines first multiplied animate power, their operations were visible and their workings analogous to physical labor. Today, modern power sources are not only inanimate, but invisible, and therefore comprehensible only to persons who have specialized knowledge.

This shift from animate to inanimate is characteristic not only of physical sources of power but of social forces as well. For example, bureaucracies are often linked to special languages, regulations, and rituals and sometimes to computer technology, centralized control, and highly specific job operations in which people are interchangeable. Information, both a coinage and a product of modernized societies, has shifted the potential distribution of social power based on specialized knowlege (privileged meaning) while at the same time threatening to establish a new basis for social stratification—from the economic haves and have nots to those who have social access to knowledge and those who do not.

The specialization of social roles and institutional functions has narrowed the functions of some institutions and expanded those of others. A conscious effort must be made to see the connections between institutions and to clarify their separate and overlapping functions. The family, for example, has been increasingly fenced in, its links to the supportive institutions of the local society weakened, and its functions gradually given over to modern service institutions and their experts. More to the point, the implicit links between family and traditional institutions—church, neighborhood, etc.—have seldom been examined critically and thus are not even discussed or planned for. In modern institutions, only what is explicated has validity, and the family is, and always has been, an institution that adapts to circumstances of individual and social life at its various stages, carrying out many essential but implicit functions, which are poorly articulated but widely shared by members of a culture.

Most parents applaud the loss of some explicit family functions to experts, teachers, doctors, television programmers, etc. It is a different sort of loss that seems to search for expression—one that we believe inheres in the loosening of links between family and traditional social institutions where they once existed, and the absence of those links in newer institutions. Lost, too, is a sense of continuity between the past world of one's fathers and a predictable future.

From infancy, people work hard to protect themselves from circumstances that would drastically alter their sense of predictability and mastery—and, in our view, they do so all their lives for reasons that are, at root, biological. There are two possibilities of loss that are rooted in human biology: *first*, loss experienced when the explanatory structures of one's life are challenged by new information, by the death of old forms and the birth of new ones, and *second*, by limited opportunities for masterful action—for effective solutions or accommodations to life's challenges that reestablish predictability and a sense of protection.

To take but one instance: it is now necessary to build into federal guidelines for social programs a requirement that parents be actively involved in the decision making and operation of programs designed to serve their children. This is one example of making explicit in new institutions once taken-for-granted links between the family (or the individual) and the institutions of public life. Another example is the hospital Child Life program referred to in the final chapter of this book, which serves to protect the psychological health of the child while restoring his physical health.

Our view of modernization was influenced primarily by Marion Levy's definition, which emphasizes the growing proportion of inanimate to animate sources of power, particularly those sources of power that are released by modern technology which in turn speed economic growth processes (Marion J. Levy, *Modernization and the Structure of Society: A Setting for International Affairs*, 2 vols. Princeton, N.J.: Princeton University Press, 1966). Daniel Bell's *The Cultural Contradictions of Capitalism*. New York: Basic Books, 1976, Godfrey Hodgson's *America in Our Time*. Garden City, N.Y.: Doubleday, 1976, and Edward Shorter's *The Making of the Modern Family*. New York: Basic Books, 1975, are recent social-historical works whose perspectives elaborate the thesis.

2. Any effort to link the forces of social institutions to the everyday life world or the child and to his mental representations of the social world

must be tentative. In addition to the sources mentioned, we relied heavily on Peter L. Berger and Thomas Luckmann, *The Social Construction of Reality: A Treatise in the Sociology of Knowledge*. Garden City, N.Y.: Doubleday, 1966, *Homeless Mind*; Berger, Berger and Kellner; Ernest G. Schactel, *Metamorphosis: On the Development of Affect, Perception, Attention, and Memory*. New York: Basic Books, 1959; and Robert Kegan, *The Evolving of Self*. Cambridge, Mass.: Harvard University Press, 1982. Several guiding premises, summarized below, became a foundation for the book. Arguments to establish their validity are not possible here, but the authors welcome communications. The premises are:

a. All knowledge is to some degree filtered through or organized by the social context in which the knower learns and recreates it. Social contents are more systematically structured and interdependent than we often admit.

b. Any functioning society has a limited number of maintenance institutions which in practice tend to shape the perimeters and parameters of life in the society. For example, a tropical agricultural community will have daily and seasonal life patterns that reflect the interdependence of economic, social, and natural growth cycles. In a highly technological society things become more humanly complicated because economic and social life can be controlled and changed by human decisions and man-made devices. One can, with some effort, argue that new technology and knowledge attract attention, mobilize interest, trigger imagination, and foster adventures that shape both a society's institutions and the consciousness of its people as they move through their now-altered daily lives.

Our everyday life world is imprinted with patterns—the ways we use our time, space, people, things—set by our work, material props, living arrangements, and social relations that are themselves shaped by the institutional structures that maintain a society. Thus the average child encounters many regular patterns that carry the residues and imprints of these institutions, i.e., their values and their influence on the texture of everyday life.

c. Communications technology, particularly television, calls attention to and reinforces the patterns of life and values of the society's major institutions. At the same time that communications technology serves its sponsors, it offers a realm of new pressures and new possibilities for "taking in" life worlds quite different from the local drama of one's life.

d. Although some families live in isolated communities where the influence of society's major institutions is muted or where television reception is limited, such communities are becoming nearly extinct. Even when families are isolated from urban life or from work in modern institutions their *consciousness* is modernized by values that pervade public life—the products and procedures of commerce, transportation, the content and style of the communications media, school books, clothing, etc.

e. Against the systematic array of messages that are woven into the patterns of daily life, parents' efforts to give a different perspective must be exceedingly powerful, vigilant, and well informed if they are to compete successfully with the dominant messages of the society.

3. See Edward T. Hall, *The Silent Language*. Garden City, N.Y.: Doubleday, 1959; Margaret Mead and Martha Wolfenstein, *Childhood in Contemporary Cultures*. Chicago: University of Chicago Press, 1955.

4. For excellent social histories of the modern family, see Kenneth Keniston et al., *All Our Children*. New York: Harcourt Brace Jovanovich, 1977, Shorter, *Modern Family*, and Christopher Lasch, *Haven in a Heartless World: The Family Besieged*. New York: Basic Books, 1977. For facts about families see Mary Jo Bane, *Here to Stay: American Families in the Twentieth Century*. New York: Basic Books, 1976. For a highly readable history of recent decades, see William Manchester, *The Glory and the Dream: A Narrative History of America, 1932–1972*. Boston: Little, Brown, 1974.

Chapter One

1. Experimental evidence supporting the contention that babies begin early to search for order and coherence in their surroundings can be found in Yvonne Brackbill, ed., *Infancy and Early Childhood: A Handbook and Guide to Human Development*. New York: Free Press, 1967; Daniel G. Freedman, *Human Infancy: An Evolutionary Perspective*. Hillsdale, N.Y.: L. Erlbaum Associates, distributed by Halsted Press, New York, 1974; Eleanor J. Gibson, *Principles of Perceptual Learning and Development*. New York: Prentice-Hall, 1969; William Kessen, Marshall M. Haith, and Philip H. Salapatek, "Infancy," *Carmichael's Manual of Child Psychology*, Paul H. Mussen, ed., 2 vols, 3d ed., New York: John Wiley, 1970, vol. 1, pp. 287–445; Daniel Stern, *The First Relationship*. Cambridge, Mass.: Harvard University Press, 1977; M. D. Vernon, *Perception Through Experience*. New York: Barnes & Noble, 1970.

On the ways the social order expresses itself in the routines and rituals of daily life, see Schutz, *Phenomenology*; Harold Garfinkel, *Studies in Ethnomethodology*. Englewood Cliffs, N.J.: Prentice-Hall, 1967; Rom Harre, "The Conditions for a Social Psychology of Childhood," *The Integration of a Child into a Social World*, M. P. M. Richards, ed. London: Cambridge University Press, 1974, pp. 245–262.

Our discussion in chapter one of children at various stages in their development is based primarily on Jean Piaget's theories of mental development in infancy and childhood. For brief summaries on his theory, see Herbert Ginsburg and Sylvia Opper, *Piaget's Theory of Intellectual De-*

velopment: An Introduction. Englewood Cliffs, N.J.: Prentice-Hall, 1969; John H. Flavell, *Cognitive Development.* Englewood Cliffs, N.J.: Prentice-Hall, 1977; and Robert Kegan, *Evolving Self.*

A number of sources aided our efforts to conceptualize how children construct reality from the phenomenal world of everyday life. Of particular interest is how they selectively invest certain events with emotional meanings that "fit" their biological predispositions, a particular family, cultural heritage, and social position. We offer a brief selection of useful sources. James Mark Baldwin, *Social and Ethical Interpretations in Mental Development: A Study in Social Psychology.* New York: Macmillan, 1897; Diana Baumrind, "The Development of Instrumental Competence Through Socialization," *Minnesota Symposium on Child Psychology,* Vol. 7, 1973, pp. 3–46; Berger and Luckman, *Social Construction;* Joan Costello and E. F. Peyton, "The Socialization of Young Children's Learning Styles," unpublished MS, 1973; Hans Peter Drietzel, ed., *Childhood and Socialization,* Recent Sociology No. 5. New York: Macmillan, 1973; Erik H. Erikson, *Childhood and Society.* New York: Norton, 1950; 2d ed., 1963; *idem, Toys and Reasons: Stages in the Ritualization of Experience.* New York: Norton, 1977; Uriel G. Foa and Edna B. Foa, *Societal Structures of the Mind.* Springfield, Ill.: Thomas, 1974; Selma H. Fraiberg, *The Magic Years: Understanding and Handling the Problems of Early Childhood.* New York: Scribner, 1959; Alex Inkeles. "Society Social Structure and Child Socialization," in John A. Clausen, ed. *Socialization and Society.* Boston: Little, Brown, 1968. Robert Kegan, *Evolving Self;* Robert D. Hess, "Social Class and Ethnic Influences on Socialization," *Carmichael's Manual of Child Psychology,* Paul H. Mussen, ed. 2 vols. 3d ed. New York: John Wiley, 1970, vol. 2, pp. 457–557; Robert D. Hess and Virginia C. Shipman, "Early Experience and the Socialization of Cognitive Modes in Children," *Child Development,* Vol. 34, 1965, pp. 869–886; A. R. Luria, *Cognitive Development, Its Cultural and Social Foundations,* Martin Lopez-Morillas and Lynn Solotaroff, trans. Cambridge: Cambridge University Press, 1974; Schactel, *Metamorphosis;* Roy Schafer, *Aspects of Internalization.* New York: International Universities Press, 1968; L. S. Vygotsky, "Play and Its Role in the Mental Development of the Child [1933]" in *Play: Its Role in Development and Evolution,* Jerome S. Bruner, Alison Jolly, and Kathy Sylva, eds. New York: Basic Books, 1976, pp. 537–554; Heinz Werner and Bernard Kaplan, *Symbol Formation: An Organismic-Developmental Approach to Language and the Expression of Thought.* New York: John Wiley & Sons, 1967; Edward F. Zigler and Irvin L. Child, *Socialization and Personality Development.* Reading, Mass.: Addison-Wesley, 1973.

2. "Life world" is a concept borrowed from Alfred Schutz, a German philosopher of the phenomenological school. In a modern society, much of the business of everyday life is linked, often directly, or at least indirectly, to the imperatives of modern economic and governmental institutions expressed in the institutions of work, markets, bureaucratic procedures,

media, school, etc. Harold Garfinkel, an American sociologist, has explored how simple exchanges, like hellos and goodbyes, express the social structures of everyday life. Edward Hall's 1983 book *The Dance of Life: The Other Dimension of Time*. New York: Anchor/Doubleday, extends his earlier work on this topic.

3. For examples, see Richard Sennett and Jonathan Cobb, *The Hidden Injuries of Class*. New York: Vintage Books, 1973; Lillian Breslow Rubin, *Worlds of Pain: Life in the Working-Class Family*. New York: Pantheon Books, 1972; Studs Terkel, *Working: People Talk about What They Do All Day and How They Feel about What They Do*. New York: Pantheon Books, 1972; Richard Balzer, *Clockwork: Life in and outside an American Factory*. Garden City, N.Y.: Doubleday, 1976; C. Robert Coles, *The Children of Crisis*. Vol. 5: *The Privileged Ones: The Well-Off and the Rich in America*. Boston: Little, Brown, 1977; Martha Wolfenstein, "French Parents Take Their Children to the Park," *Childhood in Contemporary Cultures*, Margaret Mead and Martha Wolfenstein, eds. Chicago: University of Chicago Press, 1955.

4. Leeway to play with life's possibilities may define one's sense of well-being, for both children and adults. In *Toys and Reason* Erikson develops the concept of playful leeway in a way that illuminates the links between children's efforts to make sense of their lives and the circumstances in which they grow up.

5. Selective attention—and inattention—may be the elemental processes through which the child becomes enculturated and socialized. For background on related attentional and perceptual aspects of development, see Gibson, *Perceptual Learning*, and Vernon, *Perception*. H. S. Sullivan's theory of the self is consistent with the experimental literature on perception when it posits that by age two a child has a rudimentary self system, expressed in part by his selective *inattention* to elements in his world that formerly led him to act in ways that evoked censure or punishment from important persons. Selective *attention*—as opposed to inattention—seems to function more generally as an aid to learning how to organize experience, not only to organize intimate relationships. See Harry Stack Sullivan, *Interpersonal Theory of Psychiatry*, Helen, S. Perry and Mary L. Gawel, eds. New York: Norton, 1968; Daniel Stern, *First Relationship*; and Michael I. Posner, "Cumulative Development of Attentional Theory," *American Psychologist*, vol. 37, 1982, pp. 168–179.

6. Selections from theorists and investigators of play are generously collected in Jerome S. Bruner, Alison Jolly, and Kathy Sylva, eds., *Play: Its Role in Development and Evolution*. New York: Basic Books, 1976. We have relied heavily on Erikson, Geertz, Huizinga, Piaget, Vygotsky, all represented in Bruner et al. Three additional excellent sources not represented in that collection are Erikson, *Toys and Reasons*; Susanna Millar, *The Psychology of Play*. New York: Penguin, 1968; R. E. Herron and Brian Sutton-Smith, *Child's Play*. New York: Wiley, 1971.

7. It is possible that the play of children today may be more limited—at

least with respect to play based on the direct experience of life—than it used to be because of the influence of television. Some nursery school teachers report that children now base their play on what they have seen on television, but television presents synthesized sequences of images, a very different kind of raw material from the flow of ordinary life. For some, television's images may enrich a barren life or give order to events that are in disarray in their real lives. Children may derive play themes from television, but they may be restricted in their improvisations by trying to make their play "like television"—a finished product. We do not yet know if or how television enriches or restricts the opportunity play provides for the children to construct a workable and coherent map of reality.

8. In a single play episode, an experienced observer can sometimes learn what culture and social position the child's parents represent; their prevailing values, pleasures, and the conflicts that define the intimate life of the family; the child's proclivities for learning through one or another sensory channel, his style of organization, pondering, planning, or the substance of his thoughts and feelings about things, about people, about himself. Few play episodes are starkly revealing, although play sequences observed over weeks or months almost inevitably reveal the current constructions of social and emotional reality that guide the child's actions in everyday life. For a discussion of how competence develops through mastery, see Robert W. White, "Motivation Reconsidered: The Concept of Competence," *Psychological Review*, vol. 66, 1959, pp. 297–333; and Robert W. White, "Competence as an Aspect of Personal Growth," *Primary Prevention of Psychopathology*, Martha Whalen, Kent and Jon Rolf, eds. Hanover, N.H.: University Press of New England, 1979.

9. See Edward T. Hall, *Beyond Culture*. Garden City, N.Y.: Anchor Press, 1976; Jonathan Benthall and Ted Polhems, *The Body as a Medium of Expression*. New York: E.P. Dutton, 1975.

10. A study of West Side Chicago children reared in a housing project will soon be published by Joan Costello, Jay Hirsch, and Gene Borowitz. The children were studied as preschoolers and again in their teens.

11. Even early play can be said both to express and to facilitate the child's learning about the material and social structures of life by the rules and role constraints implicit in even simple games and rituals. See, for example, J. A. Bruner and V. Sherwood, "Peekaboo and the Learning of Rule Structures," in Bruner, Jolly, and Sylva. Rules and roles are commonly used terms in the literature of child development, although definitions vary. One excellent source is Harre, "Social Psychology." Although we start with Piaget's observations and theoretical writings, e.g., Jean Piaget, *The Origins of Intelligence in Children*. New York: International Universities Press, 1952, 2nd ed. and *The Construction of Reality in the Child*. New York: Basic Books, 1954, 2nd ed., our search for a way to understand how the child maps his social world drew us to somewhat broader views,

represented, for example, by Gregory Bateson in *Steps to an Ecology of Mind: Collected Essays in Anthropology, Evolution, and Epistemology*. New York: Ballantine Books, 1975; John Grinder and Richard Bandler, "Representational Systems—Other Maps for the Same Territory," *The Structure of Magic: A Book about Language and Therapy*. 2 vols. Palo Alto, Calif.: Science and Behavior Books, 1976, vol. 2, pp. 1–26; Schachtel, *Metamorphosis;* and Alfred Korzybski, *Science and Sanity: An Introduction to Non-Aristotelian Systems and General Semantics*. 4th ed. Lakeville, Conn.: The International Non-Aristotelian Library Publishing Co., distributed by Institute of General Semantics, 1958 (originally published in 1933), pp. 58–60. Current conceptions of social cognitions, which concern themselves with questions quite similar to ours, seem to us a useful but narrow gauge for understanding children's social constructions, particularly how they develop and express their maps of reality in play; e.g., Carolyn Uhlinger Shantz, "The Development of Social Cognition," *Review of Child Development Research*, Vol. 5, E. Mavis Hetherington, ed. Chicago: University of Chicago Press, 1976. The child is not, at least in the years that most concern us, learning well-organized rules and roles in any rote sense; nor is he aware of his representations—maps—and his efforts to impose order on his experience. What we see expressed in action (and only later articulated in child-size "theories" of how and why things are as they seem) are the imperatives of the child's inner order whose limits and possibilities he is impelled to test by active experiment, i.e., in "playing around."

12. Berger and Luckmann, *Social Construction*, pp. 131–132.

13. See, for example, Marcel Proust, *Remembrance of Things Past*, 2 vols. New York: Random House, 1934. In the realm of abstract ideas, certain explanations or theories feel right to a person, "in my bones." It is often hard to accept explanations—however scientific or rationally persuasive—that run counter to in-tuition, that is the tuition of early experiences taken in as major landmarks on one's map of how things are. Although new experiences can release possibilities by destroying old barriers to thought and action, can also lead to deep sadness or anxiety as one realizes that one's first compass can not be trusted.

14. For a selection of relevant literature about babies' abilities to discriminate, or organize responses selectively, and to detect sources of power and love, see Mary D. Salter Ainsworth, *Infancy in Uganda: Infant Care and the Growth of Love*. Baltimore: Johns Hopkins Press, 1967; idem, "Object Relations, Dependency and Attachment: A Theoretical Review of the Mother-Infant Relationship," *Child Development*, Vol. 40, 1969, pp. 969–1025; Freedman, *Human Infancy*; Kessen, Haith, and Salapatek, "Infancy"; Michael Lewis and Leonard A. Rosenblum, eds., *The Effect of the Infant on Its Caregiver*. New York: Wiley, 1974; Sally Provence and Rose C. Lipton, *Infants in Institutions: A Comparison of Their Development During the First Year of Life with Family-Raised Infants*. New York: International Universities Press, 1967; Stern, *First Relationship*.

15. See Michael E. Lamb, ed., *The Role of the Father in Child Development*. New York: John Wiley & Sons, 1976.
16. See Werner and Kaplan, *Symbol Formation*.
17. It is possible that less perceptible attributes of a role lead children to be more dependent on adults for information—an advantage to some but a disadvantage to those who have a limited exchange with adults. For role play as a way of understanding self and society, see George Herbert Mead, *Mind, Self and Society*. Chicago: University of Chicago Press, 1934; Richard L. Selman, "Stages in Role-Taking and Moral Judgements as Guides to Social Intervention," *Man and Morality*, T. Likona, ed. New York: Holt, Rinehart & Winston, 1974; also Shantz, "Social Cognition," for a summary of current thinking about social cognition, and Edward E. Jones, "How Do People Perceive the Causes of Behavior?" *American Scientist*, Vol. 64, 1976, pp. 300–305, for an excellent summary of attribution theory.
18. See Harre, "Social Psychology."

Chapter Two

1. For a discussion of the social structures expressed in meeting and greeting behaviors, see Garfinkel, *Ethnomethodology* and Erving Goffman, *Interaction Ritual*. New York: Anchor Books, 1967.
2. See Alfred Schutz, *The Structures of the Life World*. London: Heinemann, 1977; Jack Douglas, ed., *Understanding Everyday Life*. Chicago: Aldine, 1970.
3. For a comparative perspective on social meeting rituals, see Hall's *Silent Language*.
4. For an extensive recent discussion of gender-based expectations, see Carol Gilligan, *In a Different Voice*. Cambridge, Mass.: Harvard University Press, 1982.
5. See chapter on handicap as a social construction in *The Unexpected Minority: Handicapped Children in America* by John Gliedman and William Roth. New York: Academic Press, 1980.
6. Children learn that acceptable "social" meanings are not always confirmed by observational evidence of what's really going on. Double messages have been studied in pathological parent-child relationships, but learning to agree that a naked emperor indeed is wearing clothes represents a universal achievement of socialization. How this begins is argued elegantly in a review paper by Daniel Stern et al., "Early Transmission of Affect: Some Research Issues," in *Frontiers of Infant Psychiatry*, Eleanor Galenson and Justin D. Call, eds. New York: Basic Books, 1983, pp. 74–85.

Chapter Three

1. Peter L. Berger and Hansfried Kellner, "Marriage and the Construction of Reality," *Facing Up to Modernity: Excursions in Society, Politics and*

Religion, Peter L. Berger, ed. New York: Basic Books, 1977. For other excellent readings on family, see Rose Laub Coser, ed. *The Family: Its Structure and Functions*. New York: St. Martin's Press, 1964; 2d ed., 1974; Theodore Lidz, *The Family and Human Adaption*. New York: International Universities Press, 1963; Marvin B. Sussman, J. Cates, and D. T. Smith, *Family and Inheritance*. New York: Russell Sage Foundation, 1970; Marvin B. Sussman and B. Cogswell, eds., *Cross-National Family Research*. Leiden: E. J. Brill, 1972; "The Family," *Daedalus* (special issue), vol. 106, no. 2, Spring 1977.

2. See Sennet, Richard, *The Fall of Public Man*. New York: Knopf, 1977, for an original and readable analysis of the changed definitions of public and private life.

3. See Edward T. Hall, *The Dance of Life; The Other Dimension of Time*, New York: Anchor/Doubleday, 1983, for a description of the choreography of social life.

4. For a description of influences on modernization see Levy, *Modernization*; and Berger, Berger and Kellner, *Homeless Mind*.

5. An excellent book on the development and implications of a "service society" is Alan Gartner and Frank Riessman's *The Service Society and the Consumer Vanguard*. New York: Harper & Row, 1974.

6. Emotional well-being seems to depend on appropriate levels of neural arousal—usually triggered by mental or physical activity. Thus, activities in which family members participate may be more basic to the maintenance of the family's sense of shared purpose than shared interests. Boredom within the family may spring from sources similar to those producing boredom in individuals—too little or too much neural stimulation. For a useful summary article, see Estelle R. Ramey, "Boredom: The Most Prevalent American Disease," *Harper's Magazine*, vol. 249, 1974, pp. 12–22.

7. See Ann Oakley, *The Sociology of Housework*. New York: Pantheon Books, 1975; and Rosalyn Baxandall, Linda Gordon, and Susan Reverby, eds., *America's Working Woman*. New York: Random House, 1976. Also, Susan Bucknell, Background papers on the history of women's work prepared for Carnegie Council members and staff, 1975 (available from Regenstein Library, Special Collections, University of Chicago).

8. Lucille J. Grow, *Early Childrearing by Young Mothers*. New York: Child Welfare League of America, 1975, pp. 9–13.

9. See Alfred J. Kahn and Sheila B. Kamerman, *Not for the Poor Alone: European Social Services*. Philadelphia: Temple University Press, 1975; and Sheila B. Kamerman and Alfred J. Kahn, *Social Services in the United States: Policies and Programs*. Philadelphia: Temple University Press, 1976.

Chapter Four

1. See Sennett, *The Fall of Public Man* and Lyn H. Lofland, *A World of Strangers: Order and Action in Urban Public Space*. New York: Basic Books, 1973, who argue that people find order, not chaos, in urban settings by imposing order and giving meaning to their experience.

2. For a comprehensive treatment, see Hannah Arendt's *The Human Condition*. Chicago: University of Chicago Press, 1958. Chapter 11, "The Labor of Our Body and the Work of Our Hands," and chapter 16, "The Instruments of Work of Our Hands," were particularly useful to us. Because child care is thought by many to be primarily physical work it often contributes little to self-esteem. Efforts to upgrade social attitudes toward child care usually include its "professionalization," often emphasizing its educational—mental—aspects. For a historical perspective, see Oakley, *The Sociology of Housework*.

3. A variety of books about work have been useful to us, although many of the examples are drawn from personal observation. Each author has a particular point of view, but all offer evidence for the importance of work to Americans' sense of themselves as worthy people and as effective parents. The first four sources are particularly pertinent: Sennett and Cobb, *The Hidden Inquiries*; Terkel, *Working*; Melvin L. Kohn, "Social Class and Parent-Child Relationships: An Interpretation," *American Journal of Sociology*, Vol. 68, 1963, pp. 471–480; Balzer, *Clockwork*. See also Rubin, *Worlds of Pain*—this book covers the same territory as Sennett and Cobb but is written from within the working class experience; Peter L. Berger et al., eds., *The Human Shape of Work: Studies in the Sociology of Occupations of Nine American Jobholders*. New York: Bantam Books, 1972; Andrew Levison, *The Working-Class Majority*. New York: Coward, McCann, and Geoghegan, 1974; Mirra Komarovsky, *Blue Collar Marriage*. New York: Random House, 1962; Walter S. Neff, *Work and Human Behavior*. New York: Atherton Press, 1968; Paul E. Mott, Floyd G. Mann, Quin McLoughlin, and Donald P. Warwick, *Shift Work: The Social, Psychological and Physical Consequences*. Ann Arbor: University of Michigan Press, 1965; Gartner and Riessman, *The Service Society*; Andrew Hacker, "What Rules America?" *New York Review of Books*, May 1, 1975, pp. 9–13 (a review of books dealing with ruling classes and corporate elites); Rosabeth Moss Kanter, *Men and Women of the Corporation*. New York: Simon and Schuster, 1977; Michael Macoby, *The Gamesman: The New Corporate Leaders*. New York: Simon and Schuster, 1967; Laura Lein, *Work and Family Life*, Center for the Study of Public Policy Report to the National Institute of Education re: Project No. 3-3094. D. R. Miller and G. E. Swanson, *The Changing American Parent*. New York: Wiley, 1958; D. G. McKinley, *Social Class and Family Life*. New York: Free Press, 1964.

4. *Work in America*, report of a Special Task Force to the Secretary of Health, Education and Welfare. Cambridge, Mass.: MIT Press, 1973, p. 13.

5. There are few studies of children's economic concepts. One useful paper is Kurt Danziger, "Children's Earliest Conceptions of Economic Relationships," *Journal of Social Psychology*, vol. 47, 1958, pp. 231–240. See also Jerome S. Bruner and C. C. Goodman, "Value and Need as Organizing Factors in Perception," *Journal of Abnormal and Social Psychology*, vol. 42, 1947, pp. 33–44.

6. Basil Bernstein, *Class, Codes and Control: Theoretical Studies Towards*

Sociology of Language. New York: Schocken Books, 1975. Bernstein argues that the class structure affects the inequitable social distribution of privileged meanings (p. 239). See also Fred Hirsch, *Social Limits to Growth*. Cambridge, Mass.: Harvard University Press, 1976.

7. In this chapter we have not touched on another form of social identification that perhaps more profoundly than any other affects a child's sense of place, power, and possibilities: membership in a subordinate social group. These groups include blacks, Hispanics, Indians, Asians, Chicanos, the handicapped, and women. Physical features, or speech characteristics, or both, identify people belonging to these groups and are an inescapable factor in their dealings with others, particularly in their working lives. Chapter six will discuss how a child is socialized into membership in such a group; the process is the same as that in which children learn about the freedoms and limitations that their parents' work and income give to their lives.

Chapter Five

1. James Youniss, *Parents and Peers in Social Development*. Chicago: University of Chicago Press, 1980.
2. For an excellent perspective on sports as an American secular liturgy and baseball as the game that best expresses American ideology, see Michael Novak, *The Joy of Sports*. New York: Basic Books, 1976.
3. Ibid., p. 59.
4. Robert J. Antonacci and Jene Barr, *Baseball for Young Champions*. New York: Whittlesey House, McGraw-Hill, 1956. Although pitchers are often the stars in baseball lore, exceptional players in other positions may be stars as well.
5. Novak, p. 58.
6. Ibid., p. 63.
7. Janet Lever, "Sex Differences in the Games Children Play," *Social Problems*, vol. 23, 1976.
8. See John Gliedman and William Roth, *Handicapped Children in America*. New York: Harcourt Brace Jovanovich, 1980.

Chapter Six

1. See chapter by Harre in Richards for concept of child's family world of home and intermediate worlds beyond it. Peter Berger developed the concept of mediating structures in modern societies in a 1975 analytic paper for the American Enterprise Institute, Washington, D.C. In briefer form the argument appears in chapter 11 of Berger's *Facing Up to Modernity: Excursions in Society, Politics, and Religion*. New York: Basic Books, 1977. Other writers who directly or indirectly develop social links between the child and intermediate institutions are Foa and Foa, *Societal Structures*; Alex Inkeles, "Society, Social Structure and Child Socialization," *Socializa-*

tion and Society, John A. Clausen, ed. Boston: Little, Brown, 1968; Schutz, *Phenomenology*; and Garfinkel, *Ethnomethodology*.

2. Although intermediate institutions are to some degree a "buffer zone" between families and the larger society, they are shaped by the major maintenance institutions of the society. Some institutions—church, neighborhood, voluntary associations—carry on traditions of the past. They are, in a sense, responsible for continuity. Other institutions—schools, medical centers, social agencies—take their cues from institutions that generate new knowledge and from the future-oriented goals of government and the economy. They are responsible for carrying people forward, for changing traditional patterns of life.

Let's take the example of a local school board whose members are business and professional leaders who expect teachers and principals to operate schools with the same efficiency and financial accountability that their business demands. Their attitudes toward "basics" versus "frills" in the curriculum will be governed by what they consider vital knowledge and skills in their own lives. They will be critical if the schools do not promote the social rules and roles which govern their daily lives. School board members may wear many hats in the course of a week or a month. In addition to their commitment to their school system they may be vestrymen at their church, sit on the board of the local bank and hospital, or be active in local politics. Their participation in a variety of roles in their community, often in the company of others who appear regularly in similar roles, leads to the reinforcement of social norms in the community as a whole.

The social norms of a particular community are shaped in part by historical, regional and local factors and by the effects of decisions taken beyond the local level of government or industry, i.e., to attract a new industry or to build a new highway. The particular industries, patterns of land use, resource exploitation, construction possibilities and transportation networks in the community are all factors in the establishment of its social norms. In a community whose economy is dominated for many years by a single industry, the people who hold prestigious positions, political office or municipal jobs will take to their jobs assumptions and experiences that incorporate the residues of long-standing encounters with the concrete economic and social events that surround that industry. Collective norms and a sense of loyalty toward them develop over time when those norms govern the public life of a community.

Those who serve in intermediate institutions may or may not share the same norms as those who govern and manage these institutions. Most of the time they will. But governors, managers and employees—school board officials, principals and school teachers, for instance—will be held accountable by their reference group outside the school and will jeopardize their social identity—their position in a social matrix—if they advance an idiosyncratic point of view or "give in" to pressure from an "outsider" group. A concrete instance might arise in the case of purchasing textbooks. A teacher will jeopardize his position if he advocates the purchase of a new textbook which violates the norms of the community. He may be criticized by colleagues if he goes along with the principal or the school board if he believes their norms interfere with good teaching. Publishing companies, well aware of this situation, generally produce only those books or educational materials for which they can find a market, that is, books that will not violate social norms defined by those who pay the bills. Thus does big business respond to and reinforce certain social norms. Only as norms change do publishers risk the mass marketing of school books which might earlier have created controversy.

Some have commented on television's paradoxical effects. On the one hand it levels the nature of social discourse and entertainment to the lowest common denominator. But on the other hand, it dissolves boundaries of privilege—opening doors to the average American that were formerly closed because he could not pay the price, travel the distance, or execute the right manner for "entrance." Everyman can see operas, ballets, plays, distant lands, the gestures of a senator as he voices a position, the uneasy expression of a public figure on a talk show.

4. Institutional religion has to compete for spiritual and social loyalty in modern times. The answers to abiding questions which people once found in religion are in competition with the rationalist formulas which are the foundation of the social, political, and economic life of the society. Individuals may resolve their personal allegiance to competing values by denying some, trying to accommodate divergent interpretations of reality, or compartmentalizing their values so that, in effect, they profess one set of beliefs on Sunday and another on Monday through Saturday, or one set at home and another at work or at play.

Children seem to adopt their parents' strategies in dealing with competing faiths and values (even if they reach different conclusions) unless temperament or critical events in their lives force a reexamination and realignment of their beliefs. However, our point here is not the child's particular course with respect to religious faith, but the fact that in growing up in contemporary society the child is exposed to competing views— competing religious faiths as well as competing secular and nonsecular points of view. In America, to bring all of experience under the same umbrella of explanation has always been difficult because the population is diverse and church and state are separate. Moreover, the relativism created by competing systems of belief means that what you believe has an element of personal choice associated with it—and therefore may not have the same quality of conviction that it would if "everybody"—that is the whole society—shared the same faith. If there is any overarching umbrella to American experience it is the belief that every individual has the right to choose his faith, his interpretation of what is real and abiding. By implication this means that every man's experience is valid, true for him; therefore when the child asks, "What is true?" he learns, at least by implication, that there are a number of truths: the truth of the rationalist, secular society, the truth of his parents' religious faith, the truth of other faiths. Because children cannot abide such relativism until the mental powers of adolescence develop, they are prone to choosing the "best."

5. See Albert Parr, "The Design of Cities," *Architectural Association Quarterly*, vol. 3, 1971, pp. 22–26.

6. The following discussion of schools is critical in tone, but it should be added that the American school system can be thought of as an overburdened and therefore vulnerable institution. Some of this excessive "burden" and vulnerability derive from the fact that school is the only social service to which all American children are entitled. It is easy for parents and communities to look to schools—most often to teachers—to fulfill all the child's needs, including those once filled by other intermediate institutions such as church, kin, and so on.

It may be that some of the jobs now done not entirely successfully by the school might be better done by television, or supplemented to a far greater degree than they are now. Television may be a more effective medium for teaching certain information and symbols skills than the usual classroom materials or teacher. It may also serve as a powerful force for displaying the social formulas necessary to adapt to the world of public affairs. As an intermediate institution, it may rival the others in its ability to organize and render new knowledge and suggest and compare courses of action.

However, emphasis on television's educational and social potential does not imply a denigration of the teacher's role or, speaking more generally, of children's need for face-to-face relationships with adults. Creative use of television could free teachers to interpret material and answer questions more fully and freely than they often have time for at present and to enter into a more satisfying partnership with parents. The complexity of modern society means that the teacher's role as interpreter—like the parent's—is a more demanding and more vital one than ever in the past.

7. See Seymour B. Sarason's *The Culture of the School and the Problem of Change*. Boston: Allyn and Bacon, 1971, and John U. Ogbu, *Minority Education and Caste: The American System in Cross-Cultural Perspective*. New York: Academic Press, 1978.

8. Schooling often appears to pay off when a society is expanding economically, although contrary to myth neither the individual payoff nor the rate of economic growth is "caused" by schooling. For more on this point of view, see Richard H. de Lone for the Carnegie Council on Children, *Small Futures: Inequality, Children and the Failure of Liberal Reform*. New York: Harcourt Brace Jovanovich, 1978, and John U. Ogbu, *Minority Education and Caste*. Also Samuel Bowles and Herbert Gintis, *Schooling in Capitalist America: Educational Reform and the Contradictions of Economic Life*. New

York: Basic Books, 1976; Pierre Bourdieu and Jean-Claude Passeron, *Reproduction in Education, Society, and Culture*. Beverly Hills, Calif: Sage, 1977. A primarily psychological or pedagogical point of view is represented by Charles E. Silberman, *Crisis in the Classroom: The Remaking of American Education*. New York: Random House, 1970; George Dennison, *The Lives of Children: The Story of the First Street School*. New York: Random House, 1969; John Holt, *How Children Fail*. New York: Dell, 1964; Jonathan Kozol, *Death at an Early Age: The Destruction of the Hearts and Minds of Negro Children in the Boston Public Schools*. Boston: Houghton Mifflin, 1967. The latter or social structural view is represented most comprehensively by Bowles and Gintis, *Schooling*. See also Christopher Jencks et al., *Inequality: A Reassessment of the Effect of Family and Schooling in America*. New York: Basic Books, 1972, and for a historical perspective, Colin Greer, *The Great School Legend: A Revisionist Interpretation of American Public Education*. New York: Basic Books, 1972.

9. Rosabeth Moss Kanter, "The Organization Child: Experience Management in a Nursery School," *Sociology of Education*, vol. 45, 1972, pp. 186–212.

10. Sara G. Zimet, ed., *What Children Read in School*. New York: Grune & Stratton, 1972.

11. This is one of many instances where children have little voice in decisions made ostensibly in the interest of their development. Dr. Seuss' books, for example, did not find a publisher for many years because adults believed his books would not interest children or serve them well!

12. Vivian, as dedicated a teacher as Florence, does not seem to be aware of the social implications implicit in her recommendations. In this regard she is like most teachers. Teachers are often unaware of the role they play in the sorting and selecting of students, a process that begins even in kindergarten. In a particularly poignant study Rist followed children from kindergarten to second grade and documented how, from their first weeks in school, they are implicitly tracked. Ray C. Rist, *The Urban School: A Factory for Failure*. Cambridge, Mass.: MIT Press, 1973. See also Robert Dreeben, *On What Is Learned in School*. Reading, Mass.: Addison-Wesley, 1968; Aaron V. Cicourel, *Cognitive Sociology*. New York: Free Press, 1974.

13. Peter Brooks, "Toward a Critical Reading of Reality," *Schoolworlds '76*, Donald N. Bigelow, ed. Berkeley, Calif.: McCutchan, 1976, pp. 54–55.

14. See Balzer, *Clockwork*, for detailed descriptions of work-talk, or Terkel, *Working*.

15. There are, however, some low-paying jobs that do involve a lot of communication and depend at least in part on the worker's ability to make his meaning clear and understand the meaning of the other or to get across information related to a particular service. Examples are the jobs of waiter, nurse's aid, domestic worker, child-care giver, or janitor in a residential building. However, the communication that these jobs require seldom calls

for a high degree of generalization or analysis. For a discussion of service jobs that build potentially reconstructive social coalitions between consumers and service, see Gartner and Riessman, *The Service Society*.

16. The Fairview educational approach permitted a strong emphasis on artistic expression of every form. A child might read folk takes, write stories, illustrate the stories she wrote, or read, sing, dance, or make up plays. The premise was that art is an important adjunct of primary education precisely because until he is six or seven the child still looks at reality in the manner of an artist. Developmentally he is not particularly well equipped for the "engineering," "component part" approach to learning. If it is the only educational diet available to him—and this is one issue at stake in the scholarization of day care and preschool education—he will almost inevitably take on, rather than take in, what is taught. He is not ready to do more than locate the new skill at some corner of his map of the social world—whereas it should serve to refine the whole map.

Art sees things whole, allowing the child to be in touch with the whole (or at least more) of his experience. It provides a "base" for knowing himself and his culture on which and out of which he can develop formal academic skills. The very nature of artistic traditions offers a coherent link to a people's way of imposing structure of making sense of reality, organizing experience, and communicating both a view and a vision, one's formal conception of events and feelings and a personal interpretation of their meaning. Florence might read her first graders a group of African folk tales. The stories might be a medium for teaching facts and figures, but at the same time they could furnish children with an avenue into their cultural heritage. The stories might be an inspiration for drawing, singing, dancing, short plays, or cooking projects; all the child's senses might be engaged in learning.

Florence might remind herself of a talk she once heard; the speaker had said that if one took Piaget seriously the arts would constitute the core curriculum of the preschool and primary school. Each sensory modality of the child and each perceptual or cognitive school skill could meet in one or other art form. And each classical or folk art tradition carries with it one or more pedagogical prescriptions—the formal disciplines upon which artistic conception and expression must rest. Thus, the arts as the core curriculum would teach children explicit skills for focusing on and increasing sensory information, organizing and reorganizing, combining, evaluating, experimenting—cognitively and expressively.

Art does not have the place of a mere "frill" or luxury in what we might call the wholistic approach to education, even, or perhaps especially, for urban minority children whom Florence is teaching. Some (like Vivian) might argue that such children "can't afford" artistic expression; it takes too much of the precious time of children who are already "behind." On the contrary, it may be a vitally important way to help children "catch up" because it helps them experience their lives, give expression to their reality, thus providing them with a base they may have lacked for the acquisition of academic skills. To use our earlier terminology, it allows them to "own" a wider range of perceptions and abilities.

The wholistic education approach waxes and wanes as a function of society's expansiveness or retrenchment on other fronts. It has always been applauded by some, denigrated by others, but largely been left as the province of private schools that can afford to experiment. If it were applied on any extensive scale, its influence on the socialization of children might be profound, for its "message" about the relationship of man and work and the nature of knowledge would be very different from the "engineering" approach. The product still counts but the process counts, too, the dancer dancing as well as the dance. Moreover, it leaves a place for knowledge that is true although not scientific, that is, not divorced from the personal. Implicitly it questions the allure of objectivity.

Finally, it must be noted that parents and teachers are usually most comfortable with educational methods that do not depart too much from the school days of their childhood. Most of us recreate the institutions we have known, with some modifications learned along the way. Teaching of the sort we have applauded requires more time, thought, and consultation, at least at the beginning, if it is to be effective and not merely clever or chaotic. Florence had perhaps the ideal "internship"—a full year of practice teaching with a skilled master teacher in a school organized to link the arts with what is known of the early stages of cognitive development. Most teachers, in their brief stint of practice teaching and in their college classrooms, learn more about pedagogical management techniques than about the cognitive and social development of children or their cultural heritage. They must inevitably fall back on tried and trusted methods unless they have the chance to work in a school where there is some leeway to experiment with help from a principal who offers creative, effective leadership. But, as we noted earlier, forces of accountability and professional tunnel vision limit everyone's initiative to the extent that safety lies in doing-what-we've-always-done. Such external forces tend to reinforce the internal tendency among human beings to stick with what's-familiar.

We portray Florence as a reflective, well-liked teacher—but she probably does not share with her colleagues the thoughts we express in the vignette; nor if her school is typical will very many teachers or even the principal spend much time in her classroom. If parents do not complain and the children do as well or better than other first graders, she may continue her approach quietly and hope to teach a few student teachers as she was taught. She has probably learned already that she cannot alone change the culture of the school. See Sarason, *Culture of the School*.

17. Murray Levine and Adeline Levine, eds., *A Social History of Helping Services: Clinic, Court, School, and Community*. New York: Appleton-

Century-Crofts, 1970. See in particular Sarason's paper which discusses, among other issues, learning to read.

18. For an extended treatment of this topic, see Ogbu, *Minority Education*. In chapter four we discussed the concept of class, a complex form of social identification that attributes values, tastes, life goals, and competencies to individuals who vary by income, education, and cultural heritage. Caste and class are mutually reinforcing ways of sorting children, but they are not the same. If a black child like Brian Mosby and a white child live comfortably with professionally successful "middle class" parents, the black child will not enjoy the privileged status of his white peer. It is clearest at the upper reaches of class status that neither income nor education erases caste marking and the social penalty associated with it.

19. Studies of new textbooks, readers, and library books suggest that although the pictures and story lines are more representative of American diversity, the underlying assumptions about who and what really matters have changed very little. See for example Sara G. Zimet, ed., *What Children Read;* G. E. Bloom, R. Waite, and Sara G. Zimet, "A Motivational Content Analysis of Children's Primers," *Basic Studies on Reading,* H. Levin and P. Williams, eds. New York: Basic Books, 1970, pp. 188–221; also Robert D. Hess, "Competence and Educational Processes," *The Growth of Competence,* Kevin Connally, ed. New York: Academic Press, 1974.

20. Daniel Scheinfeld, an anthropologist at the Institute for Juvenile Research in Chicago, has studied these matters for some time. His Ph.D. dissertation, "Dominance, Exchange and Achievement in a Lower Income Black Neighborhood" (Department of Anthropology, University of Chicago, 1973), is particularly instructive. See also Daniel R. Scheinfeld, "Family Relationships Among Boys of Lower-Income Black Families," *American Journal of Orthopsychiatry,* vol. 53, 1983, pp. 127–143.

21. For an example of one family's approach see "A Janitor Who Dreamed His Daughters Would Be Doctors," *New York Times,* June 20, 1977, p. 22.

22. A minority child deeply and intimately influenced by a parent, teacher, or special friend like Florence's mother must, in time, cross-reference two realities. Very often a member of a minority group who "makes it" in the dominant culture can switch codes, that is, operate in two or more idioms of behavior or language both literally and figuratively, with all the strain and advantage of sharpened awareness that such ability entails. He starts out with a "map of possibility"; perhaps the map points the way, as it did for Florence, toward being "someone," a teacher. For Lester, the same end implied transferring to another school as a first step. Eventually, however, the child must become fully aware of society's standard-issue map for people of his caste, one that may point the way only to work others do not want and a second-class position in society. The way may be posted with signs that read "People Like You Need Not Apply," or

there may be a sign that says "Proven Exceptions to the Rule May Enter Here." Full awareness of this second reality begins to develop when the child enters school, if it has not confronted him earlier. At school, he meets the public world of the dominant culture more completely than before and learns the course it charts for him.

If his grounding in life has been firm enough and if support continues, he may be able to steer a hopeful course—to superimpose, so to speak, on his map of the way things really are his invested map of how they might be and to strive to make that "might be" in part a reality for himself. But to do this successfully he must learn to handle the rules and codes of the dominant culture, part of which consists of mastering that culture's symbolic verbal and numerical codes. Yet it is also a matter of learning certain styles and ways of doing things many of which have to do with how to get things done when faced with impersonal, bureaucratic procedures. See *Growing Up in the Projects* by Joan Costello, Jay Hirsch, and Gene Borowitz, forthcoming.

Chapter Seven

1. See Berger, Berger, and Kellner, *Homeless Mind*; or Charles E. Lindbloom, *Politics and Markets: The World's Political-Economic Systems*. New York: Basic Books, 1977; or F. Hirsch, *Social Limits to Growth*.

2. See, for example, H. Barry, Irvin L. Child, and M. K. Bacon, "Relation of Child Training to Subsistence Economy," *American Anthropologist*, vol. 61, 1959, pp. 51–63; Yehudi A. Cohen, "The Shaping of Men's Minds: Adaptations to the Imperatives of Culture," in *Anthropological Perspectives on Education*, Murray L. Wax, Stanley Diamond, and Fred O. Gearing, eds. New York: Basic Books, 1977; Beatrice Whiting, "Work and the Family: Cross-Cultural Perspectives," *Women: 1973*, Florence Denmark, ed., A Random House Annual. New York: Random House, 1973; Inkeles, "Society, Social Structure." We omit a discussion of modern technologies' effects on the child's physical well-being, which are considered in chapter 3 of Kenneth Keniston and the Carnegie Council on Children, *All Our Children*.

3. Richard Scarry, *Richard Scarry's Busiest People Ever*. New York: Random House, 1976; Richard Scarry, *Richard Scarry's Cars and Trucks and Things That Go*. Racine, Wis.: Western Publishing, 1974.

4. James Turner, *The Chemical Feast*. New York: Grossman, 1970. Also see Fred Powledge, *Fat of the Land*. New York: Simon & Schuster, 1983.

5. Martin E. P. Seligman, *Helplessness: On Depression, Development, and Death*. San Francisco: W. H. Freeman, 1975.

6. For the importance of feeling that one has some leeway, see Erik Erikson, *Toys and Reasons*.

Bibliography

Ainsworth, Mary D. Salter. *Infancy in Uganda: Infant Care and the Growth of Love.* Baltimore: Johns Hopkins Press, 1967.

Ainsworth, Mary D. Salter. "Object Relations, Dependency and Attachment: A Theoretical Review of the Mother-Infant Relationship." *Child Development*, 1969, 40, 969–1025.

Antonacci, Robert J. and Barr, Jene. *Baseball for Young Champions.* New York: Whittlesey House, McGraw-Hill, 1956.

Arendt, Hannah. *The Human Condition.* Chicago: University of Chicago Press, 1958.

Baldwin, James. *Nobody Knows My Name.* New York: Dial Press, 1961.

Baldwin, James Mark. *Social and Ethical Interpretations in Mental Development: A Study in Social Psychology.* New York: Macmillan, 1897.

Balzer, Richard. *Clockwork: Life In and Outside an American Factory.* Garden City, N.Y.: Doubleday, 1976.

Bandura, Albert. "Self-Efficacy Mechanism in Human Agency," *American Psychologist*, 1982, 37, 122–167.

Bane, Mary Jo. *Here to Stay: American Families in the Twentieth Century.* New York: Basic Books, 1976.

Barker, Roger G. and Schoggen, Phil. *Qualities of Community Life: Measurement of Environment Behavior in an American and English Town.* San Francisco: Jossey-Bass, 1973.

Barry, H. Child, Bacon, Irvin L. and Margaret K. "Relation of Child Training to Subsistence Economy." *American Anthropologist*. 1959: 61, 51–63.

Bateson, Gregory, in *Steps to an Ecology of Mind: Collected Essays in Anthropology, Evolution, and Epistemology.* New York: Ballantine Books, 1975.

Baumrind, Diana. "The Development of Instrumental Competence Through Socialization," in *Minnesota Symposium on Child Psychology*, 1973, 7, 3–46.

Baxandall, Rosalyn, Gordon, Linda, and Reverby, Susan (eds.), *America's Working Woman.* New York: Random House, 1976.

Bell, Daniel. *The Cultural Contradictions of Capitalism.* New York: Basic Books, 1976.

Benthall, Jonathan and Polhemus, Ted. *The Body as a Medium of Expression.* New York: E.P. Dutton, 1975.

Berger, Peter L., et al., (eds.). *The Human Shape of Work: Studies in the Sociology of Occupations of Nine American Jobholders.* New York: Bantam Books, 1972.

Berger, Peter L., Berger, Brigitte, and Kellner, Hansfried. *The Homeless Mind: Modernization and Consciousness.* New York: Random House, 1973.

Berger, Peter L. and Luckmann, Thomas. *The Social Construction of Reality.* Garden City, New York: Doubleday, 1966.

Berman, Phyllis W. and Ramey, Estelle R. (eds.). *Women: Developmental Perspective.* U. S. Dept. H. H. S., NIH Pub. No. 82–2298. Washington, D.C., 1982.

Bernstein, Basil. *Class, Codes and Control: Theoretical Studies Towards a Sociology of Language.* New York: Schocken Books, 1975.

Blom, G. E., Waite, R., and Zimet, S. G. "A Motivational Content Analysis of Children's Primers," in H. Levin and P. Williams (eds.), *Basic Studies on Reading.* New York: Basic Books, 1970.

Bleuler, Manfred. *The Schizophrenic Disorders.* New Haven: Yale University Press, 1978.

Borowitz, Gene H., Costello, Joan, and Hirsch, Jay G. "Clinical Observations of Ghetto Four-Year-Olds: Organization, Involvement, Interpersonal Responsiveness, and Psychosexual Content of Play." *Journal of Youth and Adolescence,* 1972, 1, 59–79.

Bouldine, Elise. "Women as Role Models in Industrializing Societies," in Sussman, M. and Cogswell, B. (eds.), *Gross-National Family Research.* London: E. J. Brill, 1972.

Bourdieu, Pierre and Passerson, Jean-Claude. *Reproduction in Education, Society, and Culture.* Beverly Hills, Calif.: Sage, 1977.

Bowles, Samuel and Gintis, Herbert. *Schooling in Capitalist America: Educational Reform and the Contradictions of Economic Life.* New York: Basic Books, 1976.

Brackbill, Yvonne. *Infancy and Early Childhood: A Handbook and Guide to Human Development.* New York: Free Press, 1967.

Brooks, Peter. "Toward a Critical Reading of Reality," in Donald N. Bigelow (ed.), *School Worlds '76.* Berkeley, Calif.: McCutchan, 1976.

Bruner, Jerome S., Jolly, Alison, and Sylva, Kathy. (eds.). *Play: Its Role in Development and Evolution.* New York: Basic Books, 1976.

Bruner, Jerome A. and Sherwood, V. "Peekaboo and the Learning of Rule Structures," in Bruner et al., *Play: Its Role in Development and Evolution.* New York: Basic Books, 1976.

Bruner, Jerome S. and Goodman, C. C. "Value and Need as Organizing Factors in Perception." *Journal of Abnormal and Social Psychology,* 1947, 42, 33–44.

Bucknell, Susan. Background papers on the history of women's work prepared for the Carnegie Council on Children, 1975. Available from Special Collections at Regenstein Library, University of Chicago.

Carter, Elizabeth A. and McGoldrick, Monica. *The Family Life Cycle.* New York: Gardner, 1980.

Cicourel, Aaron V. *Cognitive Sociology: Language and Meaning in Social Interaction.* New York: Free Press, 1974.

Clarke-Stewart, Alison. *Child Care in the Family: A Review of Research and Some Propositions for Policy.* New York: Academic Press, 1977.
Cohen, Yehudi A. "The Shaping of Men's Minds: Adaptations to the Imperatives of Culture," in Murray L. Wax, Stanley Diamond, and Fred O. Gearing (eds.), *Anthropological Perspectives on Education.* New York: Basic Books, 1977.
Coles, C. Robert. *The Children of Crisis: The Privileged Ones: The Well-Off and Rich in America.* Boston: Little, Brown, 1977.
Coser, Rose Laub (ed.). *The Family: Its Structure and Functions.* New York: St. Martin's Press, 1964, 1974.
Costello, Joan, Hirsch, Jay G., and Borowitz, Gene. *Growing Up in the Projects.* Chicago: University of Chicago, forthcoming book.
Costello, Joan and Peyton, Ellice F. "The Socialization of Young Children's Learning Styles." Unpublished manuscript, 1973.
Costello, Joan. *Practical Child Development Knowledge for Planning Child and Family Policies.* Chicago: Child Policy Project, University of Chicago, 1984.
Daedalus (special issue), "The Family." 1977, 106.
Danziger, Kurt. "Children's Earliest Conceptions of Economic Relationships." *Journal of Social Psychology*, 1958, 47, 231–240.
DeLone, Richard H. *Small Futures: Inequality, Children and the Failure of Liberal Reform.* New York: Harcourt Brace Jovanovich, 1978.
Dennison, George. *The Lives of Children: The Story of the First Street School.* New York: Random House, 1969.
Dreitzel, Hans Peter. (ed.). *Childhood and Socialization*, Recent Sociology No. 5. New York: Macmillan, 1973.
Dreeben, Robert. *On What Is Learned in School.* Reading, Mass.: Addison-Wesley, 1968.
Erikson, Erik H. *Toys and Reasons: Stages in the Ritualization of Experience.* New York: Norton, 1977.
Erikson, Erik H. *Childhood and Society.* New York: Norton, 1950, 1963.
Flavell, John H. *Cognitive Development.* Englewood Cliffs, N.J.: Prentice-Hall, 1977.
Foa, Uriel G. and Foa, Edna B. *Societal Structures of the Mind.* Springfield, Ill.: Thomas, 1974.
Fraiberg, Selma H. *The Magic Years: Understanding and Handling the Problems of Early Childhood.* New York: Scribner, 1959.
Freedman, Daniel G. *Human Infancy: An Evolutionary Perspective.* Hillsdale, N.Y.: L. Erlbaum Associates, 1974.
Freud, Anna and Burlingham, Dorothy. *Infants Without Families.* N.Y. International Universities Press, 1944.
Garfinkel, Harold. *Studies in Ethnomethodology.* Englewood Cliffs, N.J.: Prentice-Hall, 1967.
Gartner, Alan and Riessman, Frank. *The Service Society and the Consumer Vanguard.* New York: Harper & Row, 1974.

Gibson, Eleanor J. *Principles of Perceptual Learning and Development.* New York: Prentice-Hall, 1969.

Gilligan, Carol. *In a Different Voice: Psychological Theory and Women's Development.* Cambridge, Mass.: Harvard University Press, 1982.

Ginsburg, Herbert and Opper, Sylvia. *Piaget's Theory of Intellectual Development: An Introduction.* Englewood Cliffs, N.J.: Prentice-Hall, 1969.

Gliedman, John and Roth, William. *The Unexpected Minority: Handicapped Children in America.* New York: Harcourt Brace Jovanovich, 1980.

Goffman, Erving. *Interactions Rituals: Essays on Face-to-Face Behavior.* New York: Anchor Books, 1967.

Greer, Colin. *The Great School Legend: A Revisionist Interpretation of American Public Education.* New York: Basic Books, 1972.

Grinder, John and Bandler, Richard, in *The Structure of Magic: A Book about Language and Therapy.* Palo Alto, Calif.: Science and Behavior Books, 1976.

Grow, Lucille J. *Early Childrearing by Young Mothers: A Research Study.* N.Y.: Child Welfare League of America, 19.

Hall, Edward T. *The Dance of Life: The Other Dimension of Time.* New York: Anchor Press/Doubleday, 1983.

Hall, Edward T. *Beyond Culture.* Garden City, N.Y.: Anchor Books, 1976.

Hall, Edward T. *The Silent Language.* Garden City, N.Y.: Doubleday, 1959.

Hardgrove, Carol B. and Dawson, Rosemary B. *Parents and Children in the Hospital: The Family's Role in Pediatrics.* Boston: Little, Brown, 1972.

Harre, Rom. "The Conditions for a Social Psychology of Childhood," in M.P.M. Richards (ed.), *The Integration of a Child into a Social World.* London: Cambridge University Press, 1974.

Harre, Rom. *Social Being.* London: Rowman, 1980.

Henry, Jules. *On Sham, Vulnerability and Other Forms of Self Destruction.* New York: Random House, 1973.

Hess, Robert D. "Competence and Education," in Kevin Connally (ed.), *The Growth of Competence.* New York: Academic Press, 1974.

Hess, Robert D. and Shipman, Virginia C. "Early Experience and the Socialization of Cognitive Modes in Children." *Child Development,* 1965, 34, 869–886.

Hess, Robert D. "Social Class and Ethnic Influences on Socialization," in Paul H. Mussen (ed.), *Carmichael's Manual of Child Psychology,* 2nd ed. New York: John Wiley & Sons, 1970.

Hirsch, Fred. *Social Limits to Growth.* Cambridge, Mass.: Harvard University Press, 1976.

Hirsch, Jay G., Borowitz, Gene H., and Costello, Joan. "Individual Differences in Ghetto 4-Year-Olds." *Archives of General Psychiatry,* 1970, 22, 268–276.

Hirsch, Jay G. and Costello, Joan. "School Achievers and Underachievers in an Urban Ghetto." *The Elementary School Journal,* 1970, 71, 79–85.

Hodgson, Godfrey. *America in Our Time.* Garden City, N.Y.: Doubleday, 1976.

Holt, John. *How Children Fail.* New York: Dell, 1964.
Hughes, Linda. *Childlife and Childlore.* Cooperstown, N.Y.: Cooperstown Graduate Programs, 1977.
Inkeles, Alex. "Society, Social Structure and Child Socialization," in John A. Clausen (ed.), *Socialization and Society.* Boston: Little, Brown, 1968.
Jencks, Christopher, et al. *Inequality: A Reassessment of the Effect of Family and Schooling in America.* New York: Basic Books, 1972.
Jones, Edward E. "How Do People Perceive the Causes of Behavior?" *American Scientist,* 1976, 64, 300–305.
Kahn, Alfred J. and Kamerman, Sheila B. *Not for the Poor Alone: European Social Services.* Philadelphia: Temple University Press, 1975.
Kamerman, Sheila B. and Kahn, Alfred J. *Social Services in the United States: Policies and Programs.* Philadelphia: Temple University Press, 1976.
Kamerman, Sheila B. and Kahn, Alfred J. *Child Care, Family Benefits and Working Parents.* New York: Columbia University Press, 1981.
Kanter, Rosabeth Moss. "The Organization Child: Experience Management in a Nursery School." *Sociology of Education,* 1972, 45, 186–212.
Kanter, Rosabeth Moss. *Men and Women of the Corporation.* New York: Simon and Schuster, 1977.
Kegan, Robert. *The Evolving Self: Problem and Process in Human Development.* Cambridge, Mass.: Harvard University Press, 1982.
Keniston, Kenneth. *All Our Children: The American Family Under Pressure.* New York: Harcourt Brace Jovanovich, 1977.
Kessen, William, Haith, Marshall M., and Salapatek, Philip H. "Infancy," in Paul H. Mussen (ed.), *Carmichael's Manual of Child Psychology.* New York: John Wiley & Sons, 1970.
Kohn, Melvin L. "Social Class and Parent-Child Relationships: An Interpretation." *American Journal of Sociology,* 1963, 68, 471–480.
Komarovsky, Mirra. *Blue-Collar Marriage.* New York: Random House, 1962.
Kozol, Jonathan. *Death at an Early Age: The Destruction of the Hearts and Minds of Negro Children.* Boston: Houghton Mifflin, 1967.
Korzybski, Alfred. *Science and Sanity: An Introduction to Non-Aristotelian Systems and General Semantics,* 4th ed. Lakeville, Conn.: The International Non-Aristotelian Library Publishing Co., 1958.
Lamb, Michael E. (ed.). *The Role of the Father in Child Development.* New York: John Wiley & Sons, 1976.
Lasch, Christopher. *Haven in a Heartless World: The Family Besieged.* New York: Basic Books, 1969.
Lein, Laura. *Work and Family Life.* Report to the National Institute of Education re: Project No. 3-3094. Cambridge, Mass.: Center for the Study of Public Policy, 1974.
Lessing, Doris. *The Memoirs of a Survivor.* New York: Alfred A. Knopf, 1975.
Lever, Janet. "Sex Differences in the Games Children Play." *Social Problems,* 1976, 23.

Levine, Murray and Levine, Adeline (eds.). *A Social History of Helping Services: Clinic, Court, School and Community.* New York: Appleton-Century-Crofts, 1970.

Levison, Andrew. *The Working Class Majority.* New York: Coward, McCann, & Georghegan, 1974.

Levy, Marion L. *Modernization and the Structure of Society.* Princeton, N.J.: Princeton University Press, 1966.

Lewis, Michael and Rosenblum, Leonard A. *The Effect of the Infant on Its Caregiver.* New York: John Wiley & Sons, 1974.

Lidz, Theodore. *The Family and Human Adaptation.* New York: International Universities Press, 1963.

Liljestrom, Rita. *Are Children Better Off in the "Postindustrial" Society?* New York: Swedish Information Service, November 1977.

Lindbloom, Charles E. *Politics and Markets: The World's Political-Economic Systems.* New York: Basic Books, 1977.

Lofland, Lynn H. *A World of Strangers: Order and Action in Urban Public Space.* New York: Basic Books, 1973.

Luria, A. R. *Cognitive Development, Its Cultural and Social Foundations.* Translated by Martin Lopez-Morillas and Lynn Solotaroff. London: Cambridge University Press, 1974.

Macoby, Michael. *The Gamesman: The New Corporate Leaders.* New York: Simon & Schuster, 1967.

Madge, Nicola (ed.). *Families at Risk.* London: Heineman Educational Books, 1983.

Manchester, William. *The Glory and the Dream: A Narrative History of America, 1932–1972.* Boston: Little, Brown, 1974.

Masnick, George S. and Bane, Mary Jo. *The Nation's Families: 1960–1990.* Boston: Auburn House, 1980.

McKinley, Donald D. *Social Class and Family Life.* New York: The Free Press, 1964.

Mead, George Herbert. *Mind, Self and Society.* Chicago: University of Chicago Press, 1934.

Mead, Margaret and Wolfenstein, Martha. *Childhood in Contemporary Cultures.* Chicago: University of Chicago Press, 1955.

Millar, Susanna. *The Psychology of Play.* New York: Penguin, 1968.

Miller, Donald R. and Swanson, G. *The Changing American Parent.* New York: John Wiley & Sons, 1958.

Miller, George A. "The Magical Number Seven, Plus or Minus Two: Some Limits on Our Capacity for Processing Information." *The Psychological Review*, 1956, 63, 81–96.

Mills, C. Wright. *The Sociological Imagination.* New York: Oxford University Press, 1959.

Moore, Donald, et al. *Child Advocacy and the Schools.* Chicago: Designs for Change, 1983.

Mott, Paul E., Mann, Floyd G., McLoughlin, Quin; and Warwick,

Donald P. *Shift Work: The Social, Psychological and Physical Consequences.* Ann Arbor: University of Michigan Press, 1965.

Neff, Walter S. *Work and Human behavior.* New York: Atherton Press, 1968.

Novak, Michael. *The Joy of Sports.* New York: Basic Books, 1976.

Oakley, Ann. *The Sociology of Housework.* New York: Pantheon Books, 1975.

Ogbu, John U. *Minority Education and Caste: The American System in Cross-Cultural Perspective.* New York: Academic Press, 1978.

Parr, Albert."The Design of Cities." *Architectural Association Quarterly,* 1971, 3, 22–26.

Piaget, Jean. *The Origins of Intelligence in Children,* 2nd ed. New York: International Universities Press, 1952.

Piaget, Jean. *The Construction of Reality in the Child,* 2nd ed. New York: Basic Books, 1954.

Proust, Marcel. *Remembrance of Things Past.* New York: Random House, 1934.

Provence, Sally. "Some Relationships Between Activity and Vulnerability in the Early Years," in James E. Anthony (ed.), *The Child in His Family,* Vol. 3. *Children at Psychiatric Risk.* New York: John Wiley & Sons, 1974.

Provence, Sally and Lipton, Rose C. *Infants in Institutions.* New York: International Universities Press, 1962.

Provence, Sally and Naylor, Audrey. *Working with Disadvantaged Parents and Their Children.* New Haven: Yale U. Press, 1983.

Ramey, Estelle, R. "Boredom: The Most Prevalent American Disease." *Harper's Magazine,* 1974, 249, 12–22.

Rist, Ray C. *The Urban School: A Factory for Failure.* Cambridge, Mass.: M.I.T. Press, 1973.

Rubin, Lillian Breslow. *Worlds of Pain: Life in the Working-Class Family.* New York: Pantheon Books, 1972.

Rutter, Michael. "Protective Factors in Children's Responses to Stress and Disadvantage," in Kent, M. W. and Rolf, J. E. (eds.), *Primary Prevention of Psychopathology,* vol. III. Hanover, N.H.: University Press of New England, 1979.

Sarason, Seymour B. *The Culture of the School and the Problem of Change.* Boston: Allyn & Bacon, 1971.

Scarry, Richard. *Richard Scarry's Cars and Trucks and Things that Go.* Racine, Wis.: Western Publishing, 1974.

Scarry, Richard. *Richard Scarry's Busiest People Ever.* New York: Random House, 1976.

Schactel, Ernest G. *Metamorphosis: On the Development of Affect, Perception, Attention, and Memory.* New York: Basic Books, 1959.

Schafer, Roy. *Aspects of Internalization.* New York: International Universities Press, 1968.

Scheinfeld, Daniel R. "Family Relationships and School Achievement Among Boys of Lower-Income Urban Black Families." *American Journal of Orthopsychiatry,* 1983.

Scheinfeld, Daniel R. "Dominance, Exchange and Achievement in a Lower Income Black Neighborhood." University of Chicago, Dept. of Anthropology, 1973, 53, 127–143.
Schutz, Alfred. *Phenomenology and Social Relations: Selected Writings.* Chicago: University of Chicago Press, 1970.
Schutz, Alfred. *Phenomenology and the Social World.* Evanston, Ill.: Northwestern University Press, 1967.
Schutz, Alfred. *The Structures of the Life World.* London: Heinemann, 1977.
Seligman, Martin E. P. *Helplessness: On Depression, Development, and Death.* San Francisco: W. H. Freeman, 1975.
Selman, Richard L. "Stages in Role-Taking and Moral Judgements as Guides to Social Intervention," in T. Likona (ed.), *Man and Morality.* New York: Holt, Rinehart & Winston, 1974.
Sennett, Richard. *The Fall of Public Man.* New York: Knopf, 1977.
Sennett, Richard and Cobb, Jonathan. *The Hidden Injuries of Class.* New York: Vintage Books, 1973.
Shantz, Carolyn Uhlinger. "The Development of Social Cognition," in Mavis Hetherington (ed.), *Review of Child Development Research,* vol. 5. Chicago: University of Chicago Press, 1976.
Shorter, Edward. *The Making of Modern Family.* New York: Basic Books, 1975.
Silberman, Charles E. *Crisis in the Classroom: The Remaking of American Education.* New York: Random House, 1970.
Steiner, Gilbert Y. *The Futility of Family Policy.* Washington: Brookings, 1981.
Stern, Daniel, et al. "Early Transmission of Affect: Some Research Issues," in *Frontiers of Infant Psychiatry,* Galenson, Eleanor and Call, Justin D. (eds.). New York: Basic Books, 1983.
Stern, Daniel. *The First Relationship.* Cambridge, Mass.: Harvard University Press, 1977.
Sullivan, Harry Stack. *Interpersonal Theory of Psychiatry.* Edited by Helen S. Perry and Mary L. Gawel. New York: Norton, 1968.
Suransky, Valerie Polakow. *The Erosion of Childhood.* Chicago: University of Chicago Press, 1982.
Sussman, Marvin B. and Cogswell, B. (eds.). *Cross-National Family Research.* Leiden: E. J. Brill, 1972.
Terkel, Studs. *Working: People Talk about What They Do All Day and How They Feel about What They Do.* New York: Pantheon Books, 1972.
Tizard, Barbara, Cooperman, Oliver, Joseph, Anne; and Tizard, Jack. "Environmental Effects on Language Development: A Study of Young Children in Long-Stay Residential Nurseries." *Child Development,* 1972, 43, 337–358.
Turner, James S. *The Chemical Feast: The Ralph Nader Study Group Report on Food Protection and the FDA.* New York: Grossman, 1970.
Vernon, M. D. *Perception Through Experience.* New York: Barnes & Noble, 1970.

Vygotsky, L. S. "Play and Its Role in the Mental Development of the Child (1933)," in Bruner et al., *Play: Its Role in Development and Evolution.* New York: Basic Books, 1976.

Walsh, Froma (ed.). *Normal Family Processes.* New York: Guilford, 1982.

Werner, Heinz and Kaplan, Bernard. *Symbol Formation: An Organismic-Developmental Approach to Language and the Expression of Thought.* New York: John Wiley & Sons, 1967.

White, Robert. "Motivation Reconsidered: The Concept of Competence." *Psychological Review,* 1959, 66, 297–333.

White, Robert W. "Strategies of Adaptation," in Coelho, G. V., Hamburg, D. A., and Adams, J. (eds.). *Coping and Adaptation.* New York: Basic Books, 1974.

White, Robert W. "Competence as an Aspect of Personal Growth," in Kent, M. W. and Rolf, J. E. (eds.). *Primary Prevention of Psychopathology,* vol. III. Hanover, N.H.: University Press of New England, 1979.

Whiting, Beatrice. "Work and the Family: Cross-Cultural Perspectives," in Florence Denmark (ed.)., *Women: 1973.* New York: Random House, 1973.

Wolfenstein, Martha and Mead, Margaret. (eds.). *Childhood in Contemporary Cultures.* Chicago: University of Chicago Press, 1955.

Work in America, report of a Special Task Force to the Secretary of U.S. Dept. H.E.W. Cambridge, Mass.: M.I.T. Press, 1973, p. 13.

Youniss, James. *Parents and Peers in Social Development.* Chicago: University of Chicago Press, 1980.

Zigler, Edward F. and Child, Irvin L. *Socialization and Personality Development.* Reading, Mass.: Addison-Wesley, 1973.

Zimet, Sara G. (ed.). *What Children Read in School: A Critical Analysis of Primary Reading Textbooks.* New York: Grune & Stratton, 1972.

SUBJECT INDEX

Age, stage,
  general, 12, 29
  infants and toddlers, 2, 12, 14–15, 109
  preschoolers, 3–10, 12, 16, 18–23, 41, 56, 97–110, 116, 133, 144
  schoolagers, 13, 17, 19–23, 79–88, 95, 98, 116, 125
  adolescents, 13–41, 169
  adolescent parents, 46–57
"Action for Children's Television," 150–151
Advertising, 127, 139, 150
American public values, 107–109, 118–120, 126, 155–156
Arts, 98, 169–170
Attachments,
  emotional, 9, 10, 12, 14
  to sensory landmarks, 14
Authority, modern sources, xiii

Baseball, 80–88, 164
Bridging the private-public world, 122
Bureaucracies, 41, 92, 106, 121–147, 153, 157

Caste (see also Social status), 115, 171
Childrearing,
  dilemmas, xvi, 38–42
  adolescent parents, 46–57
Choice (see also Power Opportunities), 140–141, 151
Church, religion, xiii–xvi, 89–93, 122–123, 165–167

Cognition, 10, 21, 79
Communications industry, xiii, 121–122, 155
Community, neighborhood, xiii–xvi, 8, 10, 31, 69, 82–85, 89–91
Conflicts, intrapsychic, 7
Construction of reality (see Social construction and Mapping of the social world)
Culture, cultural style, 2, 9, 12, 18–19, 29, 33, 66–68, 80, 91, 99, 115–120, 127, 170
  Black, 99, 117–120
  Public, 112

Daycare, 45–56, 79, 97–110, 116, 169

Early child bearing, 46–57
Economic institutions, xiii, 60, 74, 89–91, 121–127, 130–147, 155
The Electric Company, 95
Environment, 134–136
Everyday life structures, 61, 88, 92, 104, 112–113, 122–123, 154–155, 157, 161

Family world, xiv–xv, 7, 10, 35–58, 64–74, 79–80, 107, as social construction, 36, shared tasks, 42–43, 155, values, 93
First grade (see also Reading, Writing), 93, 95–98, 103, 110–113, 169–170, as rite of passage, 93

Friendship (*see* Peers)

Gestural signatures, 12, 55
Government institutions/ bureaucracies, xiii, 41, 89–91, 121, 131–141

Handicap, disability, 23–34, 64, 88
Helplessness, sense of powerlessness, 39, 73, 140–141
Hospitals, 90, 142–146
    child life programs, 144–146, 154
Housing, 128–130

Identity, identification, 10, 19, 61, 116, 164–165
Imitation, 15, 17
Income, 9, 51, 59–63, 68–77, 94, 114, 128, 164, 171
Information, 41–42, 56, 89–91, 111, 121, 126, 137, 154
Institutionalized order (*see also* Social messages, Social order, Social world, Rules), 105
Intermediate institutions, mediating structures, 19, 21, 89–90, 153–154, 164, 165, 167–168

Jobs (*see also* Work), 92, 111

Knowledge expansion, explosion (*see* Information), 41–44, 92

Learned helplessness (*see* Helplessness), 140–141
Life world (*see* Everyday structures, Social messages), 1, 2, 8, 10, 14, 16

Maintenance institutions, 155, 165

Mental mapping of the social world, 1–22, 29, 35, 45, 54–56, 60, 71–77, 79, 83, 91, 124, 146, 151, 154, 159–160, 169, 171–172
Marriage, as social construction, 35, 54, 161
    reconstruction as family, 37–38, 44–45
Mastery, 8, 88, 107, 127, 154
Mediating structures (*see* Intermediate institutions)
Medical centers, xiii, 41
Minority status, (*see also* Caste), 114–120, 171
Modernization, xiii, 40–46,
    definition, 154–155

Neighborhood, 89–93, 98, 100, 119, 122–125, 128–131, 165

Participation, social, 63, 88
Patterns of social reality in everyday life (*see also* Everyday life), xiv–xv, 6, 9, 35, 75
    of thought and action, 15, 121, 126, 155, 165
Peers, friendships, 79–88, 93–94, 164
    peer culture, 117–119
Perception, 13–15
Play, 3–9, 13, 18, 21, 22, 56–57, 82, 98, 109, 127, 158, 160–161, 164
    politics of play, 8–9
    game, 20, 80–88
Power, 7, 14, 17, 35, 75–77, 92, 109, 141, 149
    parents, 35
    invisible sources (technology), 40
    powerlessness, 46, 105, 125, 140
    possibilities, 76

Index

Privilege (*see also* Social status, Caste), 103, 118, 124, 153
Privileged meanings (*see* Social meanings), 76, 124, 163
Public voice, 92–93, 98, 113, 125, 139, 141, 150–151
   political voice, 93

Racial issues (*see also* Minority status), 8, 11, 88
Reading (*see also* First grade), 95–98, 103, 110–111, 113, 132, 170–171
Relationships (*see* Family), 35, 43
Religion (*see* Church)
Rituals, social and religious, 2, 6, 19, 43

Schools, xiii, 10, 22, 41, 54, 60, 64, 89–120, 165, 167–172
Self, 12, 17, 39, 44, 61–62, 71
Sex roles, 8, 11, 15, 17, 19–20, 32, 44–45, 67, 72–73, 87–88
Social agencies, xiii, 54, 90, 165
Social class, status, 112, 114–116, 129, 163, 171–172
Social construction, 88, 124, 160–161
Social exclusion, marks of, 8–9, 33, 88
Social messages, xvi, 6, 29, 33, 36, 59, 60, 72, 88, 93, 156, 170
   social meanings, 9, 12, 15, 60–62, 76, 88
   daycare and school, 105–120, 141, 152, 156
Social networks, 65, 89
Social order, 93, 121, 162

Social roles, 1, 9–22, 29, 44, 60, 79, 83–88, 116, 153, 159–161, 165
Social rules, norms, 9–22, 29, 60, 79, 83–88, 106, 125, 132, 159–160, 165, 172
Social status, 2, 7, 61–62, 75–77
Social world, 90–91, 155, 159, 169
Socialization, 10, 158, 164, 170
Societal structures and values, xiii–xv
   structures and values, xiv, 44
Specialization, specialists, experts (*see also* Modernization), 43
Sports, 80–88, 164
Stress, xiv, 38

Teachers, 41, 71, 94–96
Technology, technological change, 40, 54, 110, 121, 153, 172
Television, xv–xvi, 60, 75, 89–91, 94, 109, 112, 122, 126, 137, 155, 159, 166–167
Temperament, 6
Tracking, 102
Transportation, 128–131

Welfare, 51–55
Where the Wild Things Are, 109
Work, work roles, 9, 19, 21, 31, 37, 39–41, 44–45, 59–77, 92–94, 110–112, 125, 128, 131, 155, 157
   child "work", 98, 163–164, 168–169
Writing, 97, 110

AUTHOR INDEX

Ainsworth, Mary D. Salter 160
Antonacci, Robert J. 164
Arendt, Hannah 163
Ashton-Warner, Sylvia 96

Baldwin, James 59
Baldwin, James Mark 157
Balzer, Richard 158, 163, 168
Bandler, Richard 160
Barry, H. 172
Bateson, Gregory 160
Baumrind, Diana 157
Baxandall, Rosalyn 162
Bell, Daniel 154
Benthall, Jonathan 159
Berger, Brigitte 153, 155, 172
Berger, Peter L. 10, 153, 155, 157, 160, 161, 162, 163, 164, 172
Bernstein, Basil 163
Bloom, G. E. 171
Borowitz, Gene 159
Boulding, Elise 1
Bourdieu, Pierre 168
Bowles, Samuel 168
Brackbill, Yvonne 156
Brooks, Peter 111, 169
Bruner, Jerome S. 157, 158, 159, 163
Bucknell, Susan 162

Chicago Tribune 59
Child, Irvin L. 157, 172
Cicourel, Aaron V. 168
Clausen, John A. 157, 164
Cobb, Jonathan 158, 163
Cohen, Yehudi A. 172
Coles, Robert 158

Coser, Rose Laub 162
Costello, Joan 157, 159

Danzinger, Kurt 163
deLone, Richard H. 167
Dennison, George 168
Dickens, Charles 43
Douglas, Jack 161
Dreeben, Robert 168
Dreitzel, Hans Peter 157

Erikson, Erik H. 157, 158, 172

Flavell, John H. 157
Foa, Uriel G. and Edna B. 157, 164
Forman, Ellice Peyton 157
Fraiberg, Selma H. 157
Freedman, Daniel G. 156, 160

Garfinkel, Harold 156, 158, 161, 164
Gartner, Alan 162, 163, 169
Geertz, Clifford 158
Gibson, Eleanor J. 156, 158
Gilligan, Carol 161
Ginsberg, Herbert 156
Gintis, Herbert 168
Gliedman, John 161, 164
Grinder, John 160
Greer, Colin 168
Grow, Lucille J. 162

Hacker, Andrew 163
Haith, Marshall M. 156, 160
Hall, Edward T. 156, 158–159, 161, 162

Index

Harre, Rom 156, 159, 161, 164
Henry, Jules 121
Herron, R. E. 158
Hess, Robert D. 157, 171
Hetherington, E. Mavis 160
Hirsch, Fred 164, 172
Hirsch, Jay G. 159, 172
Hodgson, Godfrey 154
Holt, John 168
Huizinga, J. 158

Inkeles, Alex, 157, 164, 172

Jencks, Christopher 168
Jolly, Alison 157, 158
Jones, Edward E. 161

Kahn, Alfred J. 162
Kamerman, Sheila B. 162
Kanter, Rosabeth Moss 163, 168
Kaplan, Bernard 157, 160
Kegan, Robert 155, 157
Kellner, Hansfried 161, 172
Keniston, Kenneth 172
Kessen, William 156, 160
Kohn, Melvin L. 163
Komarovsky, Mirra 163
Korzybski, Alfred 160

Lamb, Michael E. 161
Lein, Laura 163
Lever, Janet 164
Levin, H. 171
Levine, Murray and Adeline 170
Levison, Andrew 163
Levy, Marion J. xiii, 89, 154, 162
Lewis, Michael 160
Lidz, Theodore 162
Lindbloom, Charles E. 172
Lipton, Rose C. 160
Lofland, Lyn H. 162
Luckmann, Thomas 10, 155, 157, 160
Luria, A. R. 157

Mabley, Jack, column 59
Macoby, Michael 163
McKinley, D. G. 163
Mead, George Herbert 161
Mead, Margaret 7, 156, 158
Millar, Susanna 158
Miller, Donald R. 163
Mills, C. Wright 79
Mott, Paul E. 163
Mussen, Paul H. 156, 157

Neff, Walter S. 163
Novak, Michael 164

Oakley, Ann 162, 163
Ogbu, John U. 167, 171
Opper, Sylvia 156

Parr, Albert 167
Passerson, Jean-Claude 168
Piaget, Jean 12, 156, 158, 159, 170
Posner, Michael I. 158
Proust, Marcel 160
Provence, Sally 160

Ramey, Estelle R. 162
Richards, M. P. M. 156
Riessman, Frank 162, 163, 169
Rist, Ray C. 168
Rosenblum, Leonard A. 160
Roth, William 161, 164
Rubin, Lillian Breslow 158

Salapatek, Philip H. 156, 160
Sarason, Seymour B. 114, 168, 171
Scarry, Richard 40, 123, 172
Schachtel, Ernest G. 23, 155, 157
Schafer, Roy 157
Scheinfeld, Daniel R. 171
Schutz, Alfred 153, 156, 157, 160, 161
Seligman, Martin E. P. 172
Selman, Richard L. 161
Sendak, Maurice 109

Sennett, Richard 158, 162, 163
Shantz, Carolyn Uhlinger 160
Shipman, Virginia C. 157
Shorter, Edward 154
Silberman, Charles E. 168
Stern, Daniel 156, 158, 160, 161
Sullivan, Harry Stack 158
Sussman, Marvin B. 162
Sutton-Smith, Brian 158
Swanson, G. E. 163
Sylva, Kathy 157

Terkel, Studs 158, 163, 168
Turner, James S. 172

Vernon, M. D. 156, 158
Vygotsky, L. S. 157, 158

Wax, Murray L. 172
Werner, Heinz 157, 160
Whalen, Martha Kent 159
White, Robert W. 159
Whiting, Beatrice 172
Wilder, Laura Ingalls 43
Wolfenstein, Martha 156, 158

Youniss, James 164

Zigler, Edward F. 157
Zimet, Sara G. 168, 171